PSYCHOLOGICAL PERSPEC I IVES ON PRAISE

Praise is perhaps the most widely used technique to influence others. When used appropriately, praise can motivate people, make them feel better, and improve their social relationships. Often, however, praise fails to work as intended and may even cause harm. *Psychological Perspectives on Praise* reviews and integrates psychological theory and research to provide an overarching perspective on praise.

With contributions from leading scholars in the field, this book amalgamates diverse theoretical and empirical perspectives on praise. The book starts with providing an overview of prominent theories that seek to explain the effects of praise, including self-enhancement theory, self-verification theory, attribution theory, and self-determination theory. It then discusses several lines of empirical research on how praise impacts competence and motivation, self-perceptions (e.g., self-esteem and narcissism), and social relationships. It does so in a range of contexts, including children's learning at school, employees' commitment at work, and people's behavior within romantic relationships. The book concludes by showing how praise can be understood in its developmental and cultural context.

Revealing that praise is a message rich in information about ourselves and our social environments, this book will be of interest to social, organizational, personality, developmental, and educational psychologists; students in psychology and related disciplines; and practitioners including teachers, managers, and counselors who use praise in their daily practice.

Eddie Brummelman is Assistant Professor at the University of Amsterdam. He obtained his PhD at Utrecht University in 2015 and was Marie Skłodowska-Curie fellow at Stanford University. His research focuses on the socialization of the self: how social feedback shapes children's self-views, such as self-esteem and narcissism. He is a recipient of awards including the National Postdoc Prize from the Royal Holland Society of Sciences and Humanities, the George Butterworth Young Scientist Award from the European Association for Developmental Psychology, and the Rising Star Award from the Association for Psychological Science.

Current Issues in Social Psychology

Series Editor: Johan Karremans

Current Issues in Social Psychology is a series of edited books that reflect the state of current and emerging topics of interest in social psychology.

Each volume is tightly focused on a particular topic and consists of seven to ten chapters contributed by international experts. The editors of individual volumes are leading figures in their areas and provide an introductory overview.

The series is useful reading for students, academics, and researchers of social psychology and related disciplines. Example topics include self-esteem, mindfulness, evolutionary social psychology, minority groups, social neuroscience, cyberbullying, and social stigma.

Mindfulness in Social Psychology
Edited by Johan C. Karremans and Esther K. Papies

Belief Systems and the Perception of Reality
Edited by Bastiaan Rutjens and Mark Brandt

Current Directions in Ostracism, Social Exclusion and Rejection Research
Edited by Selma Rudert, Rainer Greifeneder & Kipling Williams

New Directions in the Psychology of Close Relationships
Edited by Dominik Schoebi & Belinda Campos

The Psychology of Food Marketing and Overeating
Edited by Frans Folkvord

Psychological Perspectives on Praise
Edited by Eddie Brummelman

For more information about this series, please visit: https://www.routledge.com/

PSYCHOLOGICAL PERSPECTIVES ON PRAISE

Edited by Eddie Brummelman

LONDON AND NEW YORK

First published 2021
by Routledge
2 Park Square, Milton Park, Abingdon, Oxon OX14 4RN

and by Routledge
52 Vanderbilt Avenue, New York, NY 10017

Routledge is an imprint of the Taylor & Francis Group, an informa business

British Library Cataloguing-in-Publication Data
A catalogue record for this book is available from the British Library

Library of Congress Cataloging-in-Publication Data
A catalog record has been requested for this book

ISBN: 9780367347482 (hbk)
ISBN: 9780367347475 (pbk)
ISBN: 9780429327667 (ebk)

Typeset in Bembo
by codeMantra

CONTENTS

FIGURES

CONTRIBUTORS

Frederik Anseel, UNSW Business School, University of New South Wales, Australia

Mika Asaba, Department of Psychology, Stanford University, US

Ashwini Ashokkumar, Department of Psychology, The University of Texas at Austin, US

Eddie Brummelman, Research Institute of Child Development and Education, University of Amsterdam, the Netherlands

Xiaochen Chen, Department of Psychology, Renmin University of China, China

Andrei Cimpian, Department of Psychology, New York University, US

Jennifer Crocker, Department of Psychology, The Ohio State University, US

Carol S. Dweck, Department of Psychology, Stanford University, US

Lauren Eskreis-Winkler, The Wharton School, University of Pennsylvania, US

Ayelet Fishbach, Booth School of Business, The University of Chicago, US

Kayla Good, Department of Psychology, Stanford University, US

Sandra Graham, Department of Education, University of California, Los Angeles, US

Stathis Grapsas, Department of Developmental Psychology, Tilburg University, the Netherlands

Joan E. Grusec, Department of Psychology, University of Toronto, Canada

Hyowon Gweon, Department of Psychology, Stanford University, US

Jennifer Henderlong Corpus, Department of Psychology, Reed College, US

Gail D. Heyman, Department of Psychology, University of California San Diego, US

Patty Leijten, Research Institute of Child Development and Education, University of Amsterdam, the Netherlands

Edward P. Lemay, Jr., Department of Psychology, University of Maryland, College Park, US

Elena Martinescu, Department of Organization Sciences, Free University Amsterdam, the Netherlands

Florrie Fei-Yin Ng, Department of Educational Psychology, The Chinese University of Hong Kong, Hong Kong SAR, China

Janice Ng, Department of Psychology, University of Illinois at Urbana-Champaign, US

Eva M. Pomerantz, Department of Psychology, University of Illinois at Urbana-Champaign, US

Duane Rudy, Department of Human Development and Family Science, University of Missouri, US

Bart Soenens, Department of Developmental, Personality, and Social Psychology, Ghent University, Belgium

William B. Swann, Jr., Department of Psychology, The University of Texas at Austin, US

Sander Thomaes, Department of Psychology, Utrecht University, the Netherlands

Linden R. Timoney, Department of Psychology, University of Waterloo, Canada

Maarten Vansteenkiste, Department of Developmental, Personality, and Social Psychology, Ghent University, Belgium

Andrea C. Vial, Department of Psychology, New York University, US

Joanne V. Wood, Department of Psychology, University of Waterloo, Canada

FOREWORD
Praise in the egosystem and the ecosystem
Jennifer Crocker

> Undoubtedly, the most threatening aspect of praise is the obligation it puts on us to be praise-worthy people. If we accept praise, if we really believe the best about ourselves, then we are under an obligation to behave accordingly. This is deeply frightening to us. For if we really believe it when we are told that we are competent, or intelligent, or beautiful, then we are continually on the spot to *be* competent, or intelligent, or beautiful, not only in the eyes of the person who praised us but, even worse, in our own eyes. The responsibility to be continually at our best, to live up to our talents and abilities, is perhaps our most difficult problem in living—and we naturally defend against it.
>
> (Farson, 1963, p. 63)

Praise is powerful but frequently misunderstood. Although intuition suggests that praise bolsters people, empirical research shows that it sometimes undermines them. Praise can motivate, but it can also sting. Praise can strengthen social bonds or weaken them. Although praise can be a powerful reward for a job well done, excessive praise or faint praise can foster self-doubt. In light of the ability of praise to spur people on to great achievements or undermine them, it is essential to understand the many variations of praise; their consequences for motivation, self-concepts, and relationships; and what type of praise given by whom in what social context has beneficial or toxic effects. The chapters in this volume provide much needed insights, based, in empirical research, on the psychology of praise.

The power of praise results from the fact that people are social beings who survive and thrive in the context of supportive social relationships (Baumeister & Leary, 1995). Praise conveys important information about whether people have qualities that are valued by others. But people do not always accept praise at face value; people interpret the meaning of praise for themselves, their relationships, and their place in the world. Understanding the psychology of praise helps us understand human nature itself. The ability of praise to inspire or deflate, to forge connection or isolation, reveals the nature of human social motivation.

Praise given by one person to another is an inherently evaluative and interpersonal process. As the chapters in this volume amply demonstrate, praise has consequences for self-evaluations and social relationships of its recipients. Praise can convey valuable information to recipients about how others view the quality of their performance (e.g., how good was it?), the causes of good performance (e.g., effort or ability), and their competencies and characteristics (e.g., you're so good at math, smart, or such a good person). But praise also communicates information about social relationships—how discerning the provider is, the recipient's relationship to the provider (e.g., is the provider's positive regard contingent on being praise-worthy? Is the provider merely trying to ingratiate herself with the recipient?), and whether the recipient belongs in the social context. Recipients of praise are not passive; they desire, seek, interpret, and respond to praise in ways that shape their own reactions to praise and the behavior of praise providers (Brummelman & Dweck, Chapter 7, this volume; Lemay, Chapter 11, this volume).

Accordingly, praise affects and is affected by the social motivations of both the provider and the recipient of praise. Both providers and recipients of praise have a range of motivations that can affect the provision, receipt, interpretation, and consequences of praise. In this foreword, I suggest that the problematic consequences of praise emerge when praise giving or receipt is energized by egosystem motivation. I consider how egosystem motivation shapes how people give and receive praise, and its affective, motivational, and interpersonal consequences. I conclude by suggesting an alternative—ecosystem motivation—that can energize praise without these problematic consequences.

Egosystem motivation

People with egosystem motivation tend to be preoccupied with their worth and value, both in their own and in others' eyes (see Crocker & Canevello, 2012, for a review). They focus on what events, such as receiving praise or criticism, mean about them (e.g., "I can do this," or "I am a failure."). They want to see themselves and to be seen by others as having desirable qualities (e.g., smart, good-looking, funny, helpful) that make them valued by others (Anseel & Martinescu, Chapter 1, this volume). It is not enough to *have* those qualities (e.g., to *be* smart, good-looking, funny, or helpful); other people must *notice and appreciate* them. Accordingly, people with egosystem motivation often do things intended to make sure others "get" their desirable qualities and do not notice their flaws. For example, to be perceived as smart, a student might raise her hand when she knows the answer to a question, but not raise her hand to ask a question when she is confused. Raising or not raising her hand does not change how smart she is, but it could change how smart others think she is. This concern with image management develops early (Heyman, Chapter 13, this volume; Thomaes & Leijten, Chapter 15, this volume).

Because they are aware of being evaluated and judged by others, people with egosystem motivation tend to be self-conscious. Success elicits feelings of happiness, pride, and excitement. However, this emotional high of success in the egosystem tends to be short-lived. Others' positive impressions can quickly change if one's flaws or weaknesses are exposed, so the positive emotions that follow from success at image management are often soon followed by anxiety about whether the image can be maintained.

Praise as an activator of egosystem motivation

It is easy to see how receiving praise could activate egosystem motivation. Praise communicates information about others' evaluations—of specific performances, qualities of the self, or the entire person. It can be an important source of information about the self (Rudy & Grusec, Chapter 12, this volume). Praise is likely to grab the attention of recipients, especially if they have any uncertainty about these issues. Praise can also reveal what impressions others have formed of oneself, and therefore their willingness to be a means, rather than an obstacle, to satisfaction of one's needs and desires. Consider, for example, whether you would prefer to ask someone who has praised your work, or someone who has not, for a letter of recommendation.

Different types of praise may activate egosystem motivation to different degrees and for different lengths of time. Person praise (e.g., "you are brilliant!"), with its broad implications for the type of person one is and therefore one's value in a range of social contexts and relationships, may typically foster greater preoccupation with one's value and worth than praise for effort, which can have implications for a narrower range of contexts and relationships. But sometimes people who are praised for their effort or overpraised for their performance infer that they are seen as lacking ability (Corpus & Good, Chapter 5, this volume; Graham & Chen, Chapter 3, this volume).

These complexities suggest that the degree and duration of egosystem activation when people receive praise may depend on the cognitive effort required to process the meaning and implications of the praise, and integrate it into their beliefs about themselves, other people, and the world. Recipients of praise may think about whether they believe the evaluation implied by the praise, whether they trust the sincerity of the praiser (Asaba & Gweon, Chapter 8, this volume), what the praise indicates about the cause of their (good) performance, what it means about their likely future success, what they must do to sustain the praise and perhaps conceal their mistakes and weaknesses, whether the praiser's regard for them is conditional on their continued praiseworthiness, whether and how to respond to the praise, and whether they belong in the relationship or social context.

Costs of receiving praise in the egosystem

Egosystem motivation has numerous costs (see Crocker & Canevello, 2012, for a review), and praise that activates egosystem motivation is no exception. The chapters in this volume describe some of the costs of praise for its recipients. For example, by focusing attention on image management and prompting preoccupation with one's worth and value, egosystem motivation uses limited working memory capacity, reducing people's capacity to analyze situations and problems, and leads to nonoptimal judgment and decision-making (Zhang & Baumeister, 2006). Praise that activates egosystem motivation may have similar effects. Preoccupation with the meaning of praise for one's worth and value likely uses limited cognitive resources, leaving less cognitive capacity for thinking about other things, including the impact of one's behavior on others.

Moreover, because people with egosystem motivation tend to have performance goals, they lose intrinsic motivation to learn and withhold effort in the face of difficulty, which in turn impairs their task engagement and performance (Jiang, Canevello, & Crocker, 2019). Praise appears to have similar effects (Corpus & Good, Chapter 5, this volume). Thus, praise may inhibit both the motivation and the capacity to grow as a person by activating egosystem motivation.

People with egosystem motivation experience anxiety and discomfort in social interactions, contributing to negative emotional experiences (Crocker & Canevello, 2012). Their symptoms of depression and anxiety increase over time in both clinical and nonclinical samples (Crocker, Canevello, Breines, & Flynn, 2010; Erickson et al., 2018). Several chapters in this volume explain how praise can prompt anxiety about whether one can live up to it and continue to earn praise in the future. Praise may, in some cases, paradoxically contribute to low self-esteem, anxiety, and symptoms of depression (see Timoney & Wood, Chapter 9, this volume, for examples), and excessive praise may foster narcissism (Brummelman & Grapsas, Chapter 10, this volume).

Last but not least, egosystem motivation has costs for relationships. When people are motivated by the egosystem, they feel competitive with others, which in turn predicts feeling isolated, even with close relationship partners (see Crocker & Canevello, 2012, for a review). They view their relationships as working in zero-sum ways, so one person's gain must come at the expense of others. They are less supportive and responsive to others and perceive others as less supportive and responsive to them, which predicts declines in feelings of closeness, satisfaction, and commitment to relationship partners and increases in loneliness. In a longitudinal study, people high in psychological entitlement, who believe they deserve admiration and respect from others, had high self-image goals, which in turn predicted hostility and conflict in their relationships (Moeller, Crocker, & Bushman, 2009).

The costs of praise for relationships have been studied less, but several chapters included here suggest that praise can also have costs for relationships (e.g., Lemay, Chapter 11, this volume). For example, praise can communicate conditional positive regard, which threatens relationships (Soenens & Vansteenkiste,

Chapter 4, this volume). Excessive praise and praise for effort can lead members of stereotyped groups to question their belonging (Vial & Cimpian, Chapter 14, this volume). The role of praise in fostering or undermining close relationships is ripe for future investigation.

A note on praise, self-esteem, and egosystem motivation

Several of the chapters in this volume note the potential negative effects of praise—especially person praise and exaggerated praise—for people who are low in self-esteem (Ashokkumar & Swann, Chapter 2, this volume; Timoney & Wood, Chapter 9, this volume). For low self-esteem people, person praise or exaggerated praise may require more cognitive processing, and therefore prompt more preoccupation with their worth and value, than it does for high self-esteem people. High self-esteem people may typically accept praise as true, because it fits their positive self-views (see Blaine & Crocker, 1993, for a discussion). Low self-esteem people, and those with specific negative self-views, may need to think longer and harder about the meaning and implications of the praise, and how to integrate it with their beliefs about themselves, other people, and the world. They may ruminate about how to respond to the praise, the conditionality of the praiser's regard, and its implications for belonging. In particular, they may struggle with whether to accept the validity of the praise or reject it.

It is not that high self-esteem people lack egosystem motivation. Rather, egosystem motivation is likely to be activated under different circumstances for high self-esteem people. High self-esteem people tend to be surprised and wounded by criticism or rejection, which are discrepant from their positive self-views. For them, negative feedback may require more cognitive processing, and therefore more preoccupation with their worth and value (Blaine & Crocker, 1993). Faint praise, praise for effort, or praise given to other people may also require cognitive processing for high self-esteem people, because it is not as positive as expected.

In sum, although high and low self-esteem people react differently to praise and criticism or rejection, high self-esteem does not eliminate egosystem motivation. Everyone can be motivated by the egosystem under the right circumstances.

Egosystem motivation and giving praise

Although much of the research described in this volume focuses on the recipients of praise, egosystem motivation can also energize giving praise (Pomerantz, Ng, & Ng, Chapter 16, this volume). Praisers motivated by the egosystem view others as means or obstacles to satisfaction of their own needs and desires and give praise to manipulate or control others' behavior (Soenens & Vansteenkiste, Chapter 4, this volume). Parents, for example, may use praise to encourage their child to perform in ways that reflect well on the parents (Brummelman & Grapsas, Chapter 10, this volume). Praisers may give insincere or excessive praise, attempting to "manage" the recipients' insecurities, feelings, or self-esteem (Brummelman & Dweck,

Chapter 7, this volume; Lemay, Chapter 11, this volume; Rudy & Grusec, Chapter 12, this volume). These egosystem-driven reasons for giving praise may undermine recipients' trust, prompting recipients' preoccupation with their worth and value to the praiser.

Praisers' intentions may not be obvious, even to praisers, and some intentions of praisers might not clearly fit egosystem motivation. For example, when people give praise to relieve another's anxieties or insecurities, are they focused solely on what will support the recipient, or are they attempting to prove their support-iveness, or to reduce their own distress by getting the recipient to calm down?

Ecosystem motivation

In addition to having the capacity for egosystem motivation, all humans have the capacity for ecosystem motivation, which provides an alternative source of mo-tivation for giving and receiving praise, with fewer negative downstream conse-quences (Crocker & Canevello, 2012).

People with ecosystem motivation care about the well-being of others and want to act in ways that are constructive and supportive and do not harm others. They view the well-being of people in their interpersonal ecosystem as intercon-nected, so they think about events and interactions in terms of their implications for others' needs and desires in addition to their own. They view relationships as working in non-zero-sum ways, so what is good for another person is ultimately good for the ecosystem and therefore the self. In this system, it is not sufficient to appear supportive; people with ecosystem motivation want to provide sup-port that maintains, enhances, and protects others' well-being. Thus, ecosystem motivation predicts supportive and responsive (i.e., understanding, caring, and validating) behaviors, and increases in these behaviors over time.

The desire to act in ways that are constructive and supportive does not mean that people simply want to avoid conflict, please others, or be liked by others. As parents, teachers, and medical personnel know, acting in ways that support oth-ers' well-being sometimes involves giving constructive negative feedback, pre-venting others from harming themselves, and having limits or giving treatments that others resist or dislike (Zaki, 2014). Ecosystem motivation predicts raising issues and concerns with others, but in constructive ways—listening, trying to understand others' perspectives, identifying root causes of problems and difficul-ties, and feeling a sense of shared responsibility for resolving the issue (Canevello, Crocker, Lewis, & Hartsell, 2019). Thus, the goal to be constructive and sup-portive should not be confused with the goal to be positive or liked.

Praise as an activator of ecosystem motivation

Previous research shows that ecosystem motivation can be contagious—one person's ecosystem motivation predicts increases in their partner's ecosystem motivation over time (Canevello & Crocker, 2010). One mechanism for the contagion of ecosystem motivation is responsiveness; people with ecosystem motivation are understanding, caring, and validating of others. Others notice and are responsive in return, and they develop greater intentions to be support-ive and constructive. This suggests that when praise is given with the intention to be supportive and constructive, rather than with the intention to manipu-late or control another's behavior or emotions, praise may activate ecosystem motivation.

Benefits of ecosystem motivation

Ecosystem motivation has numerous benefits and few discernable costs (Crocker & Canevello, 2012). People with ecosystem motivation feel more cooperative with others, which in turn predicts feeling calm, clear, connected, and loving. They are more supportive and responsive to others and perceive others as more sup-portive and responsive to them, which predicts increased feelings of closeness, satisfaction, and commitment to relationship partners. They become more se-cure in their relationships over time. Ecosystem motivation predicts decreased symptoms of depression and anxiety over time in both clinical and nonclinical samples, in part because of positive effects on relationships (Crocker et al., 2010; Erickson et al., 2018). Thus, praise in the context of ecosystem motivation may benefit one's own and others' well-being and relationships.

Moreover, people with ecosystem motivation tend to be growth-oriented and have learning goals in achievement settings (Crocker & Canevello, 2012). Thus, praise that activates ecosystem motivation may foster both the motivation and the capacity to grow as a person. Not least, by focusing attention on what would be constructive and supportive of others, praise that activates ecosystem motivation may reduce preoccupation with one's worth and value, potentially freeing up cognitive capacity to analyze situations and problems, leading to more optimal judgment and decision-making.

Receiving praise in the ecosystem

What does it mean to receive praise in the ecosystem? This issue has not yet been explored in research, but extrapolation from previous research suggests some hypotheses. With ecosystem motivation, recipients view praise not as an attempt to manipulate or control them, but rather as help and support with their goals (Eskreis-Winkler & Fishbach, Chapter 6, this volume). Recipients might ask for more information about specific strengths and weaknesses in their work, or in themselves, so they can learn and grow. Praise can provide information about the difference recipients can make for others, and what they can do in the service of others (Rudy & Grusec, Chapter 12, this volume). Recipients may think not about what the praise means their worth or value, but rather about what it means for what they can contribute to the well-being of others and their interpersonal ecosystem in ways that are good for themselves.

In the ecosystem, recipients should respond to praise in ways that are good for themselves and others. For example, they may respond with gratitude for the support and feedback they receive, which may inspire acts of generosity, such as wanting to give support to others. Praise received with ecosystem motivation should build trust, closeness, and connections with others by communicating what the praiser appreciates about the recipient.

In sum, praise received in the ecosystem is viewed not as indicating one's worth and value, but rather as information about how one can make a difference for others. Learning to shift from thinking about what praise means about one's own worth and value to thinking about what praise means for the contributions people can make may enable people to learn and benefit from praise without the downsides of egosystem motivation. Praise that activates the ecosystem may be especially beneficial for people who are low in self-esteem and who tend to be especially preoccupied with the meaning of praise for their worth and value (Marigold, Holmes, & Ross, 2007).

Giving praise in the ecosystem

How can people give praise with ecosystem motivation? First and foremost, when people have ecosystem motivation, they intend to give praise that is constructive and supportive of the recipient's goals. Praise given with ecosystem motivation is responsive, caring, and validating. It is authentic and vulnerable, and communicates the difference the recipient has made to the praiser. Praise given with ecosystem motivation should foster ecosystem motivation in the recipient, potentially creating virtuous cycles that enhance well-being and relationships.

Conclusion

An integrative theoretical perspective promises not only to knit together the various threads of the research findings described in this volume but also to raise important questions not yet addressed and new avenues for research on praise. Here I offer one such integrative framework. I suggest that because people are social beings, the power of praise to be beneficial or toxic results from the social motivations that energize people when they give and receive praise. Specifically, I suggest that praise is toxic when it is energized by egosystem motivation, fostering preoccupation with the recipient's worth and value in their own and others' eyes. More speculatively, I suggest that praise may be most beneficial when it is energized by ecosystem motivation, focusing people's attention on how they can make a positive difference for others. From this perspective, the motivational, emotional, and interpersonal difficulties associated with praise result not just from the praise itself, or even from the specific type of praise (e.g., person praise or effort praise) provided. Rather, the intentions of praiser and the recipient can result in the same praise having very different effects.

REFERENCES

Baumeister, R. F., & Leary, M. R. (1995). The need to belong: Desire for interpersonal attachments as a fundamental human motivation. *Psychological Bulletin, 111*, 497–529.

Blaine, B., & Crocker, J. (1993). Self-esteem and self-serving biases in reactions to positive and negative events: An integrative review. In R. F. Baumeister (Ed.), *Self-esteem: The puzzle of low self-regard* (pp. 55–85). Hillsdale, NJ: Erlbaum.

Canevello, A., & Crocker, J. (2010). Creating good relationships: Responsiveness, relationship quality, and interpersonal goals. *Journal of Personality and Social Psychology, 99*, 78–106.

Canevello, A., Crocker, J., Lewis, K., & Hartsell, J. (2019). Compassionate goals, constructive approaches to interpersonal problems, and upset feelings in relationships. Manuscript in preparation.

Crocker, J., & Canevello, A. (2012). Consequences of self-image and compassionate goals. In P. Devine & A. Plant (Eds.), *Advances in experimental social psychology* (Vol. 45, pp. 229–277). San Diego, CA: Academic Press.

Crocker, J., Canevello, A., Breines, J. G., & Flynn, H. (2010). Interpersonal goals and change in anxiety and dysphoria in first-semester college students. *Journal of Personality and Social Psychology, 98*, 1009–1024.

Erickson, T. M., Granillo, M. T., Crocker, J., Abelson, J. L., Reas, H. E., & Quach, C. M. (2018). Compassionate and self-image goals as interpersonal maintenance factors in clinical depression and anxiety. *Journal of Clinical Psychology, 74*, 608–625.

Farson, R. E. (1963). Praise reappraised. *Harvard Business Review, 41*, 61–66.

Jiang, T., Canevello, A., & Crocker, J. (2019). How relationships foster thriving: Associations among compassionate goals in relationships, growth seeking, and academic self-regulation. Unpublished manuscript.

Marigold, D. C., Holmes, J. G., & Ross, M. (2007). Fostering relationship resilience: An intervention for low self-esteem individuals. *Journal of Experimental Social Psychology, 45*, 624–630.

Moeller, S. J., Crocker, J., & Bushman, B. J. (2009). Creating hostility and conflict: Effects of entitlement and self-image goals. *Journal of Experimental Social Psychology, 45*, 448–452.

Zaki, J. (2014). Empathy: A motivated account. *Psychological Bulletin, 140*, 1608–1647.

Zhang, L., & Baumeister, R. F. (2006). Your money or your self-esteem: Threatened egotism promotes costly entrapment in losing endeavors. *Personality and Social Psychology Bulletin, 32*, 881–893.

PART I

Central theories

1

PRAISE FROM A SELF-ENHANCEMENT PERSPECTIVE

More, I want more?

Frederik Anseel and Elena Martinescu

> How defenseless we are in the face of flattery.
> (Milan Kundera, *The Unbearable Lightness of Being*, 1984)

One of the earliest and most fundamental insights in the human psyche is that information about the self is not processed in a neutral or objective way. The self is the central point of reference for thinking, feeling, and making decisions. How people feel and think about themselves plays a crucial role in how they navigate their lives (e.g., Allport, 1937; James, 1890). An extensive stream of research in social psychology has systematically examined how selecting, processing, remembering, and reacting to information about the self is driven by an intricate combination of motives. Perhaps the strongest motive to drive information processing is self-enhancement. People have an innate tendency to evaluate themselves favorably and have a strong desire to maintain favorable feelings about themselves. Various human attitudes, cognitions, and behaviors can be traced back to this basic self-enhancement motive (for an overview of empirical findings, see Sedikides & Gregg, 2008), with praise probably being the most visible manifestation of the self-enhancement motive. In this chapter, we aim to summarize how self-enhancement theory advances our understanding of the psychology of praise. In doing so, we briefly review theoretical debates and real-world manifestations of praise. By identifying boundary conditions to self-enhancement-driven praise, we contribute to our understanding of when and why praise might have adaptive and maladaptive effects.

Praise through a self-enhancement lens

The self-enhancement motive

In an early review on how people react to appraisals about themselves, Shrauger (1975) was one of the first to coin the term "self-enhancement," as the desire of people to think favorably of themselves. The desire to think well of oneself has emerged as one of the strongest human motivations, deeply wired in the brain and observed in most cultures (Cai, Wu, Shi, Gu, & Sedikides, 2016). Once formed, the self-concept is fairly stable and generally positive. Because maintaining positive evaluations about the self is adaptive and helps people maintain their mental health (Taylor, Kemeny, Reed, Bower, & Grunewald, 2000), people will go out of their way to acquire information that sustains these positive self-conceptions and try to protect their self-concept from negative information. Given that self-enhancement research has mostly focused on how people deal with the positivity or negativity of self-relevant information, the self-enhancement literature should be particularly relevant in understanding the psychology of praise. More specifically, because such self-relevant information is often encountered in the form of feedback, the psychology of praise is perhaps best understood by examining how people seek, react to, and process feedback (e.g., Anseel, Beatty, Shen, Lievens, & Sackett, 2015; Anseel, Lievens, & Levy, 2007). Feedback is generally defined as "actions taken by (an) external agent(s) to provide information regarding some aspect(s) of one's task performance" (Kluger & DeNisi, 1996, p. 255). Feedback information is not neutral to the feedback receiver; by its very nature, it contains information that signals positive and negative aspects about the self, and as such, feedback might promote or hurt one's feelings of self-worth. To avoid threats to the self-concept, people tend to embrace positive feedback and dismiss or avoid negative feedback. Studies on feedback–seeking behavior have shown that individuals prefer interaction partners that are expected to give positive rather than negative feedback, for example, by seeking less feedback from managers who are known to give harsh evaluations (Steelman, Levy, & Snell, 2004). People with low performance expectations refrain from seeking feedback more than those with high expectations, to avoid the drop in self-worth associated with negative feedback (Tsui, Ashford, St. Clair, & Xin, 1995). More generally, people shape their social environments to increase the likelihood of receiving praise (e.g., Hepper, Hart, Gregg, & Sedikides, 2011). Furthermore, people process positive self-relevant information faster than negative self-relevant information and spend more time reading favorable information (for reviews, see Anseel et al., 2007; Sedikides & Strube, 1997). Thus, reactions to praise and its counterpart, criticism, are typically based on a simple, almost reflex-like cognitive appraisal of the feedback message: "If feedback is negative, then dismiss it as inaccurate, but if feedback is positive, then embrace it as the truth" (Anseel & Lievens, 2006).

As praise is not always easily given, people develop different strategies to acquire positive information about themselves, even if this does not involve explicit feedback from others. For instance, people connect with or distance themselves from others to put themselves in a favorable light and, when cued to remember a performance event, will report having been praised, while in reality no feedback was given at all (Sedikides & Gregg, 2008). Furthermore, in the absence of public praise, gossip or talking informally about others who are not present is a covert strategy for self-enhancement. People are especially interested in gossip about others who are similar to themselves, as they can draw relevant social comparisons from this gossip. Hearing negative gossip about others is self-enhancing, making people feel they are doing better than the target (Martinescu, Janssen, & Nijstad, 2014). People use gossip to self-enhance by denigrating their competitors and increasing perceptions of their own attractiveness (Reynolds, Baumeister, & Maner, 2018). Furthermore, being praised by others through positive gossip feels good, to the same extent as receiving direct positive feedback (Martinescu, Janssen, & Nijstad, 2019).

Positivity, consistency, or accuracy?

Self-enhancement is pervasive when dealing with feedback, suggesting that this motive is all-overpowering. For instance, an early study on praise described people as being driven to think about themselves "as favorably as they can get away with" (Smith, 1968). Are people insatiable when it comes to praise? Do people only want more positive feedback?

This question has been the subject of a fierce scientific debate in the past few decades, examining the primacy of self-enhancement. How people process information appears to be determined by self-enhancement but also various other self-evaluation motives, which nuances the seemingly overpowering human need for praise. For instance, a self-verification motive may drive people to maintain consistency between their self-views and new self-relevant information, even when those self-views are negative, sometimes motivating people to prefer negative feedback over praise (Swann, Rentfrow, & Guin, 2002). Similarly, people may seek diagnostic self-relevant information that can reduce uncertainty about an aspect of the self (Trope & Neter, 1994). According to the self-assessment motive, people seek diagnostic information, regardless of its positive or negative implications for the self and regardless of whether the information affirms or challenges existing self-conceptions. Although self-enhancement is dominant, the other self-motives have adaptive value and work in concert to determine cognition, emotion, and behavior (Sedikides & Strube, 1997).

Boundaries to embracing praise

Studying the interplay between different self-evaluation motives has been instrumental in identifying those conditions wherein people may refrain from their quest for praise, in favor of other adaptive behaviors. The urge to seek praise is especially strong in psychologically "unsafe" environments, where individuals' positive self-concept is threatened (e.g., by the mere prospect of receiving negative information). To reestablish a feeling of overall positivity, individuals are likely to exhibit behaviors that reaffirm the self (Campbell & Sedikides, 1999). However, research has shown that self-enhancement can be curtailed. For instance, seeking and receiving praise is limited by cognitive constraints. If people feel accountable, by anticipating that they have to explain their self-views to an audience or will be individually assessed by others, they are more likely to acknowledge weaknesses (Sedikides, Herbst, Hardin, & Dardis, 2002). Seeking and embracing praise also becomes less likely when people are asked to elaborate on their feedback or generate reasons for why they might perhaps not be doing as well as they initially thought (Anseel, Lievens, & Schollaert, 2009). Similarly, when cognitive resources are plentiful or people are encouraged to reconsider, the self-assessment motive often prevails (Trope, 1986), leading people to seek out accurate instead of positive feedback. Finally, individual differences such as a learning goal orientation or a growth mind-set may lead people to seek negative feedback instead of praise (VandeWalle, 2003), because negative feedback is more instrumental for learning than praise.

Identifying the boundaries of embracing praise is crucial to our understanding of learning and development. Negative feedback is a key aspect of how employees regulate their efforts and performance in sports, in education, or at work (Kluger & DeNisi, 1996). People need information about their current performance to signal how actual performance levels may be discrepant from their goals or perceived performance levels and guide and adjust their effort, work strategies, or their goals. Thus, identifying the boundaries of self-enhancement strivings is important if we want to understand how praise may not only satisfy self-enhancement needs but also regulate learning and development.

New developments

Current theoretical issues

A theoretical issue that has remained on the research agenda is the adaptive value of self-enhancement relative to potential negative consequences. Recent research supports the idea that self-enhancement is generally beneficial, because it increases psychological resilience and adjustment (Dufner, Gebauer, Sedikides, & Denissen, 2019). For example, after self-enhancement on a task-relevant aspect of the self, people have higher beliefs in their ability to complete the task, increasing effort and performance (O'Mara & Gaertner, 2017).

However, when self-enhancement is disconnected from reality and rationality or is not believable, it can contribute to maladjustment. Baumeister and colleagues (2003) warn that indiscriminate praise promotes narcissism, whereas praise should be used sparingly as a reward for progress or for socially desirable behavior. For example, business leaders who receive high levels of praise and few disagreeing opinions make more biased strategic decisions, ultimately harming their performance (Park et al., 2011). Inflated praise makes children emotionally vulnerable and has been found to harm their self-efficacy beliefs (Brummelman et al., 2014). Similarly, overly positive self-assessments may instigate psychological distress and vulnerability to depression (Kim & Chiu, 2011).

Thus, one important question is how to balance the benefits and drawbacks of seeking praise and self-enhancement. Self-affirmation research suggests that once people reach an adequate level of positive self-regard, they cope better with self-threats (Steele, 1988). Therefore, self-enhancement might be a maintenance motive rather than an unstoppable driver for more positivity: once we have self-enhanced, we may be better equipped to withstand challenges to the self-concept.

However, not all self-enhancing information genuinely reflects one's qualities, progress, good behavior, or praiseworthy results. Others who feed individuals' self-enhancement desires may have ulterior motives, such as manipulating their needs, attitudes, and consumption behaviors. For example, social media platforms, which offer vast opportunity for self-enhancement, have been suggested to deliver instant gratification and to be addictive, with an estimated 210 million people who are compulsive, pathological Internet users (Longstreet & Brooks, 2017). Presumably partly driven by the quest for praise, employees and students are increasingly drawn to social media for "likes" and "views," which results in lower focus and performance, as well as higher anxiety and mental health issues (Gupta & Irwin, 2016; Li & Lin, 2019). Due to the abundance of unfavorable social comparisons people can draw between themselves and others in online environments, people might feel worse about themselves and experience loneliness, low self-worth, body shame, and poor mental health (Hanna et al., 2017). Online self-enhancement risks introducing a vicious cycle: When people are hungry for praise, they post self-flattering content. If these posts do not receive the amount of praise they hoped for, this might further fuel their need for self-enhancement.

Social media has become embedded in current society and culture, making it difficult to discontinue usage, in fear of becoming disconnected from others, and missing out on important news and invitations (Bullinger & Vie, 2017). Therefore, an interesting public debate and research topic that is taking shape is whether institutional policies should regulate or nudge the use of these platforms in certain contexts, acknowledging that individuals themselves may not be best equipped to do so.

"Real-world" applications

The abundant research on self-enhancement has generated a wide range of applications. Knowledge that people who feel accepted by others are less likely to feel threatened by negative feedback and are more receptive to criticism (Trope & Neter, 1994) has led to the development of the "sandwich feedback technique," where negative feedback is delivered alongside praise. Although somewhat contested (Brown, Farnham, & Cook, 2002), this is a widely popular way of delivering performance feedback.

Marketers and advertisers rely heavily on self-enhancement insights. Advertisers strive to create campaigns that will be shared online, helping them reach target audiences through electronic word of mouth. People are inclined to share content that makes them look well informed, helpful, or funny (Berger & Milkman, 2012). Self-enhancement applications also include fundraising and crowdsourcing on social media. Facebook users have raised over 1 billion US dollars between 2015 and late 2018 (Facebook, 2018). By donating money to fundraisers set up by their contacts or by calling for donations for noble causes themselves, people signal socially desirable behavior and are likely to receive praise and support. This is in line with evidence showing that self-enhancement motivates acting morally in public, but not necessarily in private (Dong, van Prooijen, & van Lange, 2019).

In sum, self-enhancement is a powerful driver of behavior, which is manifested in ever-more diverse ways, as new communication technologies arise. Although maintaining a positive and optimistic self-view is essential for well-being, promoting psychological resilience and self-efficacy, the pursuit of praise and self-enhancement can also fuel negative self-views, anxiety, and vulnerability to addiction or manipulation. In a sense, our relationship with praise can be summarized by the famous dictum of physicist Paracelsus: "All substances are poisons; there is none of which is not a poison. The right dose differentiates a poison from a remedy" (Bernoulli, 1994). The self-enhancement literature seems to have attained a mature stage, allowing it to make more specific predictions and refined recommendations about the exact inflection points where positive self-enhancement effects may turn into maladjusted cognition and behaviors that ultimately hurt one's life satisfaction and mental health.

References

Allport, G. W. (1937). *Personality: A psychological interpretation.* New York, NY: Holt.

Anseel, F., Beatty, A. S., Shen, W., Lievens, F., & Sackett, P. R. (2015). How are we doing after 30 years? A meta-analytic review of the antecedents and outcomes of feedback-seeking behavior. *Journal of Management, 41,* 318–348.

Anseel, F., & Lievens, F. (2006). Certainty as a moderator of feedback reactions? A test of the strength of the self-verification motive. *Journal of Occupational and Organizational Psychology, 79,* 533–551.

Anseel, F., Lievens, F., & Levy, P. E. (2007). A self-motives perspective on feedback-seeking behavior: Linking organizational behavior and social psychology research. *International Journal of Management Reviews, 9,* 211–236.

Anseel, F., Lievens, F., & Schollaert, E. (2009). Reflection as a strategy to enhance task performance after feedback. *Organizational Behavior and Human Decision Processes, 110,* 23–35.

Baumeister, R. F., Campbell, J. D., Krueger, J. I., & Vohs, K. D. (2003). Does high self-esteem cause better performance, interpersonal success, or healthier lifestyles? *Psychological Science in the Public Interest, 4*(1), 1–44.

Berger, J., & Milkman, K. (2012). What makes online content viral? *Journal of Marketing Research, 49*, 192–205.

Bernoulli, R. (1994). Paracelsus—physician, reformer, philosopher, scientist. *Cellular and Molecular Life Sciences, 50*, 334–338.

Brown, J. D., Farnham, S. D., & Cook, K. E. (2002). Emotional responses to changing feedback: Is it better to have won and lost than never to have won at all? *Journal of Personality, 70*, 127–141.

Brummelman, E., Thomaes, S., Orobio de Castro, B., Overbeek, G., & Bushman, B. J. (2014). "That's not just beautiful—that's incredibly beautiful!": The adverse impact of inflated praise on children with low self-esteem. *Psychological Science, 25*, 728–735.

Bullinger, C., & Vie, S. (2017). After a decade of social media: Abstainers and ex-users. In D. M. Walls & S. Vie (Eds.), *Social writing/social media: Publics, presentations, and pedagogies* (pp. 69–88). Fort Collins, CO: University Press of Colorado.

Cai, H., Wu, L., Shi, Y., Gu, R., & Sedikides, C. (2016). Self-enhancement among Westerners and Easterners: A cultural neuroscience approach. *Social Cognitive and Affective Neuroscience, 11*, 1569–1578.

Campbell, W. K., & Sedikides, C. (1999). Self-threat magnifies the self-serving bias: A meta-analytic integration. *Review of General Psychology, 3*, 23–43.

Dong, M., van Prooijen, J-W., & van Lange, P. A. M. (2019). Self-enhancement in moral hypocrisy: Moral superiority and moral identity are about better appearances. *PLOS ONE, 14*, e0219382.

Dufner, M., Gebauer, J. E., Sedikides, C., & Denissen, J. J. (2019). Self-enhancement and psychological adjustment: A meta-analytic review. *Personality and Social Psychology Review, 23*, 48–72.

Facebook. (2018). People raise over $1 billion for the causes they care about on Facebook. Retrieved from https://newsroom.fb.com/news/2018/11/people-raise-over-1-billion/

Gupta, N., & Irwin, J. D. (2016). In-class distractions: The role of Facebook and the primary learning task. *Computers in Human Behavior, 55*, 1165–1178.

Hanna, E., Ward, L. M., Seabrook, R. C., Jerald, M., Reed, L., Giaccardi, S., & Lippman, J. R. (2017). Contributions of social comparison and self-objectification in mediating associations between Facebook use and emergent adults' psychological well-being. *Cyberpsychology, Behavior, and Social Networking, 20*, 172–179.

Hepper, E. G., Hart, C. M., Gregg, A. P., & Sedikides, C. (2011). Motivated expectations of positive feedback in social interactions. *The Journal of Social Psychology, 151*, 455–477.

James, W. (1890). *The principles of psychology.* New York, NY: Henry Holt.

Kim, Y., & Chiu, C. (2011). Emotional costs of inaccurate self-assessments: Both self-effacement and self-enhancement can lead to dejection. *Emotion, 11*, 1096–1104.

Kluger, A. N., & DeNisi, A. (1996). The effects of feedback interventions on performance: A historical review, a meta-analysis, and a preliminary feedback intervention theory. *Psychological Bulletin, 119*, 254–284.

Li, L., & Lin, T. T. C. (2019). Smartphones at work: A qualitative exploration of psychological antecedents and impacts of work-related smartphone dependency. *International Journal of Qualitative Methods, 18*, 1–12.

Longstreet, P., & Brooks, S. (2017). Life satisfaction: A key to managing internet & social media addiction. *Technology in Society, 50*, 73–77.

Martinescu, E., Janssen, O., & Nijstad, B. A. (2014). Tell me the gossip: The self-evaluative function of receiving gossip about others. *Personality and Social Psychology Bulletin, 40*, 1668–1680.

Martinescu, E., Janssen, O., & Nijstad, B. A. (2019). Emotional and behavioral responses to gossip about the self. *Frontiers in Psychology, 9*, 2603.

O'Mara, E. M., & Gaertner, L. (2017). Does self-enhancement facilitate task performance? *Journal of Experimental Psychology: General, 146*, 442–455.

Park, S., Westphal, J., & Stern, I. (2011). Set up for a fall: The insidious effects of flattery and opinion conformity toward corporate leaders. *Administrative Science Quarterly, 56*, 257–302.

Reynolds, T., Baumeister, R. F., & Maner, J. K. (2018). Competitive reputation manipulation: Women strategically transmit social information about romantic rivals. *Journal of Experimental Social Psychology, 78*, 195–209.

Sedikides, C., Herbst, K. C., Hardin, D. P., & Dardis, G. J. (2002). Accountability as a deterrent to self-enhancement: The search for mechanisms. *Journal of Personality and Social Psychology, 83*, 592–605.

Sedikides, C., & Gregg, A. P. (2008). Self-enhancement: Food for thought. *Perspectives on Psychological Science, 3*, 102–116.

Sedikides, C., & Strube, M. J. (1997) Self-evaluation: To thine own self be good, to thine own self be sure, to thine own self be true, and to thine own self be better. In L. Berkowitz, (Ed.), *Advances in experimental social psychology*, (Vol. 29, pp. 209–269). New York, NY: Academic Press.

Shrauger, J. S. (1975). Responses to evaluation as a function of initial self-perceptions. *Psychological Bulletin, 82*, 581–596.

Smith, M. B. (1968). The self and cognitive consistency. In R. P. Abelson, E. Aronson, W. J. McGuire, T. M. Newcomb, M. J. Rosenberg, & P. H. Tannenbaum (Eds.), *Theories of cognitive consistency: A sourcebook* (pp. 366–373). Chicago, IL: Rand McNally.

Steele, C. M. (1988). The psychology of self-affirmation: Sustaining the integrity of the self. In L. Berkowitz (Ed.), *Advances in experimental social psychology* (Vol. 21, pp. 261–302). San Diego, CA: Academic Press.

Steelman, L. A., Levy, P. E., & Snell, A. F. (2004). The feedback environment scale: Construct definition, measurement and validation. *Educational and Psychological Measurement, 64*, 165–184.

Swann Jr, W. B., Rentfrow, P. J., & Guinn, J. (2002). Self-verification: The search for coherence. In M. Leary & J. Tangney, (Eds.), *Handbook of self and identity* (pp. 367–383). New York, NY: Guilford Press.

Taylor, S. E., Kemeny, M. E., Reed, G. M., Bower, J. E., & Gruenewald, T. L. (2000). Psychological resources, positive illusions, and health. *American Psychologist, 55*, 99–109.

Trope, Y. (1986). Self-enhancement and self-assessment in achievement behavior. In Y. Trope (Ed.), *Handbook of motivation and cognition: Foundations of social behavior* (pp. 350–378). New York, NY: Guilford Press.

Trope, Y., & Neter, E. (1994). Reconciling competing motives in self-evaluation: The role of self-control in feedback seeking. *Journal of Personality and Social Psychology, 66*, 646–657.

Tsui, A. S., Ashford, S. J., St. Clair, L., & Xin, K. R. 1995. Dealing with discrepant expectations: Response strategies and managerial effectiveness. *Academy of Management Journal, 38*, 1515–1543.

VandeWalle, D. (2003). A goal orientation model of feedback-seeking behavior. *Human Resource Management Review, 13*, 581–604.

2

THE SABOTEUR WITHIN

Self-verification strivings can make praise toxic

Ashwini Ashokkumar and William B. Swann, Jr.

> Praise was a poison to me; I choked on it. I wanted the professor to shout at me, wanted it so deeply I felt dizzy from the deprivation. The ugliness of me had to be given expression.
>
> (Westover, 2018, p. 277)

Unexpected praise was terrifying to Tara Westover, author of the award-winning memoir, *Educated*. Although few people develop such an extreme aversion to praise, most feel wary when they receive praise that challenges their firmly held self-views. In this chapter, we use self-verification theory (Swann, 1983, 2012) to illuminate this phenomenon. The theory proposes that people want to be seen as they see themselves, even if their self-views are negative. As a result, people with negative self-views recoil at evaluations that seem overly positive and embrace evaluations that seem appropriately negative. We begin by considering why this pattern emerges.

The function of self-knowledge and self-verification strivings

Humans are born with an instinctual preference for social approval. As early as 4.5 months, infants prefer voices that have the melodic contours of acceptance rather than rejection (Fernald, 1989). Similarly, 5-month-olds prefer gazing at smiling faces over non-smiling ones (Shapiro, Eppler, Haith, & Reis, 1987). Later during development, children endorse positive views of themselves before embracing negative self-views (e.g., Benenson & Dweck, 1986). Among adults, there is widespread consensus that people prefer praise, at least in Western societies. Support for this belief comes from evidence that people report liking positive feedback more than negative feedback, even when the feedback seems overly positive (Kwang & Swann, 2010).

But if people are fundamentally motivated to acquire positive evaluations, why do individuals like Tara eschew such evaluations? The answer emerges from a consideration of how children form their self-views. From a very early age, children learn that others evaluate them on the basis of their personal characteristics, abilities, and so on. Children carefully note these evaluations and use them to form self-views (Mead, 1934). Once formed, these self-views serve as proxies for how people fit into the social hierarchy (Leary & Baumeister, 2000). Individuals who suffer from maltreatment as children often conclude that they are at the bottom of this hierarchy. In extreme cases like Tara's, they may even decide that they are worthless.

Yet if it is clear why people might form negative self-views, it is less obvious why they should wish to preserve these self-views. After all, working to preserve negative self-views will clearly frustrate people's desire for praise. If the self-enhancement motive is as fundamental as some theorists claim it is (Alicke & Sedikides, 2009), why did Tara report feeling "dizzy from the deprivation" when the professor praised her?

To understand Tara's desire for self-verification, consider the important role that self-views play in mental life. Prominent self-theorist Howard Murphy once noted that self-knowledge "serves as the chart by which the individual navigates. If it is lost, he can make only impulsive runs in fair weather. The ship drifts helplessly whenever storms arise" (1947, p. 715). A case study reported by the neurologist Oliver Sacks (1985) shows how losing a stable sense of self can cause an individual to feel adrift. Due to chronic alcohol abuse, patient William Thompson suffered from memory loss so profound that he forgot who he was. Lacking stable self-views, Thompson did not know how to act toward people and was unable to maintain meaningful relationships with them. His case study illustrates why mechanisms designed to stabilize identities would have been selected for during human evolutionary history: stable identities are required for harmonious relationships, which in turn facilitate effective division of labor and accomplishment of objectives.

Stable self-views may not only serve the pragmatic function of helping people regulate their social relationships but also serve the epistemic function of enabling people to make predictions about their worlds. This will reassure people that things are as they should be, fostering a sense of coherence and place. In fact, firmly held self-views will serve as the centerpiece of knowledge systems and thus determine the viability of that system. It is thus unsurprising that by mid-childhood, a preference for evaluations that confirm and stabilize self-views emerges (e.g., Cassidy, Ziv, Mehta, & Feeney, 2003). This preference will have a profound impact on people's reactions to praise.

The fleeting gleam of praise

The preference for praise that all humans seem to be born with is intrinsically simple. That is, as soon as people recognize that an evaluation is positive, they develop an affinity for it. Self-verification strivings, however, are more complex. For self-verification to occur, in addition to recognizing an evaluation as positive or negative, people must also compare it to their self-view to determine whether the evaluation is self-verifying or non-verifying. This comparison process leads to a subsequent preference for self-verifying evaluations that may override the initial preference for a positive evaluation. The foregoing logic suggests that if people with low self-esteem are prevented from fully processing praise, they may embrace it because they have not yet realized that it is not self-verifying. That is, people with negative self-views may find praise appealing immediately after receiving it, but this appeal may be short-lived and fragile. The results of three studies support this reasoning.

One study employed a "think aloud" methodology (Swann, Stein-Seroussi, & Giesler, 1992). People with positive and negative self-views thought out loud into a tape recorder as they chose to interact with either an evaluator who provided positive evaluations or one who provided negative evaluations. Analyses of the tape recordings revealed that even people with negative self-views were initially smitten by the favorable evaluation before becoming wary of it:

> I like the [favorable] evaluation but I am not sure that it is, ah, correct, maybe. It _sounds_ good, but [the negative evaluator]… seems to know more about me.

Consistent with self-verification theory, people with negative self-views tended to ultimately choose the negative evaluator. Comments by people with negative self-views revealed that they were drawn by the match between the partner's evaluation and their own self-view:

> I think that's pretty close to the way I am. [The negative evaluator] better reflects my own view of myself, from experience.

Follow-up studies experimentally tested the idea that positivity strivings occur before verification strivings. When forced to choose between two evaluators quickly, participants selected the positive evaluator regardless of their self-view. Only when given time to ponder their decision did participants with negative self-views choose negative, self-verifying partners. Similarly, depriving people of cognitive resources by having them rehearse a phone number while they chose an interaction partner had a similar effect of short-circuiting self-verification strivings. As a result, even persons with negative self-views chose positive partners while resource-deprived (Swann, Hixon, Stein-Seroussi, & Gilbert, 1990).

In naturally occurring relationships, wherein people have plenty of time to process the evaluations they receive from others, self-verification strivings should cause people with negative self-views to eschew praise. One set of researchers (Kille, Eibach, Wood, & Holmes, 2017) examined the role of self-verification in response to compliments from romantic relationship partners. Consistent with self-verification theory, individuals with negative self-views devalued their partners' compliments, citing discrepancies between the positive information conveyed in the compliment and their own self-views. Similarly, when people received overly positive feedback regarding their group identities, they responded to this non-verifying feedback by derogating those who delivered the feedback (Vázquez, Gomez, & Swann, 2018).

Self-verification strivings may cause people with low self-esteem to not only express ambivalence about praise but also withdraw from persons who praised them. In two independent investigations (De La Ronde & Swann, 1998; Swann, De La Ronde & Hixon, 1994), married persons rated themselves and their partner on a series of qualities (e.g., intelligence) and then rated the quality of their relationships. Consistent with the idea that the gleam of praise is fleeting for people with negative self-views, such individuals were less committed to spouses who appraised them positively. Later studies revealed that individuals whose negative self-views were not verified by their partner were especially likely to divorce their partners (e.g., Burke & Harrod, 2005). Apparently, people preferred self-verifying evaluations to non-verifying evaluations even when the self-verifying evaluations were negative.

One reason underlying the counterintuitive finding that people with negative self-views prefer self-verifying, negative evaluations could be that self-verifying negative evaluations are reassuring, while non-verifying evaluations provoke anxiety. For example, researchers (Wood, Heimpel, Newby-Clark, & Ross, 2005) contrasted the reactions of high and low self-esteem participants to success. Whereas high self-esteem persons reacted quite favorably to success, low self-esteem participants reported being anxious and concerned, apparently because they found success to be surprising and unsettling. Similarly, others (Ayduk, Gyurak, Akinola, & Mendes, 2013) observed participants' cardiovascular responses to positive and negative evaluations. When people with negative self-views received positive feedback, their cardiovascular reactions (i.e., blood pressure reactivity as well as negative facial expressions and body posture) indicated that they felt "threatened." In contrast, when participants with negative self-views received negative feedback, their cardiovascular reactions indicated that they were "galvanized" (i.e., aroused in a manner associated with approach motivation). The opposite pattern emerged for people with positive self-views.

How can we get individuals with negative self-views to embrace praise?

Even though people with negative self-views prefer self-verifying negative evaluations, it may not always be adaptive for them to eschew praise. For example, self-verification strivings may thwart positive change and cause people with negative self-views to tolerate poor treatment from others ranging from disparaging marriage partners (Swann & Predmore, 1985) to exploitative employers (Wiesenfeld, Swann, Brockner, & Bartel, 2007). The story of Tara Westover with which we opened this chapter represents a case in point. Decades of abuse by family members convinced her that she was worthless, and it took years of support from key people in her life, psychotherapy, and success in her career to reverse the effects of her early experiences. Yet, in many respects, she was very fortunate, as her many talents and guidance from those who loved her enabled her to extricate herself from a horrific life situation. In Tara's case and similar ones, a key challenge is bringing people with negative self-views to accept praise.

Given that persons with low self-esteem perceive praise as toxic because it feels self-discrepant, reducing perceptions of being misunderstood should help them benefit from praise. A potential solution may be to simultaneously verify a person's perception of themselves (e.g. "I agree that you may have some negative qualities that don't matter to me") but also encourage them to recognize positive aspects of themselves. Some studies have in fact shown that successes and compliments can be reframed in ways that make them less threatening. For example, Zunick and colleagues (Zunick, Fazio, & Vasey, 2015) identified a way to enable people with low self-esteem benefit from positive evaluations based on their past successes. Their studies introduced a "directed abstraction" writing task, wherein participants considered a past success (e.g., in public speaking) and then wrote about "why" they were successful. By presupposing that people were responsible for their success, the manipulation was able to direct those with negative self-views to generalize from that success, report higher ability levels, and even persist in the face of subsequent failure. Marigold, Holmes, and Ross (2007) focused on compliments in romantic relationships. They discovered that reframing a partner's past compliments in an abstract manner (e.g., by writing about "why" their partner "admired" them) led persons with low self-esteem to report increased happiness, state self-esteem, and evaluations of their relationship. In fact, these effects were still evident two weeks after the intervention. Follow-up studies discovered that the reframing manipulation also decreased negative behavioral responses to relationship threats among low self-esteem individuals (Marigold, Holmes, & Ross, 2010). Apparently, reflecting on the meaning and significance of a compliment persuaded these participants to perceive their partner's positive evaluation as enduring (e.g., "She appreciates that I am thoughtful") rather than as a one-time incident (e.g., "She said I was thoughtful"). Importantly, these researchers warn that such abstract reframing interventions will be effective only insofar as they "direct those with negative self-views towards positive generalizations" (Zunick et al., 2015, p. 16). This means that some types of abstract reframing can backfire. For example, abstract reframing of the content of the compliment itself (i.e., conceptualizing it at an abstract manner that focuses on meaning) can be harmful because it may trigger a conflict between the compliment and the individual's self-views. In contrast, concrete construal of the compliment (i.e., conceptualizing it at a concrete, behavioral level) allows for processing the compliment in isolation and avoiding integration with the individual's self-theories (Kille et al., 2017). As a result, persons with low self-esteem who processed a compliment in a concrete (vs. abstract) way were just as gratified by the praise as persons with high self-esteem.

In short, it is possible to detoxify praise for persons with negative self-views by framing it in ways that minimize the threat to their self-theories. Carefully framed praise may allow those with negative self-views to benefit from praise, but such interventions have so far been shown to have only short-term effects. Given that the toxicity of praise experienced by some is produced by their negative self-views, perhaps the ultimate solution would be to actually change their self-theories. One possibility begins by leveraging naturally occurring contexts in which people with negative self-views tolerate praise. Consider dating relationships. Although married people display a clear preference for self-verifying partners, people who are dating display a preference for positive partners, even when they have negative self-views (Swann et al., 1994). Apparently, while dating, people are most concerned with keeping the relationship alive, but this unalloyed desire for positive evaluations is replaced by a desire for self-verification as they grow more confident that the partner is "hooked" (Campbell, Lackenbauer, & Muise, 2006; Swann et al., 1994). Conceivably, people with negative self-views could be convinced to continue to suspend their desire for self-verification until they actually come to internalize relatively positive self-views through a self-perception process (Bem, 1972).

Conclusion

As we have highlighted here, praise can have counterintuitive effects when it contradicts one's firmly held self-views. Non-verifying praise is particularly harmful to people who suffer from low self-esteem and depression because it threatens their firmly held negative self-views. For these individuals, praise is not just ineffective, it can be toxic. They may therefore habitually avoid praise and instead select contexts and relationship partners that raise the chances that they will receive verification for their unfounded negative self-views. As a result, they may get trapped in a perpetual cycle of life experiences that feel safe and predictable despite being objectively problematic. Fortunately, recent work suggests that it *is* possible to detoxify praise for persons with low self-esteem, at least in the short term, by framing it in ways that minimize threat. Yet, for those with low self-esteem, the ultimate end to harmful self-verifying cycles may require improving their self-esteem. It is sobering that decades after self-verification theory was first introduced, we still know precious little about how to achieve lasting improvements in self-esteem, which perhaps reflects the difficulty of this endeavor. Yet, as stories like Tara's demonstrate, it is clearly possible for people who harbor negative conceptions of self to enjoy dramatic improvements in their conceptions of self. A key challenge for future researchers will be to engineer interventions that make Tara's extraordinary odyssey commonplace.

References

Alicke, M. D., & Sedikides, C. (2009). Self-enhancement and self-protection: What they are and what they do. *European Review of Social Psychology, 20*(1), 1–48.

Ayduk, Ö., Gyurak, A., Akinola, M., & Mendes, W. B. (2013). Consistency over flattery: Self-verification processes revealed in implicit and behavioral responses to feedback. *Social Psychological and Personality Science, 4*, 538–545.

Bem, D. J. (1972). Self-perception theory. In L. Berkowitz (Ed.), *Advances in experimental social psychology* (Vol. 6, pp. 1–62). New York, NY: Academic Press.

Benenson, J. F., & Dweck, C. S. (1986). The development of trait explanations and self-evaluations in the academic and social domains. *Child Development, 57*, 1179–1187.

Burke, P. J., & Harrod, M. M. (2005). Too much of a good thing? *Social Psychology Quarterly, 68*, 359–374.

Campbell, L., Lackenbauer, S. D., & Muise, A. (2006). When is being known or adored by romantic partners most beneficial? Self-perceptions, relationship length, and responses to partner's verifying and enhancing appraisals. *Personality and Social Psychology Bulletin, 32*, 1283–1294.

Cassidy, J., Ziv, Y., Mehta, T. G., & Feeney, B. C. (2003). Feedback seeking in children and adolescents: Associations with self-perceptions, attachment representations, and depression. *Child Development, 74*, 612–628.

De La Ronde, C., & Swann, W. B. Jr. (1998). Partner verification: Restoring shattered images of our intimates. *Journal of Personality and Social Psychology, 75*, 374–382.

Fernald, A. (1989). Intonation and communicative intent in mothers' speech to infants: Is the melody the message? *Child Development, 60*, 1497–1510.

Kille, D. R., Eibach, R. P., Wood, J. V., & Holmes, J. G. (2017). Who can't take a compliment? The role of construal level and self-esteem in accepting positive feedback from close others. *Journal of Experimental Social Psychology, 68*, 40–49.

Kwang, T. & Swann, W. B., Jr. (2010). Do people embrace praise even when they feel unworthy? A review of critical tests of self-enhancement versus self-verification. *Personality and Social Psychology Review, 14*, 263–280.Leary, M. R., & Baumeister, R. F. (2000). The nature and function of self-esteem: Sociometer theory. In M. P. Zanna (Ed.), *Advances in experimental social psychology* (Vol. 32, pp. 1–62). New York, NY: Academic Press.

Marigold, D. C., Holmes, J. G., & Ross, M. (2007). More than words: Reframing compliments from romantic partners fosters security in low self-esteem individuals. *Journal of Personality and Social Psychology, 92*, 232–248.

Marigold, D. C., Holmes, J. G., & Ross, M. (2010). Fostering relationship resilience: An intervention for low self-esteem individuals. *Journal of Experimental Social Psychology, 46*, 624–630.

Mead, G. H. (1934). *Mind, self and society.* Chicago, IL: University of Chicago Press.

Murphy, G. (1947). *Personality: A biosocial approach to origins and structure.* New York, NY: Harper and Brothers.

Sacks, O. (1985). *The man who mistook his wife for a hat and other clinical tales.* New York, NY: Simon and Shuster.

Shapiro, B., Eppler, M., Haith, M., & Reis, H. (1987, April). *An event analysis of facial attractiveness and expressiveness.* Paper presented at the meeting of the Society for Research in Child Development, Baltimore, MD.

Swann, W. B., Jr. (1983). Self-verification: Bringing social reality into harmony with the self. In J. Suls & A. G. Greenwald (Eds.), *Psychological perspectives on the self* (Vol. 2, pp. 33–66). Hillsdale, NJ: Erlbaum.

Swann, W. B., Jr. (2012). Self-verification theory. In P. Van Lang, A. Kruglanski, & E. T. Higgins (Eds.), *Handbook of theories of social psychology* (pp. 23–42). London, England: Sage.

Swann, W. B., Jr., De La Ronde, C., & Hixon, J. G. (1994). Authenticity and positivity strivings in marriage and courtship. *Journal of Personality and Social Psychology, 66*, 857–869.

Swann, W. B., Hixon, J. G., Stein-Seroussi, A., & Gilbert, D. T. (1990). The fleeting gleam of praise: Cognitive processes underlying behavioral reactions to self-relevant feedback. *Journal of Personality and Social Psychology, 59*, 17–26.

Swann, W. B., & Predmore, S. C. (1985). Intimates as agents of social support: Sources of consolation or despair? *Journal of Personality and Social Psychology, 49*, 1609–1617.

Swann, W. B., Stein-Seroussi, A., & Giesler, R. B. (1992). Why people self-verify. *Journal of Personality and Social Psychology, 62*, 392–401.

Vázquez, A., Gómez, Á., & Swann, W. B. (2018). You just don't get us! *Social Psychology, 49*, 231–242.

Westover, T. (2018). *Educated: A memoir.* New York, NY: Random House.

Wiesenfeld, B. M., Swann W. B., Jr., Brockner, J., & Bartel, C. A. (2007). Is more fairness always preferred? Self-esteem moderates reactions to procedural justice. *Academy of Management Journal, 50*, 1235–1253.

Wood, J. V., Heimpel, S. A., Newby-Clark, I. R., & Ross, M. (2005). Snatching defeat from the jaws of victory: Self-esteem differences in the experience and anticipation of success. *Journal of Personality and Social Psychology, 89*, 764–780.

Zunick, P. V., Fazio, R. H., & Vasey, M. W. (2015). Directed abstraction: Encouraging broad, personal generalizations following a success experience. *Journal of Personality and Social Psychology, 109*, 1–19.

3

AN ATTRIBUTIONAL APPROACH TO TEACHER PRAISE

Sandra Graham and Xiaochen Chen

Consider this experiment. Two students just completed a math test. The teacher hands back the tests, and both students got the same score—seven out of ten problems correct. To one student (Student A), the teacher says, "Great job! I am very pleased with your tests results." To the other student (Student B), the teacher just returns the test and does not say anything. Which student (A or B) does the teacher think tried harder? Which student (A or B) does the teacher think is smarter?

If you try this little experiment with students older than about 10 years of age, most (beyond chance) will probably say that the teacher thought the praised Student A tried harder, but that the neutral feedback Student B was smarter. Why would this be? What theoretical principles might explain why praise, compared to neutral feedback, might be related to more perceived effort but lower perceived ability? In our view, a good theory has a set of interrelated constructs, linked together with an operational language, able to account for a broad array of phenomena, and with a set of reference experiments that always work (see Weiner, 2006). We believe that this simple praise study is one such reference experiment that fits within a general theory of motivation based on causal attributions.

In this chapter, we present an attributional perspective on praise as a cue to attributions about ability and effort. We begin by outlining the basic principles of an attributional theory of motivation, focusing on those most relevant to the attributional cue function of teacher praise. In the next section, we describe studies on teacher feedback including praise and its relation to ability and effort attributions. Included here are developmental studies that draw on basic principles about children's emerging understanding of the characteristics of ability and effort. In the final section, we consider implications of this research for teacher feedback to vulnerable populations, particularly ethnic minority youth.

Attribution theory

Attributions are answers to "why" questions, such as "Why did I fail the test?" or "Why is the teacher so angry with this student?" Note that we make attributions about ourselves and about other people. There is no one unifying attribution theory, but rather a collection of approaches that began with the seminal work of Heider (1958) and was then further developed by prominent social psychologists in the following decades (e.g. Kelley, 1973; Weiner, 1986). Although distinct, these approaches all shared a concern with three central issues: specifying the perceived causes of outcomes, identifying the antecedents of those causes, and linking particular causes with unique psychological and behavioral consequences. In this chapter, we organize our causal analysis around an attributional theory of motivation as formulated by Weiner and colleagues (Weiner, 1986, 2006) because that theory provides the most complete approach to the three issues noted above.

In the achievement domain, where most attribution research within the Weiner framework has been carried out, success and failure often are attributed to an ability factor that includes both aptitude and acquired skills, an effort factor that can be either temporary or sustained, the difficulty of the task, luck, mood, and help or hindrance from others. Among these causal ascriptions, in Western cultures at least, ability and effort are the most dominant perceived causes of success and failure. When explaining achievement outcomes, individuals attach the most importance to how smart they or others are and how hard they or others try.

Because specific attributional content will vary between motivational domains as well as between individuals within a domain, attribution theorists have focused on the underlying dimensions or properties of causes in addition to specific causes per se. Here we ask, for example, how are ability and effort similar and how are they different? Are there other attributions that share the overlapping and nonoverlapping properties of ability and effort? Three underlying properties, labeled causal dimensions, have been identified. These are *locus*, or whether a cause is internal or external to the individual; *stability*, which designates a cause as constant or varying over time; and *controllability*, or whether a cause is subject to volitional influence. All causes theoretically are classified into one of the eight cells of a locus × stability × controllability dimensional matrix. For example, ability is typically perceived as internal, stable, and uncontrollable. When we attribute our failure to low ability (aptitude), we tend to see this as a characteristic of ourselves, enduring over time, and beyond personal control. Effort, on the other hand, is also internal, but unstable and controllable. Failure attributed to insufficient effort indicates a personal characteristic that is modifiable by one's own volitional behavior.

These conceptual distinctions between causes are central to an attributional theory of motivation because each dimension is uniquely related to a set of cognitive, emotional, and behavioral consequences. The locus dimension of causality is related to self-esteem and esteem-related emotions like pride and shame. We feel more pride when our successes are attributed to internal causes and less shame if our failures are attributed to external causes. The stability dimension affects subjective expectancy about future success and failure. When failure is attributed to stable causes like low ability, we are more likely to expect failure to continue than when the same outcome is attributed to unstable causes such as insufficient effort. As the third dimension of causality, causal controllability relates largely to perceived responsibility in *others* and therefore is linked to a set of interpersonal consequences that are directed toward other people. For example, when someone's failure is perceived as caused by an uncontrollable factor such as low ability, perceivers feel sympathy and they desire to help the failing individual. In contrast, failures attributed to controllable causes like low effort tend to evoke anger and the withholding of help. Thus, at the very heart of this attributional model of motivation is the specification of complex interrelationships between causal thinking, feeling, and acting.

Praise (and blame) as attributional cues

Praise from an attributional perspective is particularly relevant when we think about attributional antecedents. How do students know, for example, whether they failed a test because they are low in ability or because they did not try hard enough? Early attribution research identified a number of antecedent cues, such as prior performance history and social norm information, that influence self-ascriptions (Kelley, 1973). If a student has been doing poorly in a course all semester, or if she fails a test and everyone else gets an "A," both of these are very salient sources of information that might then be used by the student to infer low ability as the cause for failure.

Another source of attributional information about effort and ability is feedback from teachers. Teachers no doubt often directly tell their students that they did not put forth enough effort, for trying hard is compatible with the work ethic espoused in school. Although teachers typically do not directly tell their students that they are low in ability, this attributional information may be subtly, indirectly, and even unknowingly conveyed. Two attribution principles are relevant to how praise might function as a subtle and unintended low-ability cue. First, praise is related to perceived effort expenditure in that the successful student who tries hard is maximally rewarded, while the lazy student is maximally punished (Weiner, 1986). Second, effort and ability are often perceived as compensatory causes of achievement. One cause can compensate, or make amends for, the absence of another cause such that high effort can make amends for low ability (Heider 1958). From the perceiver's perspective, the higher one's effort, the lower one's perceived ability, and vice versa. Thus, if two students achieve the same outcome, often the one who tries harder (and is praised) is perceived as lower in ability.

In a series of studies, Meyer and colleagues were the first to document the attributional cue function of both praise for success and blame for failure (Meyer, Bachmann, Hempelmann, Plöger, & Spliier, 1979). In that study, college students were given information that two students had identical outcomes on a test that was described as easy or difficult. Test difficulty was crossed with whether the two students succeeded at or failed the test. In the success conditions, one student was praised by a teacher for the outcome, and the other student received neutral feedback. In the failure conditions, one student was criticized for the outcome (blamed), and the other student received neutral feedback. Participants then inferred how smart the teacher thought each student was. Across easy and difficult tasks, results showed that the praised student was inferred to be lower in ability than the unpraised student. Given failure, the neutral feedback student was inferred to be lower in ability than the blamed student. In subsequent laboratory studies examining the robustness of the findings, college-age participants made inferences about their own ability or the ability of hypothetical students following teacher feedback in which various features of the context were manipulated such as teachers' knowledge of the students' ability or whether praise and blame elicited inferences about the likeability of students (Meyer, Mittag & Engler, 1986; Meyer, Reisenzein, & Dickhäuser, 2004). It could be that the ability-implicating messages of evaluative feedback are only evident when teachers actually know how smart their students are or whether students use the compensatory schema as opposed to a liking schema. These factors were shown to be significant moderators of the praise and blame effects. The offering of praise and the withholding of blame can function as low-ability cues especially when teachers know their students' ability and when respondents do not view praise, blame, or their absence as cues to how much teachers like their students.

Developmental patterns

The attributional analysis of praise and blame presumes a complex reasoning process from evaluative feedback about one cause (effort) to judgments about a second cause (ability). It was not clear whether young children have the cognitive capacity to undertake such reasoning. Indeed, the six Meyer et al. (1979) experiments included children as young as age 8 in the first two studies, but the hypothesized effects of praise and blame were only documented in participants older than age 12. Based on the developmental attribution literature at the time, Barker and Graham (1987) proposed two developmental hypotheses about praise as an indirect low-ability cue. First, the meaning of effort would be understood earlier than the meaning of ability. Many developmental attribution studies by the 1980s documented that young children reward high effort and punish low effort much like adults do (see Graham, 1990). But progressing from judgments about effort to inferences about ability using a compensatory rule may require more advanced cognitive reasoning. For example, Kun (1977) documented that up to about age 10, children expect effort and ability to positively covary. The student who tries harder is expected to be smarter, a phenomenon that Kun labeled the halo schema (see also Nicholls, 1978). Applied to the cue function of praise and blame, if young children perceive effort as high in response to praise and low in response to blame, the same pattern would prevail for their inferences about ability.

Barker and Graham (1987) investigated these developmental hypotheses in a study modeled after the Meyer et al. (1979) research. Children between the ages of 4 and 12 watched videotaped teaching sessions depicting a pair of students solving a set of easy math problems. One student was praised by the teacher with positive statements like "Great job!" The other student received neutral feedback of "Correct." In the second videotape, both students failed the easy problems, but one student was criticized, while the other was told simply that their answers were incorrect. Participants then rated the effort and ability of the students in each vignette on five-point scales.

The results were as we predicted. For all age groups, effort ratings varied systematically as a function of praise or blame, with the praised student inferred to be higher in effort and the blamed student lower in effort than their neutral feedback peers. With ability ratings, however, the expected developmental trend emerged. With 4–5-year-olds, effort and ability ratings positively covaried (Kun's halo schema), with the praised student judged as high in effort and ability and the blamed student low in the two attributions. Only the 10–12-year-old children inferred lower ability for the student praised after success and not blamed after failure. The 8–9-year-olds fell somewhere in between, with no systematic pattern to their inferences about ability. The correlations between effort and ability across the four hypothetical students were $r = 0.84$ for 4–5-year-olds, $r = 0.24$ for 8–9-year-olds, and $r = -0.79$ for 10–12-year-olds, indicating use of the compensatory schema only among the oldest children.

In sum, young children were not as susceptible to the ability-implicating messages of praise and blame. We suggest that this is because they do not yet perceive a compensatory relationship between effort and ability. Use of a compensatory schema is likely an important cognitive prerequisite to processing attribution-related information about effort and ability.

As interest in age-related differences in the function of praise began to receive more attention, the pattern of findings documented by Barker and Graham (1987) was replicated by other developmental researchers interested in the boundary conditions for understanding teacher feedback as attributional cues. Some of these conditions were whether the feedback occurred for one student across different subject matters (e.g., Math and English), whether it occurred repeatedly across time, and the impact of individual differences in beliefs about the inverse relationship between ability and effort (Lam, Ying, & Ng, 2008; Miller & Hom, 1997; Möller, 2005). In all of these studies, children older than about age 10 perceived praise as a low-ability cue across multiple subject matters and especially when they perceived effort and ability to be inversely related. Underscoring the larger meaning of the paradoxical effects of praise, participants beyond middle childhood also reported that they would rather be like the non-praised and blamed student (Miller & Hom, 1997).

We focus on growth and change in cognitive capacities of children to explain age-related differences in the attributional cue function of praise and blame. That is, we emphasized changes in children's understanding of the meaning (causal properties) of ability and effort to argue that as they got older, they processed attributional information in a more adultlike or "logical" way. But paralleling age-related cognitive growth are systematic grade-related changes in how schools, classrooms, and instructional activities are organized. As children transition from middle childhood to early adolescence (e.g., elementary school to middle school in the U.S. context), there is an increasing focus on testing, accountability, academic tracking, and other public displays of individual differences in ability (e.g., Eccles & Roesser, 2011). All of these practices operate to enhance a conception of ability where being smart means being smarter than others but having to try less hard. Integrating both cognitive growth and environmental changes in the way schools are organized, it could be that early adolescence is in fact the developmental period in which youth are most susceptible to the paradoxical effects of teacher feedback (Amemiya & Wang, 2018).

More teacher feedback that can communicate low ability

Drawing on other attribution principles, researchers have identified additional teacher behaviors that, like praise, can indirectly function as low-ability cues (Graham, 1990). Earlier we stated that failure attributed to uncontrollable factors like low ability elicits sympathy from others, and sympathy, in turn, promotes offers of help. This is in contrast to failure attributed to controllable causes like insufficient effort which tends to evoke anger and the withholding of help. Now suppose that a teacher does respond with sympathy as opposed to anger toward a failing student or with an unsolicited offer of help rather than neglect. It might be the case that the student will then use these affective and behavioral displays to infer, first, the teacher's attribution, and second, his or her own self-ascription for failure. Attribution researchers have documented paradoxical effects of sympathy and unsolicited offers of help on low-ability attributions in older children and college students (Graham, 1990). Hence, there may a prevalent set of teacher behaviors that share in common the fact that they are positively motivated types of feedback that can indirectly and unintentionally function as low-ability cues.

Implications for feedback to vulnerable students

The attributional research reviewed in this chapter began over 40 years ago and has been largely conducted with nondiverse samples of white participants or with samples in which the race/ethnicity of participants was not specified. Such restricted sampling may have been a function of the time and the belief that the research was guided by general attribution principles that apply to a broad segment of the population. Yet we suggest that the findings reported here are especially relevant today for understanding some of the motivational challenges of ethnic minority children, adolescents, and young adults who experience racial achievement disparities at every educational level. In fact, the teacher practices highlighted here may be especially directed toward at-risk minority students as a means to protect their self-esteem. Other contemporary research programs have documented how misguided or excessive praise can hurt the achievement of youth with low self-esteem (Brummelman, Crocker, & Bushman, 2016).

Too much praise and, by implication, too little criticism for poor performance seem to be particularly directed toward ethnic minority students. Although not grounded in attributional analyses, Harber and colleagues documented a "positive feedback bias," defined as a tendency for teachers to provide less critical comments to African American and Latino students compared to White students with the same low achievement (Harber et al., 2012). The teachers in Harber's research appear to have been motivated by egalitarian concerns and the desire to protect the self-esteem of vulnerable minority students. But the minority students were not the beneficiaries of ability-confirming feedback that communicated high expectations and more clarity about where and when to exert effort.

Recent experimental research with ethnic minority college students also uncovered negative consequences of positive feedback. For example, Lawrence, Crocker, and Blanton (2011) reported that praise from a White but not a same-race evaluator led African American students to perceive that the evaluator had low expectations that they would succeed. Similarly, Major et al. (2016) reported that praise from a White but not a same-race evaluator given to Latino women evoked attributional ambiguity about why the praise was offered. Such uncertainty led some Latinas to question the evaluators' motives. Many were suspicious that the praise was only offered because the evaluators felt pity or wanted to appear non-prejudiced, in which case the Latina targets felt threatened and experienced a drop in self-esteem. Such differential reactions by evaluator race are of particular concern when applied to the K-12 context in this country, where more than 80% of the teachers are White in an increasingly racially/ethnically diverse school system (Geiger, 2018).

Of course, we are not suggesting that teachers of ethnic minority youth should never help their students or that they should always be angry rather than sympathetic or critical as opposed to complimentary. The appropriateness of any communication will depend on many factors, including the characteristics of both students and teachers. Social psychological research informed by attributional analyses suggests that feedback should be *wise*: It should be appropriately critical while also communicating high expectations, assurances that students have the requisite ability, and strategies for improving their performance (Cohen, Steele, & Ross, 1999; Yeager et al., 2014). Unbuffered praise or criticism by itself is rarely effective at warding off mistrust of teachers or self-blaming tendencies. Our general message is that attribution principles can facilitate our understanding of how some well-intentioned teacher behaviors can have unexpected negative effects on the motivation of vulnerable students.

References

Amemiya, J., & Wang, M. T. (2018). Why effort praise can backfire in adolescence. *Child Development Perspectives, 12*, 199–203.

Barker, G., & Graham, S. (1987). A developmental study of praise and blame as attributional cues. *Journal of Educational Psychology, 79*, 62–66.

Brummelman, E., Crocker, J., & Bushman, B. J. (2016). The praise paradox: When and why praise backfires in children with low self-esteem. *Child Development Perspectives, 10*, 111–115.

Cohen, G., Steele, C., & Ross, L. (1999). The mentor's dilemma: Providing critical feedback across the racial divide. *Personality and Social Psychology Bulletin, 25*, 1302–1318.

Eccles, J. S., & Roeser, R. W. (2011). Schools as developmental contexts during adolescence. *Journal of Research on Adolescence, 21*, 225–241.

Geiger, A. (2018). *America's public school teachers are far less racially and ethnically diverse than their students*. Washington, DC: Pew Research Center.

Graham, S. (1990). Communicating low ability in the classroom: Bad things good teachers sometimes do. In S. Graham & V. Folkes (Eds.), *Attribution theory: Applications to achievement, mental health, and interpersonal conflict* (pp. 17–36). Hillsdale, NJ: Lawrence Erlbaum.

Harber, K., Gorman, J., Gengaro, F., Butisingh, S., Tsang, W., & Ouellette, R. (2012). Students' race and teachers' social support affect the positive feedback **bias** in public schools. *Journal of Educational Psychology, 104*, 1149–1161.

Heider, F. (1958). *The psychology of interpersonal relations*. New York, NY: John Wiley.

Kelley, H. (1973). The process of causal attribution. *American Psychologist, 28*, 107–128.

Kun, A. (1977). Development of the magnitude-covariation and compensation schemata in ability and effort attributions of performance. *Child Development, 48*, 862–873.

Lam, S., Yim, P., & Ng, Y. (2008). Is effort praise motivational? The role of beliefs in the effort-ability relationship. *Contemporary Educational Psychology, 33*, 694–710.

Lawrence, J., Crocker, J., & Blanton, H. (2011). Stigmatized and dominant cultural groups differentially interpret positive feedback. *Journal of Cross Cultural Psychology, 42*, 165–169.

Major, B., Kunstman, J., Malta, B., Sawyer, P., Townsend, S., & Mendes, W. (2016). Suspicion of motives predicts minorities' responses to positive feedback in interracial interactions. *Journal of Experimental Social Psychology, 62*, 75–88.

Meyer, W., Bachmann, M., Hempelmann, M., Plöger, F., & Spiler, H. (1979). The informational value of evaluative behavior. Influences of praise and blame on perceptions of ability. *Journal of Educational Psychology, 71*, 259–268.

Meyer, W., Mittag, W., & Engler, U. (1986). Some effects of praise and blame on perceived ability and affect. *Social Cognition, 4*, 293–303.

Meyer, W., Reisenzein, R., & Dickhäuser, O. (2004). Inferring ability from blame: Effects of effort- versus liking-oriented cognitive schemata. *Psychology Science, 46*, 281–293.

Miller, A., & Hom, H. (1997). Conceptions of ability and the interpretation of praise, blame, and material rewards. *Journal of Experimental Education, 65*, 163–177.

Möller, J. (2005). Paradoxical effects of praise and criticism: Social, dimensional, and temporal comparisons. *British Journal of Educational Psychology, 75*, 275–295.

Nicholls, J. (1978). The development of concepts of effort and ability, perception of own attainment, and the understanding that difficult tasks require more ability. *Child Development, 49*, 800–814.

Weiner, B. (1986). *An attributional theory of motivation and emotion*. New York, NY: Springer.

Weiner, B. (2006). *Social motivation, justice, and the moral emotions*. Mahwah, NJ: Lawrence Erlbaum.

Yeager, D. S., Purdie-Vaughns, V., Garcia, J., Apfel, N., Brzustoski, P., Master, A., … & Cohen, G. L. (2014). Breaking the cycle of mistrust: Wise interventions to provide critical feedback across the racial divide. *Journal of Experimental Psychology: General, 143*, 804–824.

4

UNDERSTANDING THE COMPLEXITY OF PRAISE THROUGH THE LENS OF SELF-DETERMINATION THEORY

Bart Soenens and Maarten Vansteenkiste

At a first glance, praise appears to be a powerful and even self-evident strategy to enhance individuals' motivation. Almost every parent or teacher would agree that being appreciative of individuals' achievements, skill development, or ability will increase individuals' confidence and boost their motivation. However, the effects of praise on motivation are surprisingly complex, with certain forms of praise failing to promote desirable outcomes and others even yielding boomerang effects (Henderlong & Lepper, 2002). To better understand this complexity, it is important to gain insight in the psychological processes accounting for the potential benefits and pitfalls of praise.

One informative theory providing a detailed account of the processes involved in praise is self-determination theory (SDT; Ryan & Deci, 2017). According to SDT, the effectiveness of any potentially motivating strategy needs to be considered against the background of its linkage with individuals' basic psychological needs for autonomy (i.e., the need to experience psychological freedom and volition), competence (i.e., the need to feel effective and skilled), and relatedness (i.e., the need to feel closely connected to others). While satisfaction of these needs is essential for individuals' high-quality motivation and flourishing, frustration of these needs undermines motivation and increases risk for amotivation and ill-being (Ryan & Deci, 2017).

SDT's theoretical perspective on praise and intrinsic motivation

Initial SDT-based research on praise (Deci, 1971) examined its effect on intrinsically motivated behaviors, that is, behaviors enacted for activities that are experienced as inherently interesting, challenging, and enjoyable (Ryan & Deci, 2017). Praise has the potential to increase intrinsic motivation because it conveys trust in individuals' capacity to effectively engage in the activity at hand, which contributes to their interest and enjoyment of the activity. In a classic experiment, Deci (1971, Study 3) had college students work on intrinsically motivating Soma puzzles, with participants receiving either positive feedback (e.g., "That's very good" and "That's much better than average") or no feedback after solving a series of puzzles. Participants could then freely choose between solving more puzzles and reading magazines during a free-choice period, with the behavioral free-choice behavior signaling their continued interest in the activity. Participants who received positive feedback spent significantly more time making additional puzzles than those in the control condition, suggesting that praise fostered intrinsic motivation.

Deci's (1971) findings were replicated in numerous experimental studies using the free-choice persistence paradigm. A meta-analysis summarizing these studies revealed an overall effect size (Cohen's d) of 0.33 (Deci, Koestner, & Ryan, 1999). At the same time, moderation analyses indicated significant heterogeneity around this effect, suggesting that praise is more effective for some individuals than for others. A follow-up analysis for instance showed that the effect of experimentally manipulated praise was significant among college students but not among children. Deci et al. (1999) reasoned that, with increasing age, individuals increasingly see the relevance of praise for their sense of competence, with developmental research confirming this reasoning (Pomerantz & Eaton, 2000). Gender was also found to moderate the effects of praise, with positive feedback increasing intrinsic motivation more strongly among men than among women (Deci, 1972; Koestner, Zuckerman, & Koestner, 1987). According to Koestner, Zuckerman, and Olsson (1990), women would be taught to attach more importance to dependency than men, who value more strongly individualism and independent achievement. As a consequence, women might be more likely to interpret praise as a controlling attempt to maintain their dependence, while men would be inclined to see praise as a positive evaluation of their independence and individual achievements.

The finding that the effects of praise are heterogeneous points to the importance of examining individuals' *appraisals* of praise. Within cognitive evaluation theory (CET), a mini-theory within SDT dealing with contextual influences on intrinsic motivation (Ryan & Deci, 2017), it is argued that contextual events (including praise, but also the provision of choice, rewards, deadlines, and surveillance) can be given at least two different meanings. When the *informational value* of praise is most salient in a person's appraisal (Deci & Ryan, 1987), praise is experienced as conveying relevant and positive information about one's strengths and points for growth. With such an appraisal, individuals are likely to feel more confident about their capacities and to know better how to deal effectively with future challenges. In contrast, when the *evaluative value* of praise is more salient, people feel controlled by praise. Praise is then perceived as a manipulative strategy aimed at directing people's behavior and pressuring them to act in accordance with externally imposed expectations or standards, thereby thwarting their need for autonomy.

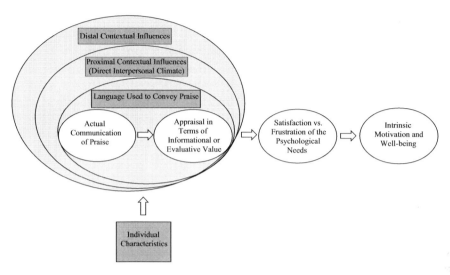

FIGURE 4.1 Conceptual model of factors involved in the appraisal of praise and its consequences for motivation and well-being.

As displayed in Figure 4.1, several factors are likely to influence individuals' appraisal of praise. One important factor is the way in which praise is conveyed or, in other words, the language used to communicate praise. When the communication of praise involves pressuring language (e.g., words such as "have to," "must," and "expect"), praise is more likely to be perceived in evaluative terms. When praise is communicated in a more neutral and descriptive fashion (ideally with reference to specific positive behaviors and strategies), its informational value is likely to increase. Another potential source of influence is the proximal interpersonal climate within which praise is provided. People may interpret praise in more benign ways when they feel a close and genuine sense of connection with the person providing praise. The degree to which the person giving praise is perceived as having adequate expertise in the domain of praise may also affect the credibility and informational value of the praise. Finally, the degree to which socialization figures are generally autonomy-supportive (vs. more controlling) may affect the appraisal of praise, with positive feedback being perceived as more informational when occurring within a generally autonomy-supportive interpersonal climate and as more evaluative within a more controlling climate.

More distal contextual factors (beyond the direct interpersonal climate between the provider and the recipient of praise) may also color individuals' interpretation of praise. For instance, in a school or a sports club with a highly competitive atmosphere, praise is more likely to be perceived in evaluative terms. Ultimately, even cultural orientation may have an effect on praise (Henderlong & Lepper, 2002). Because praise, and in particular praise for independent achievements, may be less common in Eastern (compared to Western) cultures and may be at odds with collectivist values such as interdependence and modesty (Wang, Wiley, & Chiu, 2008), (certain forms of) praise may be seen in a less positive light in Eastern cultures.

Finally, next to all of these contextual influences on praise, individual characteristics of the recipients of praise can also play a role in individuals' perception of praise. Such factors include, for instance, individuals' age, gender, and personality. Although all factors displayed in Figure 4.1 have the potential to affect the consequences of praise, research has focused most on the role of individual characteristics such as age and gender (see before) and on the language used to convey praise.

SDT-based empirical research on praise

The notion that praise contributes to intrinsic motivation to the extent it has informational value, thereby fostering a sense of competence, has received substantial empirical support. In one of the earlier experiments, Vallerand and Reid (1984) provided positive feedback, negative feedback, or no feedback to students engaging in a motor task. Participants receiving positive feedback reported higher intrinsic motivation compared to those in the other conditions, an effect that was mediated by perceived competence. Similar evidence for the explanatory role of competence in the relation between manipulated positive feedback and intrinsic motivation has been established in laboratory studies (e.g., Vansteenkiste & Deci, 2003) and in field experiments (e.g., De Muynck et al., 2017; Fransen, Vansteenkiste, Vande Broek, & Boen, 2018; Mabbe, Soenens, De Muynck, & Vansteenkiste, 2018), with intrinsic motivation, in turn, relating to various desirable outcomes in a motivational sequence, including enhanced concentration (Grouzet, Vallerand, Thill, & Provencher, 2004), vitality (Mouratidis, Vansteenkiste, Lens, & Sideridis, 2008), and greater challenge seeking (Mabbe et al., 2018). In addition to experimental evidence, correlational studies have shown that the effects of self-reported positive feedback received from socialization figures, such as coaches (Mouratidis et al., 2008), teachers (Koka & Hein, 2005), and parents (Jacquez, Cole, & Searle, 2004), on motivation and mental health are mediated by competence need satisfaction.

While praise has the potential to contribute to competence need satisfaction and subsequent intrinsic motivation, it can also have an evaluative connotation, especially if communicated in a more controlling way. In an experiment with undergraduate students working on a puzzle task, Ryan (1982) showed that (mostly positive) feedback communicated in a more evaluative and controlling way (e.g., "Good, you are doing as you *should*") relative to an informational fashion (simply indicating that they performed better than average) undermined participants' free-choice persistence (see also Ryan, Mims, & Koestner, 1983, for similar results).

Complementing this experimental research, Reeve and Jang (2006) observed teacher-student interactions and coded a variety of teaching practices, including teachers' informational and controlling ways of communicating praise.

Only teachers' observed use of informational praise was related positively to students' perceived autonomy, with perceived autonomy in turn relating to more engagement and better performance. In a diary study with athletes, Carpentier and Mageau (2016) reported that a daily informational style of providing feedback, which involved an appreciative and descriptive (rather than directive) way of providing positive feedback ("During today's training, when my coach told me that he was satisfied with my performance, he took the time to describe the specific things that I had done well"), related positively to athletes' daily self-confidence and satisfaction of the needs for autonomy and competence.

In contrast, physical education teachers' perceived use of controlling praise (e.g., "My teacher only uses praise so that I stay focused on tasks during the lesson") was found to relate to students' amotivation, albeit only among boys (Koka & Sildala, 2018). Also relevant in this regard is research on the concept of positive conditional regard, which is characteristic of parents (but potentially also other socialization figures) who provide more love and appreciation than usual when children meet certain expectations or standards (Roth, Assor, Niemiec, Deci, & Ryan, 2009). Praise can be considered one key practice through which parents convey positive conditional regard, thereby expressing heightened appreciation when a child behaves as expected or achieves a certain standard for achievement. The seemingly benign practice of positive conditional regard was shown to predict developmental problems, including test anxiety (Otterpohl, Lazar, & Stiensmeier-Pelster, 2019), suppressive emotion regulation (Israeli-Halevi, Assor, & Roth, 2015), fragile self-worth (Wouters, Colpin, Luyckx, & Verschueren, 2018), and rigid over-investment in learning (Assor & Tal, 2012). These findings suggest that praise is likely to backfire when it is used in the context of conditionally approving communication. Within such a context, praise represents not only an autonomy-suppressing strategy but also a threat to the need for relatedness. Praise is then used to manipulate the parent-child bond, with children feeling that their parents' love is inauthentic: parental love needs to be earned, and praise is deserved only when children meet parental standards.

An SDT-based perspective on different types of praise

Overall, SDT-based research has shown rather convincingly that the effectiveness of praise depends on its functional significance, that is, the degree to which it is perceived as having informational value or a more evaluative connotation (Deci & Ryan, 1987). The SDT perspective may also help to understand the effects of different types of praise distinguished in other theoretical models, including person (vs. process) praise and inflated (vs. realistic praise).

Person versus process praise

While person praise involves a positive evaluation of an individual's stable characteristics (such as personality or intelligence), process praise involves a positive evaluation of the means through which individuals achieved an outcome (such as effort or the use of adequate strategies). These two forms of praise, which have been studied extensively in the context of Dweck's (1999) theory on mindsets, have been found to affect individuals' motivation and engagement differently. Experimental studies with both elementary school children (Mueller & Dweck, 1998) and preschoolers (Kamins & Dweck, 1999) showed that children who received person praise (rather than process praise) after an initial success engaged less in challenge-seeking. When confronted with a subsequent failure, children who received person praise displayed more helplessness. Correlational studies corroborated these experimental findings. Pomerantz and Kempner (2013) showed that mothers' daily use of person (but not process) praise was predictive of elementary school children's adoption of an entity theory (i.e., the belief that ability is fixed) and reduced preference for challenge in school. Longitudinal research demonstrated that children who received more process praise in toddlerhood developed a stronger desire for challenge in preschool (Gunderson et al., 2013) and performed better in elementary school (Gunderson et al., 2018).

Considered from the SDT perspective, process praise has relatively more informational value than person praise because it points out the efforts and strategies used by individuals to achieve an outcome. When confronted with setbacks, this information is potentially helpful because individuals may know better how to deal with the setback (e.g., by increasing effort or by trying out better strategies). Thus, process praise can strengthen individuals' sense of competence because they feel better able to cope with challenges. In contrast, with person praise there is a risk that individuals feel compelled to prove their worth as a person when completing achievement-related tasks, thereby investing their self-esteem in task performance (Kamins & Dweck, 1999). Such an ego-involved orientation pressures individuals from within and thwarts the need for autonomy (Ryan, 1982; Van der Kaap-Deeder et al., 2016). Thus, the differential motivational effects of person and process praise might be accounted for by their different associations with the needs for competence and autonomy, a possibility that could be addressed more explicitly in future research.

Inflated versus realistic praise

Similar to the effects of person praise, research indicates that inflated praise is also motivationally detrimental (Brummelman, Crocker, & Bushman, 2016). Brummelman, Nelemans, Thomaes, and Orobio de Castra (2017) rated parents' use of statements reflecting inflated praise (i.e., praise containing an extremely positive evaluation including words such as *extremely, incredibly, amazing,* and *fantastic*) toward 7–11-year-old children during in-home observations. Parental inflated praise predicted decreases in children's self-esteem in a four-wave longitudinal study. Interestingly, Brummelman, Thomaes, Orobio de Castro, Overbeek, and Bushman (2014; Study 1 and Study 2) showed that parents are particularly inclined to give inflated praise when children have low-esteem, presumably because they hope to compensate for their children's low self-worth by doing so. Ironically, however, an experimental study showed that inflated praise is particularly harmful to motivation among children with low self-esteem (Brummelman et al., 2014, Study 3). These children displayed the steepest decrease in challenge-seeking after having received inflated praise for a painting.

Findings on inflated praise thus suggest that parents and children risk getting caught in a negative vicious cycle. Although inflated praise may represent a well-meant attempt to boost children's confidence, such praise may fail to yield the desired effects because it reinforces children's insecurity, especially among those suffering from low self-worth. From an SDT perspective, this undermining effect may occur because inflated praise carries little informational value. Such praise likely comes across as insincere and overly general, thereby failing to contribute to a deep and authentic sense of competence. Inflated praise may even convey high and unrealistic expectations for future performance, thereby coming across as fairly evaluative and pressuring, especially among those suffering from low self-worth.

Conclusion

SDT provides a nuanced perspective on the effects of praise, arguing that the effects of praise depend on its functional significance. When individuals interpret praise primarily in terms of its informational value, their need for competence is supported, and praise is likely to contribute to high-quality motivation. However, when individuals interpret praise more as an evaluative and pressuring practice, their need for autonomy is thwarted. In close relationships (e.g., parent-child relationships), such evaluative and manipulative praise may also be perceived as an instrument that threatens individuals' need for relatedness. When praise threatens individuals' psychological needs, it is likely to backfire and to undermine (rather than to support) individuals' motivation and well-being.

References

Assor, A., & Tal, K. (2012). When parents' affection depends on child's achievement: Parental conditional positive regard, self-aggrandizement, shame and coping in adolescents. *Journal of Adolescence, 35*, 249–260.

Brummelman, E., Crocker, J., & Bushman, B. J. (2016). The praise paradox: When and why praise backfires in children with low self-esteem. *Child Development Perspectives, 10*, 111–115.

Brummelman, E., Nelemans, S. A., Thomaes, S., & Orobio de Castro, B. (2017). When parents' praise inflates, children's self-esteem deflates. *Child Development, 88*, 1799–1809.

Brummelman, E., Thomaes, S., Orobio de Castro, B., Overbeek, G., & Bushman, B. J. (2014). "That's not just beautiful—that's incredibly beautiful!" The adverse impact of inflated praise on children with low self-esteem. *Psychological Science, 25*, 728–735.

Carpentier, J., & Mageau, G. A. (2016). Predicting sport experience during training: The role of change-oriented feedback in athletes' motivation, self-confidence and needs satisfaction fluctuations. *Journal of Sport and Exercise Psychology, 38*, 45–58.

Deci, E. L. (1971). Effects of externally mediated rewards on intrinsic motivation. *Journal of Personality and Social Psychology, 18*, 105–115.

Deci, E. L. (1972). Intrinsic motivation, extrinsic reinforcement, and inequity. *Journal of Personality and Social Psychology, 22*, 113–120.

Deci, E. L., Koestner, R., & Ryan, R. M. (1999). A meta-analytic review of experiments examining the effects of extrinsic rewards on intrinsic motivation. *Psychological Bulletin, 125*, 627–668.

Deci, E. L., & Ryan, R. M. (1987). The support of autonomy and the control of behavior. *Journal of Personality and Social Psychology, 53*, 1024–1037.

De Muynck, G. J., Vansteenkiste, M., Delrue, J., Aelterman, N., Haerens, L., & Soenens, B. (2017). The effects of feedback valence and style on need satisfaction, self-talk, and perseverance among tennis players: An experimental study. *Journal of Sport and Exercise Psychology, 39*, 67–80.

Dweck, C. S. (1999). *Self-theories: Their role in motivation, personality, and development.* New York, NY: Psychology Press.

Fransen, K., Vansteenkiste, M., Broek, G. V., & Boen, F. (2018). The competence-supportive and competence-thwarting role of athlete leaders: An experimental test in a soccer context. *PLOS ONE, 13*, e0200480.

Grouzet, F. M., Vallerand, R. J., Thill, E. E., & Provencher, P. J. (2004). From environmental factors to outcomes: A test of an integrated motivational sequence. *Motivation and Emotion, 28*, 331–346.

Gunderson, E. A., Gripshover, S. J., Romero, C., Dweck, C. S., Goldin-Meadow, S., & Levine, S. C. (2013). Parent praise to 1-to 3-year-olds predicts children's motivational frameworks 5 years later. *Child Development, 84*, 1526–1541.

Gunderson, E. A., Sorhagen, N. S., Gripshover, S. J., Dweck, C. S., Goldin-Meadow, S., & Levine, S. C. (2018). Parent praise to toddlers predicts fourth grade academic achievement via children's incremental mindsets. *Developmental Psychology, 54*, 397–409.

Henderlong, J., & Lepper, M. R. (2002). The effects of praise on children's intrinsic motivation: A review and synthesis. *Psychological Bulletin, 128*, 774–795.

Israeli-Halevi, M., Assor, A., & Roth, G. (2015). Using maternal conditional positive regard to promote anxiety suppression in adolescents: A benign strategy? *Parenting, 15*, 187–206.

Jacquez, F., Cole, D. A., & Searle, B. (2004). Self-perceived competence as a mediator between maternal feedback and depressive symptoms in adolescents. *Journal of Abnormal Child Psychology, 32*, 355–367.

Kamins, M. L., & Dweck, C. S. (1999). Person versus process praise and criticism: Implications for contingent self-worth and coping. *Developmental Psychology, 35*, 835–847.

Koestner, R., Zuckerman, M., & Koestner, J. (1987). Praise, involvement, and intrinsic motivation. *Journal of Personality and Social Psychology, 53*, 383–390.

Koestner, R., Zuckerman, M., & Olsson, J. (1990). Attributional style, comparison focus of praise, and intrinsic motivation. *Journal of Research in Personality, 24*, 87–100.

Koka, A., & Hein, V. (2005). The effect of perceived teacher feedback on intrinsic motivation in physical education. *International Journal of Sport Psychology, 36*, 91–106.

Koka, A., & Sildala, H. (2018). Gender differences in the relationships between perceived teachers' controlling behaviors and amotivation in physical education. *Journal of Teaching in Physical Education, 37*, 197–208.

Mabbe, E., Soenens, B., De Muynck, G. J., & Vansteenkiste, M. (2018). The impact of feedback valence and communication style on intrinsic motivation in middle childhood: Experimental evidence and generalization across individual differences. *Journal of Experimental Child Psychology, 170*, 134–160.

Mouratidis, A., Vansteenkiste, M., Lens, W., & Sideridis, G. (2008). The motivating role of positive feedback in sport and physical education: Evidence for a motivational model. *Journal of Sport and Exercise Psychology, 30*, 240–268.

Mueller, C. M., & Dweck, C. S. (1998). Praise for intelligence can undermine children's motivation and performance. *Journal of Personality and Social Psychology, 75*, 33–52.

Otterpohl, N., Lazar, R., & Stiensmeier-Pelster, J. (2019). The dark side of perceived positive regard: When parents' well-intended motivation strategies increase students' test anxiety. *Contemporary Educational Psychology, 56*, 79–90.

Pomerantz, E. M., & Eaton, M. M. (2000). Developmental differences in children's conceptions of parental control: "They love me, but they make me feel incompetent". *Merrill-Palmer Quarterly, 46*, 140–167.

Pomerantz, E. M., & Kempner, S. G. (2013). Mothers' daily person and process praise: Implications for children's theory of intelligence and motivation. *Developmental Psychology, 49*, 2040–2046.

Reeve, J., & Jang, H. (2006). What teachers say and do to support students' autonomy during a learning activity. *Journal of Educational Psychology, 98*, 209–218.

Roth, G., Assor, A., Niemiec, C. P., Ryan, R. M., & Deci, E. L. (2009). The emotional and academic consequences of parental conditional regard: Comparing conditional positive regard, conditional negative regard, and autonomy support as parenting practices. *Developmental Psychology, 45*, 1119–1142.

Ryan, R. M. (1982). Control and information in the intrapersonal sphere: An extension of cognitive evaluation theory. *Journal of Personality and Social Psychology, 43*, 450–461.

Ryan, R. M., & Deci, E. L. (2017). *Self-determination theory: Basic psychological needs in motivation, development, and wellness.* New York, NY: Guilford.

Ryan, R. M., Mims, V., & Koestner, R. (1983). Relation of reward contingency and interpersonal context to intrinsic motivation: A review and test using cognitive evaluation theory. *Journal of Personality and Social Psychology, 45*, 736–750.

Vallerand, R. J., & Reid, G. (1984). On the causal effects of perceived competence on intrinsic motivation: A test of cognitive evaluation theory. *Journal of Sport Psychology, 6*, 94–102.

Van der Kaap-Deeder, J., Wouters, S., Verschueren, K., Briers, V., Deeren, B., & Vansteenkiste, M. (2016). The pursuit of self-esteem and its motivational implications. *Psychologica Belgica, 56*, 143–168.

Vansteenkiste, M., & Deci, E. L. (2003). Competitively contingent rewards and intrinsic motivation: Can losers remain motivated? *Motivation and Emotion, 27*, 273–299.

Wang, Y. Z., Wiley, A. R., & Chiu, C. Y. (2008). Independence-supportive praise versus interdependence-promoting praise. *International Journal of Behavioral Development, 32*, 13–20.

Wouters, S., Colpin, H., Luyckx, K., & Verschueren, K. (2018). Explaining the relationship between parenting and internalizing symptoms: The role of self-esteem level and contingency. *Journal of Child and Family Studies, 27*, 3402–3412.

PART II
Competence and motivation

5

THE EFFECTS OF PRAISE ON CHILDREN'S INTRINSIC MOTIVATION REVISITED

Jennifer Henderlong Corpus and Kayla Good

> Praise out of season, or tactlessly bestowed, can freeze the heart as much as blame.
> (Pearl S. Buck, *To My Daughters, with Love, 1967*)

How does praise affect children's intrinsic motivation? The answer is tremendously complex, with evidence that praise can enhance motivation, undermine it, and do everything in between. In order to make sense of this complexity, Henderlong and Lepper (2002) identified a set of conceptual variables that appear to govern the effects of praise. Assuming praise is perceived as sincere, they argued that praise will enhance intrinsic motivation when it "encourages performance attributions to controllable causes, promotes autonomy, enhances competence without an overreliance on social comparisons, and conveys attainable standards and expectations" (p. 774). The goal of this chapter is to revisit these four conceptual variables in light of research from the past two decades and to reconsider their utility as an organizational framework for the literature on praise and motivation.

Performance attributions

One key characteristic of praise is its potential to communicate messages about the causes of success. *Process praise* (e.g., "What a clever approach!") highlights controllable, unstable attributions for performance (e.g., effort, strategy) and tends to produce adaptive motivational beliefs and behaviors, such as enjoyment, persistence, learning goals, and achievement. *Person praise* (e.g., "What a smart child!"), by contrast, highlights uncontrollable, stable attributions (e.g., ability) and leaves children vulnerable to maladaptive motivational beliefs and behaviors in the face of future setbacks, such as challenge avoidance and learned helplessness. Person praise may lead children to reason that, if success meant they were smart, failure must mean they are dumb. Mueller and Dweck's (1998) seminal research showed that fifth graders praised for intelligence exhibited a cascade of maladaptive beliefs and behaviors, especially when later confronted with failure. Those praised for effort, by contrast, exhibited a far more adaptive response, consistent with the robust body of research on attribution theory.

More recent work has shown that person praise creates motivational vulnerabilities in part because of its generic linguistic form (e.g., "You are good at math"), which implies that performance results from stable traits that are an essential part of one's nature (Cimpian, Arce, Markman, & Dweck, 2007). The use of generics raises the stakes for performance, which may bring about defensive reactions and feelings of helplessness. Process praise, by contrast, is a nongeneric form (e.g., "You did a good job in math"), which applies to particular instances, carries fewer expectations, and encourages persistence.

This evidence joins research over the past two decades showing that person praise is detrimental and/or process praise is beneficial across a broad set of outcomes including enjoyment, challenge-seeking, error vigilance, cheating, and shame following failure (e.g., Brummelman, Thomaes, Overbeek et al., 2014; Haimovitz & Corpus, 2011; Zhao, Heyman, Chen, & Lee, 2017). However, not all forms of process praise are equally beneficial. Effort praise has the potential to be seen as a consolation prize or signal of low ability, especially among adolescents (Amemiya & Wang, 2018), and it appears to be effective primarily among students who believe effort and ability to be positively, rather than inversely, related (Lam, Yim, & Ng, 2008). The most effective praise, therefore, is that which focuses on other process-oriented factors, such as strategy use.

Another significant development in the literature is the extension to more naturalistic, non-laboratory contexts. This work has shown that parents do embed attributional content into praise, with 42% of mothers in one study doing so as they reminisced about their child's past successes (Goodvin & Rolfson, 2014). Moreover, these attributions have long-term consequences. Process praise given at home during the toddler years, for example, predicted adaptive motivational frameworks and strong academic achievement in fourth grade (Gunderson et al., 2018), and person praise for children's daily schoolwork predicted challenge avoidance and fixed mind-sets six months later (Pomerantz & Kempner, 2013).

Taking a more contexualized view of praise raises fascinating questions for future research. First, how do the multiple and perhaps conflicting attributional messages children receive through praise impact motivation? Zentall and Morris (2010) found that the *ratio* of process to person praise kindergarteners received for a laboratory task was linearly related to adaptive motivational outcomes, with even a small proportion (25%) of person praise negatively impacting their persistence. How might such combinations of praise, delivered by known adults, impact intrinsic motivation in the real world?

Second, praise may impact not only children themselves but also others who inhabit the same social context. For example, how does praise from teachers affect parents' beliefs about their children? In a study examining parental reactions to teachers' comments on hypothetical report cards, parents' beliefs about their children were less strongly affected by person versus process praise than children's beliefs about themselves tend to be (Good & Corpus, 2017). Future research should address this topic more thoroughly given that parental beliefs are key predictors of their children's motivation.

Perceived autonomy

In addition to shaping children's beliefs about the causes of their success, praise also impacts their views about their reasons for engagement. As posited by self-determination theory, perceiving autonomy over one's own choices is crucial for facilitating and maintaining intrinsic motivation (Ryan & Deci, 2000). Praise can support autonomy by encouraging a focus on self-determined reasons for engaging in a task rather than reasons driven by others (e.g., "Wow—it looks like you really enjoyed that project!"). Such autonomy-supportive praise has been shown to predict enjoyment, engagement, and performance in an academic context (Reeve & Jang, 2006) and both persistence and positive affect in an athletic context (Mouratidis, Lens, & Vansteenkiste, 2010).

While autonomy supportive praise tends to enhance intrinsic motivation, controlling praise tends to undermine it (e.g., "If you keep that up, you'll be a math superstar!"). Interviews with elementary school students revealed frustration with overly directive feedback that took away from their sense of agency (Hargreaves, 2013). These same students, however, reported a desire for praise that pointed to specific strategies likely to be useful in the future. Thus, the most effective praise would appear to include specific information delivered in a noncontrolling manner, perhaps best achieved within the context of a positive teacher-student relationship (Bear, Slaughter, Mantz, & Farley-Ripple, 2017).

Another sense in which praise may be controlling comes from an emerging body of research on praise addiction. Repeated exposure to praise has the potential to create a psychological dependency including a "tolerance" of the effects of praise followed by "withdrawal" and, eventually, "cravings" for more (Baumeister & Vohs, 2001). In order to satisfy a praise addiction, students may come to engage in behaviors for the sole purpose of eliciting praise regardless of whether or not those behaviors have intrinsic value. This process may help to explain why college students value affirmations of self-esteem more than other appealing rewards, such as sex, food, and money (Bushman, Moeller, & Crocker, 2011). Praise may also serve to control behavior by introducing contingencies of self-worth, which similarly dampens intrinsic motivation (Brummelman, Thomaes, Castro, Overbeek, & Bushman, 2014).

While praise can function like a controlling reward, it is important to note that praise and tangible rewards are distinct and are associated with different motivational consequences. Unlike tangible rewards, praise does not have a detrimental effect on intrinsic motivation for prosocial behavior among young children (Ulber, Hamann, & Tomasello, 2016). Indeed, children's initial stages of learning a new skill may be a time during which praise is perceived as particularly supportive rather than controlling. For instance, younger infants, but not older infants, helped more often when given encouragement and praise for helping (Dahl et al., 2017). It will be important for future research to determine how praise given to older children may serve to scaffold learning across time in schooling contexts.

Competence beliefs

Praise can also influence children's beliefs about whether they are capable of succeeding in the future. When praise conveys positive information about competence, self-efficacy and intrinsic motivation are enhanced. This is sometimes communicated through social comparison (e.g., "That's the best score in the class!"), which at least temporarily enhances achievement emotions such as performance satisfaction (Gaines, Duvall, Webster, & Smith, 2005). Subsequent work has shown, however, that social-comparison praise is detrimental to children's intrinsic motivation in the long term because it teaches them to judge their own success primarily in relation to others. By contrast, praise emphasizing individual mastery (e.g., "You've really learned how to solve these problems!") builds a more resilient sense of competence that does not depend on outperforming one's peers (Corpus, Ogle, & Love-Geiger, 2006).

The effects of social-comparison information also depend on the relevance of the performance dimension being evaluated and the extent to which one feels similar to or psychologically close with the target of the comparison (Dijkstra, Kuyper, van der Werf, Buunk, & van der Zee, 2008). These moderators may be particularly consequential for older children, who tend to use social-comparison information in a more nuanced way. For instance, 9- to 10-year-olds, but not 5- to 6-year-olds, reported lower self-evaluations when they were outperformed by a peer with less expertise in a given task domain (Lapan & Boseovski, 2017). While younger children do not appear to use social comparisons to form their self-evaluations, they may use such information to suit their age-specific needs (e.g., to figure out if they are doing a novel task correctly; Dijkstra et al., 2008). Indeed, even preschool-age children are capable of engaging in social comparisons in familiar contexts (Cimpian, 2017). Future research must examine the effects of competence-related feedback, including social-comparison praise, across a variety of age groups.

In a broader sense of context, evidence from college students in the United States and China suggests that praise, and particularly social-comparison information, might be a more impactful source of efficacy for students from collectivist cultures (Lin, Fong, & Wang, 2017). This is interesting to consider in light of the practice of high-stakes testing across cultures, which likely renders normative comparisons more salient and has the potential to perpetuate the view that competence is a fixed entity that can only be assessed by comparing oneself to others

(Cimpian, 2017). How culture may moderate the effects of such practices as well as children's interpretation of feedback more broadly is an important question for future research.

Standards and expectations

A final conceptual variable relates to the standards and expectations embedded in praise. There is growing evidence that praise enhances intrinsic motivation when it provides specific information about what it means to do well and communicates reasonable expectations for performance. This information is essential so that children may appropriately direct their efforts and regulate future task engagement. Indeed, the absence of information about standards and expectations is one reason that a bias to deliver globally positive feedback to minority students may rob them of the tools needed for success (Harber et al., 2012).

Standards can be communicated through specific, descriptive praise. In a field experiment conducted during elementary school math lessons, for example, specific praise led to more on-task behavior and higher self-concept than general praise (Chalk & Bizo, 2004). This is consistent with the practical parenting literature, which advocates for nonevaluative *describing praise* (e.g., "Look at that! You combined colors to create different shades of brown."; Nordling, 2016).

Accuracy in praise also appears to be important. When children believed their parents' praise to either over- or understate their performance, depression and lower achievement followed (Lee, Kim, Kesebir, & Han, 2017). Parental overaspiration also tends to undermine learning (Murayama, Pekrun, Suzuki, Marsh, & Lichtenfeld, 2016), which invites the question of whether overaspirations communicated via praise may similarly undermine intrinsic motivation. A fascinating new line of research suggests that this may well be the case for children with low self-esteem: when given *inflated* praise (e.g., "That's an incredibly beautiful drawing"), they tend to avoid challenge and develop contingent self-worth, presumably because of the impossibly high standard implied by such praise (Brummelman, Thomaes, Castro et al., 2014). Perhaps ironically, children with low self-esteem also seem to *elicit* inflated praise from adults, thus creating a downward spiral. This highlights not only the need for transactional models when considering the effects of praise but also the issue of whether standards and expectations communicated by praise are appropriately matched to the child's self-perceptions (Brummelman, Crocker, & Bushman, 2016).

In fact, there is ample evidence that characteristics of the child influence how praise impacts motivation. For example, maternal praise given to adolescents with major depressive disorder elicited an atypical brain response compared to that of their nondepressed peers, presumably because of a mismatch between the praise and adolescents' self-perceptions (Silk et al., 2017). Even among adults, praise led to negative emotions when there was a mismatch between the learner's experience of the task and the standards and expectations implied by the praise

(Fong, et al., 2018). Taken together, these findings nicely echo a claim made by Henderlong and Lepper (2002, p. 775):

> ...praise is not a simple one-way transmission from the evaluator to the recipient but rather a complex social communication in which the role of the recipient is just as critical as the role of the evaluator. That is, the effects of praise vary depending not only on the content of the praise but also on the context in which it is delivered, the array of potential meanings it may convey, and the characteristics and interpretations of the recipient.

Conclusion

As indicated above, the conceptual variables identified by Henderlong and Lepper (2002) continue to provide a useful framework for organizing the literature on praise and motivation. Research over the past two decades indicates that praise enhances motivation and perseverance when it (a) implies that success is the result of controllable, malleable forces (e.g., strategy, effort); (b) minimizes perceptions of external control and promotes autonomy; (c) builds a resilient sense of competence; and (d) provides specific, accurate information about the quality of performance.

Moreover, a number of the most pressing issues for future research raised by Henderlong and Lepper (2002) are now actively being addressed: a wider range of outcome variables and domains tested, a move to more naturalistic contexts, and a recognition of child-driven effects and transactional processes. There has also been a growing focus on understanding moderators and mediators, such as children's self-concepts, their relationship with the evaluator, and the broader cultural context. We hope this important work continues.

At the same time, there are unexplored areas that must be part of the research agenda for the coming decades, such as the development of preventive interventions to help children interpret praise in a more productive manner. We would also advocate for more contextualized approaches, perhaps making use of microdevelopmental methods for assessing the effects of praise as they play out over time. In any case, we eagerly await the next two decades of research to illuminate further how this complex social communication impacts children's motivational processes.

References

Amemiya, J., & Wang, M-T. (2018). Why effort praise can backfire in adolescence. *Child Development Perspectives, 12,* 199–203.

Baumeister, R. F., & Vohs, K. D. (2001). Narcissism as addiction to esteem. *Psychological Inquiry, 12,* 206–210.

Bear, G. G., Slaughter, J. C., Mantz, L. S., & Farley-Ripple, E. (2017). Rewards, praise, and punitive consequences: Relations with intrinsic and extrinsic motivation. *Teaching and Teacher Education, 65,* 10–20.

Brummelman, E., Crocker, J., & Bushman, B. J. (2016). The praise paradox: When and why praise backfires in children with low self-esteem. *Child Development Perspectives, 10*, 111–115.

Brummelman, E., Thomaes, S., Castro, B. O. de, Overbeek, G., & Bushman, B. J. (2014). "That's not just beautiful—that's incredibly beautiful!" The adverse impact of inflated praise on children with low self-esteem. *Psychological Science, 25*, 728–735.

Brummelman, E., Thomaes, S., Overbeek, G., Orobio de Castro, B., van den Hout, M. A., & Bushman, B. J. (2014). On feeding those hungry for praise: Person praise backfires in children with low self-esteem. *Journal of Experimental Psychology: General, 143*, 9–14.

Bushman, B. J., Moeller, S. J., & Crocker, J. (2011). Sweets, sex, or self-esteem? Comparing the value of self-esteem boosts with other pleasant rewards. *Journal of Personality, 79*, 993–1012.

Chalk, K., & Bizo, L. A. (2004). Specific praise improves on-task behaviour and numeracy enjoyment: A study of year four pupils engaged in the numeracy hour. *Educational Psychology in Practice, 20*, 335–351.

Cimpian, A. (2017). Early reasoning about competence is not irrationally optimistic, nor does it stem from inadequate cognitive representations. In A. J. Elliot, C. S. Dweck, D. S. Yeager (Eds.), *Handbook of competence and motivation: Theory and application* (pp. 387–407). New York, NY: Guilford Press.

Cimpian, A., Arce, H.-M. C., Markman, E. M., & Dweck, C. S. (2007). Subtle linguistic cues affect children's motivation. *Psychological Science, 18*, 314–316.

Corpus, J. H., Ogle, C. M., & Love-Geiger, K. E. (2006). The effects of social-comparison versus mastery praise on children's intrinsic motivation. *Motivation and Emotion, 30*, 335–345.

Dahl, A., Satlof-Bedrick, E. S., Hammond, S. I., Drummond, J. K., Waugh, W. E., & Brownell, C. A. (2017). Explicit scaffolding increases simple helping in younger infants. *Developmental Psychology, 53*, 407–416.

Dijkstra, P., Kuyper, H., van der Werf, G., Buunk, A. P., & van der Zee, Y. G., (2008). Social comparison in the classroom: A review. *Review of Educational Research, 78*, 828–879.

Fong, C. J., Williams, K. M., Williamson, Z. H., Lin, S., Kim, Y. W., & Schallert, D. L. (2018). "Inside out": Appraisals for achievement emotions from constructive, positive, and negative feedback on writing. *Motivation and Emotion, 42*, 236–257.

Gaines, L. M., Duvall, J., Webster, J. M., & Smith, R. H. (2005). Feeling good after praise for a successful performance: The importance of social comparison information. *Self and Identity, 4*, 373–389.

Good, K., & Corpus, J. H. (2017, October). *The effect of praise type and linguistic cues on parents' beliefs about their children.* Poster presented at the biennial meeting of the Cognitive Development Society, Portland, OR.

Goodvin, R., & Rolfson, J. (2014). Mothers' attributions in reminiscing conversations about children's successes and failures: Connections with children's self-evaluations. *Merrill-Palmer Quarterly, 60*, 24–52.

Gunderson, E. A., Sorhagen, N. S., Gripshover, S. J., Dweck, C. S., Goldin-Meadow, S., & Levine, S. C. (2018). Parent praise to toddlers predicts fourth grade academic achievement via children's incremental mindsets. *Developmental Psychology, 54*, 397–409.

Haimovitz, K., & Corpus, J. H. (2011). Effects of person versus process praise on student motivation: Stability and change in emerging adulthood. *Educational Psychology, 31*, 595–609.

Harber, K. D., Gorman, J. L., Gengaro, F. P., Butisingh, S., Tsang, W., & Outllette, R. (2012). Students' race and teachers' social support affect the positive feedback bias in public schools. *Journal of Educational Psychology, 104,* 1149–1161.

Hargreaves, E. (2013). Inquiring into children's experiences of teacher feedback: Reconceptualising assessment for learning. *Oxford Review of Education, 39,* 229–246.

Henderlong, J., & Lepper, M. R. (2002). The effects of praise on children's intrinsic motivation: A review and synthesis. *Psychological Bulletin, 128,* 774–795.

Lam, S., Yim, P., & Ng, Y. (2008). Is effort praise motivational? The role of beliefs in the effort–ability relationship. *Contemporary Educational Psychology, 33,* 694–710.

Lapan, C., & Boseovski, J. J. (2017). When peer performance matters: Effects of expertise and traits on children's self-evaluations after social comparison. *Child Development, 88,* 1860–1872.

Lee, H. I., Kim, Y.-H., Kesebir, P., & Han, D. E. (2017). Understanding when parental praise leads to optimal child outcomes: Role of perceived praise accuracy. *Social Psychological and Personality Science, 8,* 679–688.

Lin, S., Fong, C. J., & Wang, Y. (2017). Chinese undergraduates' sources of self-efficacy differ by sibling status, achievement, and fear of failure along two pathways. *Social Psychology of Education, 20,* 361–386.

Mouratidis, A., Lens, W., & Vansteenkiste, M. (2010). How you provide corrective Feedback makes a difference: The motivating role of communicating in an autonomy-supporting way. *Journal of Sport and Exercise Psychology, 32,* 619–637.

Mueller, C. M., & Dweck, C. S. (1998). Praise for intelligence can undermine children's motivation and performance. *Journal of Personality and Social Psychology, 75,* 33–52.

Murayama, K., Pekrun R., Suzuki, M., Marsh, J. W., & Lichtenfeld, S. (2016). Don't aim too high for your kids: Parental overaspiration undermines students' learning in mathematics. *Journal of Personality and Social Psychology, 111,* 766–779.

Nordling, J. (2016). *Caring discipline: Practical tools for nurturing happy families and classrooms* (5th ed.). Portland, OR: Parent Support Center.

Pomerantz, E. M., & Kempner, S. G. (2013). Mothers' daily person and process praise: Implications for children's theory of intelligence and motivation. *Developmental Psychology, 49,* 2040–2046.

Reeve, J., & Jang, H. (2006). What teachers say and do to support students' autonomy during a learning activity. *Journal of Educational Psychology, 98,* 209–218.

Ryan, R. M., & Deci, E. L. (2000). Self-determination theory and the facilitation of intrinsic motivation, social development, and well-being. *American Psychologist, 55,* 68–78.

Silk, J. S., Lee, K. H., Elliott, R. D., Hooley, J. M., Dahl, R. E., Barber, A., & Siegle, G. J. (2017). "Mom - I don't want to hear it": Brain response to maternal praise and criticism in adolescents with major depressive disorder. *Social Cognitive and Affective Neuroscience, 12,* 729–738.

Ulber, J., Hamann, K., & Tomasello, M. (2016). Extrinsic rewards diminish costly sharing in 3-year-olds. *Child Development, 87,* 1192–1203.

Zentall, S. R., & Morris, B. J. (2010). "Good job, you're so smart": The effects of inconsistency of praise type on young children's motivation. *Journal of Experimental Child Psychology, 107,* 155–163.

Zhao, L., Heyman, G. D., Chen, L. L., & Lee, K. (2017). Praising young children for being smart promotes cheating. *Psychological Science, 28,* 1868–1870.

6

WHEN PRAISE—VERSUS CRITICISM—MOTIVATES GOAL PURSUIT

Lauren Eskreis-Winkler and Ayelet Fishbach

To motivate behavior, is it better to give praise or criticism? Are people more motivated when they consider successfully completed actions or actions at which they have yet to succeed? A teacher trying to goad a student to work harder can focus on either what the student has done right or what the student has done wrong. Which is the more effective strategy?

Works of several decades (e.g., Dweck & Leggett, 1988; Fishbach & Dhar, 2005; Monin & Miller, 2001) suggest there is no universal answer. How negative versus positive feedback (e.g., feedback that emphasizes missing vs. completed actions) affects motivation *depends* on other factors. One of these psychological factors is the meaning the actor ascribes to the action—whether the actor represents his or her action as a sign of commitment or a sign of progress (Fishbach & Dhar, 2005). People "highlight" a goal—they consistently strive towards that same goal over multiple opportunities—when they believe their actions signal commitment. In contrast, people balance, or juggle between goals, when they see their actions as a sign of progress.

In this chapter, we focus on how this basic insight can be used to understand the motivational power of feedback. Whether the actor sees feedback as a sign of commitment or a sign of progress determines the extent to which positive—versus negative—feedback is motivating. Specifically, positive feedback motivates goal pursuit when it signals an increase in goal commitment, whereas negative feedback motivates goal pursuit when it signals insufficient goal progress.

First, we review the dynamics of motivation. Second, we discuss how these dynamics explain the motivational power of feedback. Finally, we discuss implications.

The dynamics of motivation

Action representations affect motivation. An action representation is an individual's interpretation of his or her own behavior, and specifically, whether he or she interprets an action as a sign of commitment or a sign of progress. Commitment is one's sense that the goal is attainable and valuable (Fishbein & Ajzen, 1974). Progress is the sense that one has reduced the gap between the present state and goal completion (Carver & Scheier, 1998).

What do commitment and progress representations look like? People who make commitment representations look at their actions to discern their commitment. They ask, "Does my behavior suggest I am committed to this goal?" They evaluate their confidence in their success as well as their personal attraction to the goal. Following a successful goal-directed action, people who adopt a commitment representation tend to highlight that goal by engaging in further consistent, motivated action. They do this because they believe they are committed, and thus wish to continue to exhibit their commitment towards the goal.

In contrast, people who make progress representations look at their actions to discern their progress. They ask, "Does my behavior indicate I have made sufficient progress?" They assess whether they have done enough or need to keep going. People who estimate progress tend to balance in the aftermath of success (Fishbach, Dhar, & Zhang, 2006; Fishbach, Koo, & Finkelstein, 2014), replacing the current goal with a different one. The successful action leads people to infer they have made sufficient progress, and thus licenses a switch to an unrelated goal (Mullen & Monin, 2016; Khan & Dhar, 2006).

As an example, people exercise and eat well in order to stay healthy. In one study (Zhang, Fishbach, & Dhar, 2007), gym-goers were shown to have commitment or progress representations of their workouts. Some perceived their workouts as a sign of their commitment to staying healthy, whereas others perceived their workouts as a sign that they were making progress towards the same goal. These different representations predicted people's eating choices. Gym-goers who perceived exercise as a commitment tended to highlight by eating foods that were healthy. In contrast, those who viewed workouts as progress tended to balance by eating foods that were less healthy.

The dynamics of motivation applied to feedback

We propose that the impact of feedback, like the impact of past actions, depends on action representations. Interestingly, this proposal runs counter to some motivational theories, which suggest, universally, that positive or negative feedback is more motivating.

Past theories

According to several past motivation theories, positive feedback is universally more motivating than negative feedback (Atkinson, 1964; Bandura & Cervone,

1983; Weiner, 1974; Zajonc & Brickman, 1969). These theories propose that positive feedback, more than negative feedback, increases confidence, outcome expectancies, and commitment, and as a result, motivates behavior. For example, because people desire to be consistent (Bem, 1972), self-perception theory argues that once an action is successfully carried out, this increases the likelihood that it will be carried out again in the future. Self-efficacy theory suggests something similar: that positive feedback increases the individual's sense of competence, or efficacy, and that this, in turn, increases motivation (Bandura, 1991). For example, in the academic context, successful academic experiences increase students' self-efficacy, and self-efficacy predicts students' future academic performance, even after accounting for other key predictors, such as the student's previous academic performance and other people's expectations for the student (Bandura, Barbaranelli, Gian, & Concetta, 2001).

Other theories predict the opposite. According to these competing theories, motivation arises as a result of the gap between one's present achievements and the desired end state (Carver & Scheier, 1998; Higgins, 1987; Kluger & DeNisi, 1996; Locke & Latham, 1990; Miller, Galanter, & Pribram, 1960). Positive feedback, which narrows this gap, is therefore less motivating than negative feedback, which (psychologically) accentuates it. Indeed, according to Cybernetic theory, negative feedback is a more effective motivator than positive feedback because it draws attention to the difference between current and desired states of achievement.

A more nuanced alternative

In contrast to past theories, we propose a more nuanced view. Based on insights from the dynamics of motivation described above, we argue that the motivational power of positive and negative feedback *depends* on whether it is interpreted as a sign of commitment or a sign of progress. When people interpret feedback as a sign of commitment, positive feedback is more motivating than negative feedback. In contrast, when people interpret feedback as a sign of progress, negative feedback is more motivating than positive feedback (Fishbach et al., 2006).

Why is this? Consider a student whose teacher praises them for their performance on a Spanish oral. If this student interprets the feedback as a sign that they are good at Spanish, and committed to excelling in Spanish, then this positive feedback ought to motivate further studying and Spanish achievement. By contrast, if the student interprets the positive feedback as a sign that they have made sufficient progress, then they will invest less effort in subsequent Spanish assignments, redirecting their efforts towards other goals.

By this same logic, negative feedback ought to increase motivation when it signals progress, but ought to decrease motivation when it signals commitment. Continuing with the same example, a Spanish student whose teacher criticizes them for their performance on a Spanish oral, and interprets the feedback as a sign that insufficient progress has been made, will be motivated to redouble their efforts in order to make further progress. Yet interpreting the same negative feedback as a reflection of one's commitment will have the opposite effect. Students who interpret negative feedback to mean that they lack commitment—that is, the ability to achieve a goal or the desire to do so—will withdraw effort.

Among other factors, individual differences in commitment and expertise often determine whether individuals see their actions as a signal of commitment or progress (Finkelstein & Fishbach, 2012; Koo & Fishbach, 2008). Because uncommitted individuals and novices feel uncertain about their level of commitment, they use feedback to infer whether they are committed. These individuals ask about commitment and take their successful actions as a signal of commitment (i.e., that they value the goal and can achieve it). Committed individuals and experts, in contrast, already know they are committed, and, therefore, they use feedback to infer progress; that is, they take their action as a signal that progress has been made.

Indeed, empirical evidence demonstrates that among individuals with low commitment—that is, among individuals who tend to adopt a commitment frame—positive feedback is more motivating. In one study, students who studied for a pass/fail exam to which commitment was low were more motivated when considering the class materials they covered successfully than when they considered the materials they had not yet covered (Koo & Fishbach, 2008). In contrast, among individuals who are highly dedicated—individuals who tend to adopt a progress frame—negative feedback was more motivating than positive feedback. Students who studied for an important exam, and were therefore committed to doing well, reported higher levels of motivation after they considered the materials they have not yet covered versus materials they had covered (Koo & Fishbach, 2008). This pattern has also been found among adults in the workforce. Adults with high professional commitment who receive criticism subsequently demonstrate higher performance on work tasks than those who are praised (Brunstein & Gollwitzer, 1996). Indeed, as people gain expertise—which is to say, as they become more secure in their commitment, and therefore more attuned to progress—they shift from being more motivated by positive feedback to being more motivated by negative feedback. Across one series of studies, people who were less expert in academic subjects, environmental behavior, and beauty regimens were more motivated by positive feedback, yet as expertise increased, people were more motivated by negative feedback than by positive feedback (Finkelstein & Fishbach, 2012).

Other times, praise or criticism is phrased such that it prompts people to interpret their actions as indicative of either commitment or progress (Fishbach & Dhar, 2005). For example, asking people "Do you feel committed" or "Do you feel you made progress" prompted people to generate commitment versus progress representations. Similarly, praise that expresses commitment (e.g., "You're so good at this," "That's not for you") could potentially encourage people to adopt such an action representation, whereas criticism that expresses progress (e.g., "You're falling behind") could likely encourage people to adopt a progress representation.

When praise is more motivating than criticism

Past research suggests that when people are in a commitment frame, praise will be more motivating than criticism, yet when people are in a progress frame, criticism is more motivating than praise. As noted above, nonexperts tend to spontaneously adopt a commitment frame, whereas experts tend to adopt a progress frame. Indeed, nonexperts will generally be more motivated by praise than by criticism.

More recent research has tested how positive versus negative feedback affects people's motivation to learn from the failed or successful experience itself. Thus, whereas previous research examined how feedback affected subsequent goal-related motivation, this more recent research has tested whether feedback affects people's motivation to continue learn—versus tune out—in an ongoing learning experience. In particular, this research has examined the degree to which praise versus criticism promotes engagement versus disengagement. The general finding is that nonexperts learn more—they stay on task, pay attention, and demonstrate higher levels of learning—when they receive positive feedback, as compared to negative feedback (Eskreis-Winkler & Fishbach, 2019, 2020).

To test the relative motivational power of praise versus criticism on in-task motivation, in one study, participants answered a series of binary-choice questions on a new language (Eskreis-Winkler & Fishbach, 2019). In these questions, participants saw a symbol and had to guess the meaning of the symbol when presented with two possibilities. After each question, the participant received randomly determined feedback ("correct" or "incorrect"). Because each question had only two possible answers, the informational value of success and failure feedback was equivalent: both allowed the participant to determine the correct answer. Despite this, participants demonstrated higher levels of learning following praise (positive feedback) than following criticism (negative feedback). Often, those receiving criticism were subsequently paying so little attention that they performed no better than chance level on the recall task. The result of criticism was tuning out and low task commitment.

In another study, telemarketers at a US company completed a series of binary-choice trivia questions on the topic of customer service (Eskreis-Winkler & Fishbach, 2019). Telemarketers who received feedback on correct answers—praise—learned from the feedback at a rate above chance (as demonstrated by learning levels on a posttest). In contrast, telemarketers who received feedback on incorrect answers—criticism—did not learn at a rate that exceeded change—which is to say, they tuned out and did not learn anything from negative feedback at all. This differential effect on learning replicated across other content domains (i.e., linguistic content, social content) and across different samples (field, online). People continued to learn more from praise than from criticism, even when learning from criticism was redesigned to be less cognitively taxing than learning from praise (requiring fewer mental inferences), and even when learning from both praise and criticism was incentivized.

In sum, praise and criticism not only influence subsequent motivation but also on-task motivation—the degree to which people tune in versus let their mind wander off task. The motivational power of praise and criticism depends on how they are interpreted. Given that praise is more motivating in a commitment frame, and a commitment frame is prevalent among nonexperts—it stands to reason that many people, most of the time, are more motivated by praise than by criticism.

Implications

The insights above suggest specific recommendations for teachers, coaches, mentors, parents, and anyone else with an interest in motivating others. Supervisors who are unsure whether praise or criticism will be more motivating ought to consider the action representation the target is likely to adopt. Targets in a commitment framework are likely to be more motivated by praise, whereas targets in a progress framework are likely to be more motivated by criticism. To the extent that targets are nonexperts, and thus more likely to adopt a commitment frame, praise will be more motivating than criticism.

While the above analysis has clear implications for leadership, one limitation of these recommendations is that using only praises to motivate people with a commitment framework may lead them to miss out on valuable critical information. Indeed, as the experiments above demonstrated, people in a commitment framework often tune out and fail to learn from criticism (Eskreis-Winkler & Fishbach, 2019). Not sharing such information could further increase their blind spot. Criticism often offers qualitatively unique information that is not available in praise—for example, information on missed opportunities, missing actions, gaps, and discrepancies. Praise, which tells people what they are doing right, offers none of this information. Thus, unlike the binary-choice paradigm cited above, in which praise and criticism were manipulated to offer similar information on the "correct" answer, it is often the case that qualitatively different types of information are present in praise versus criticism. Thus, one clear drawback of "matching" feedback to a person's action representation is that crucial—typically, critical—information will not be shared or learned from.

Is there a way around this problem? In our research, we found one potential answer. In one study, we found that novices—those ostensibly with a commitment framework—were able to learn just as much from criticism as from praise when the criticism was given to someone else (Eskreis-Winkler & Fishbach, 2019). Participants in this study completed the same binary-choice questions described above, following which they were randomized to see positive or negative feedback. We examined whether participants learned more from positive versus negative feedback when it was delivered to the self, as well as whether they learned more from positive versus negative feedback when they observed it being given to someone else. We found that participants learned less from failure (vs. success) feedback when the feedback was on their own performance (replicating the effects described above), but they learned just as much from negative (vs. positive) feedback when they were third-party observers, observing the feedback being delivered to someone else. These results suggest an initial solution to the problem of how to get commitment-minded individuals to pay attention to and learn from criticism, just as much as they pay attention and learn from praise.

Surely, there are also others. Another potential solution would be to shift people's action representations to accommodate the feedback that needs to be delivered. For example, people could be primed to adopt a commitment frame when the coach wants to deliver positive feedback and primed to adopt a progress frame when the coach wants to deliver negative feedback. Above, we discussed several factors that influence action representation (individual differences in level of commitment or expertise, framing questions). Action representations are also influenced by whether people construe their actions abstractly versus concretely (Fishbach, Dhar, & Zhang, 2006). When people construe their actions abstractly, they are more likely to perceive their actions as expressing commitment, and when people construe their actions concretely, they are more likely to infer progress. It follows that praises will be more motivating when they are presented abstractly (e.g., "you've excelled your first year med school"), whereas criticism will be more motivating when it is presented concretely ("you've failed a specific exam").

Conclusion

In sum, the motivating power of positive and negative feedback depends on factors outside of the feedback. Praise tends to be more motivating when it is interpreted as a sign of commitment. In contrast, criticism tends to be more motivating when it is interpreted as a sign of insufficient progress. These effects determine overall task engagement as well as the degree to which people tune in (or out) during the specific task on which they are getting feedback.

References

Atkinson, J. W. (1964). *An introduction to motivation.* Oxford, England: Van Nostrand.

Bandura, A. (1991). Social cognitive theory of self-regulation. *Organizational Behavior and Human Decision Processes, 50,* 248–287.

Bandura, A., Barbaranelli, C., Caprara, G. V., & Pastorelli, C. (2001). Self-efficacy beliefs as shapers of children's aspirations and career trajectories. *Child Development, 72,* 187–206.

Bandura, A., & Cervone, D. (1983). Self-evaluative and self-efficacy mechanisms governing the motivational effects of goal systems. *Journal of Personality and Social Psychology, 45,* 1017–1028.

Bem, D. J. (1972). Self-perception theory. In L. Berkowitz (Ed.), *Advances in experimental social psychology* (Vol. 6, pp. 1–63). New York, NY: Academic Press.

Brunstein, J. C., & Gollwitzer, P. M. (1996). Effects of failure on subsequent performance: The importance of self-defining goals. *Journal of Personality and Social Psychology, 70,* 395–407.

Carver, C. S., & Scheier, M. F. (1998). *On the self-regulation of behavior.* New York, NY: Cambridge University Press.

Dweck, C. S., & Leggett, E. L. (1988). A social-cognitive approach to motivation and personality. *Psychological Review, 95*, 256–273.

Eskreis-Winkler, L., & Fishbach, A. (2019). Not learning from failure—the greatest failure of all. *Psychological Science, 30*, 1733–1744.

Eskreis-Winkler, L., & Fishbach, A. (2020). Hidden failures. *Organizational Behavior and Human Decision Processes, 157*, 57–67.

Fishbach, A., & Dhar, R. (2005). Goals as excuses or guides: The liberating effect of perceived goal progress on choice. *Journal of Consumer Research, 32*, 370–377.

Fishbach, A., Dhar, R., & Zhang, Y. (2006). Subgoals as substitutes or complements: The role of goal accessibility. *Journal of Personality and Social Psychology, 91*, 232–242.

Finkelstein, S. R., & Fishbach, A. (2012). Tell me what I did wrong: Experts seek and respond to negative feedback. *Journal of Consumer Research, 39*, 22–38.

Fishbach, A., Koo, M., & Finkelstein, S. R. (2014). Motivation resulting from completed and missing actions. *Advances in Experimental Social Psychology, 50*, 257–307.

Fishbein, M., & Ajzen, I. (1974). Attitudes towards objects as predictors of single and multiple behavioral criteria. *Psychological Review, 81*, 59–74.

Higgins, E. T. (1987). Self-discrepancy: A theory relating self and affect. *Psychological Review, 94*, 319–340.

Khan, U., & Dhar, R. (2006). Licensing effect in consumer choice. *Journal of Marketing Research, 43*, 259–266.

Kluger, A. N., & DeNisi, A. (1996). The effects of feedback interventions on performance: A historical review, a meta-analysis, and a preliminary feedback intervention theory. *Psychological Bulletin, 119*, 254–284.

Koo, M., & Fishbach, A. (2008). Dynamics of self-regulation: How (un)accomplished goal actions affect motivation. *Journal of Personality and Social Psychology, 94*, 183–195.

Locke, E. A., & Latham, G. P. (1990). *A theory of goal setting and task performance.* Englewood Cliffs, NJ: Prentice-Hall.

Miller, G. A., Galanter, E., & Pribram, K. H. (1960). *Plans and the structure of behavior.* New York, NY: Henry Holt.

Monin, B., & Miller, D. T. (2001). Moral credentials and the expression of prejudice. *Journal of Personality and Social Psychology, 81*, 33–43.

Mullen, E., & Monin, B. (2016). Consistency versus licensing effects of past moral behavior. *Annual Review of Psychology, 67*, 363–385.

Weiner, B. (1974). *Achievement motivation and attribution theory.* Morristown, NJ: General Learning Press.

Zajonc, R. B., & Brickman, P. (1969). Expectancy and feedback as independent factors in task performance. *Journal of Personality and Social Psychology, 11*, 148–156.

Zhang, Y., Fishbach, A., & Dhar, R. (2007). When thinking beats doing: The role of optimistic expectations in goal-based choice. *Journal of Consumer Research, 34*, 567–578.

7

PARADOXICAL EFFECTS OF PRAISE

A transactional model

Eddie Brummelman and Carol S. Dweck

Modern parents and teachers often feel responsible for their children's self-esteem and motivation. While they are not wrong that their words and actions are consequential, their ideas about how to instill self-esteem and motivation may sometimes be misguided. In the past few decades, much of the burden of instilling self-esteem and motivation has been placed on the practice of praising children. Indeed, it seems quite intuitive that saying positive things about children—about what they have done and what their qualities are—would make them feel good about themselves and would motive them to take on challenges and persist in the face of setbacks.

This belief in the power of praise has spread through Western society. Self-help books state, "Be generous with your praise. Find as many opportunities to sincerely praise your children as you can" (McKay, 1992, p. 243). Posters, such as "101 Ways to Praise a Child," provide parents and teachers with inspiration for how to praise, ranging from "Good," "Well done," and "Nice work" to "Excellent," "Outstanding," and "You're spectacular." Parenting and educational interventions often use praise as their core component, and, in fact, praise can often be effective (O'Mara, Marsh, Craven, & Debus, 2006). Unsurprisingly, then, many Western adults use praise to boost children's self-esteem and to make them feel confident about their abilities (Miller & Cho, 2018). However, research is suggesting that these well-intentioned efforts are not always successful. In this chapter, we will examine *when* and *why* praise may sometimes instead undermine children's self-esteem and motivation. In doing so, we will propose a transactional model to shed light on these paradoxical effects of praise.

Transactional model

To date, praise has primarily been studied as a unidirectional process, with children being shaped by adults' praise (Henderlong & Lepper, 2002). Yet, every evaluative event is a transaction between the people involved. In this view, children are not mere recipients of praise; they may draw praise from others, which may, in turn, shape them. In recent years, researchers have developed models to understand these transactions involving praise (Brummelman, Crocker, & Bushman, 2016; Haimovitz & Dweck, 2017). These models do not focus exclusively on how children are being shaped by adults' praise, but on transactions between the praiser (the adult) and the praisee (the child). They describe how such transactions may arise out of adults' well-intentioned attempts to increase children's self-esteem (Brummelman et al., 2016) and motivation (Haimovitz & Dweck, 2017). Here, we bridge these models to provide a transactional model of praise that addresses both self-esteem and motivation.

According to our model (Figure 7.1), especially in Western societies, adults' lay theories typically hold that praise is an effective way of raising children's self-esteem and motivation (step 1). In order to accomplish this desired outcome, adults may be especially inclined to give *person praise*, such as "You're so smart!" or *inflated praise*, such as "You did incredibly well!" (step 2). These forms of praise—while often quite pleasant in the moment—may, in some cases, inadvertently jeopardize self-esteem and motivation in the longer run, as they may make children concerned about upholding the positive evaluation, both in their own eyes and in the eyes of others. This concern can make children vulnerable to future challenges or setbacks, both actual and feared (step 3). A child's lowered self-esteem or motivation may, in turn, further motivate adults to offer praise, establishing an undesirable cycle (step 4). We will discuss each of these steps in detail.

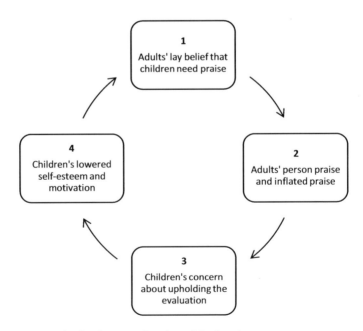

FIGURE 7.1 Hypothesized transactional model of praise.

Step 1: Why do adults praise?

Most parents and teachers want what is best for their children, and many believe, correctly, that they play a key role in supporting the child's self-esteem and motivation. In addition to this general stance, there may also be particular events that signal to parents and teachers that this would be a good time to play that supportive role. One such example may be when the child has had a success. At these times, it may seem almost obligatory to offer praise.

Socialization practices, including praise, may be driven by adults' *lay theories* (also known as *implicit theories, naïve theories, ethnotheories,* or *folk theories*). Lay theories reflect the core beliefs that people have about themselves and others, and they can guide information processing and decision making (Plaks, Levy, & Dweck, 2009). Among such lay theories are those that adults hold about child-reaing. Many Western adults believe that self-esteem is key to children's motivation and that self-esteem can be raised effectively through praise (Miller & Cho, 2018). In fact, most Western adults believe that children need praise to feel satisfied with themselves (Brummelman & Thomaes, 2011) and to be confident about their abilities (Mueller & Dweck, 1998). Such culture-specific beliefs may translate into concrete parenting behaviors. Compared to their non-Western counterparts, Western adults are more likely to praise children for their successes (Ng, Pomerantz, & Lam, 2007). Thus, lay theories may inspire adults to bestow praise on children.

Step 2: How do adults praise?

Praise can vary in its focus and its extremity. In terms of focus, praise can be directed at the child's personal qualities (*person praise,* e.g., "You're really smart at this") or the process through which the child achieved success (*process praise,* e.g., "You found a good way to do it"; Kamins & Dweck, 1999; see also Mueller & Dweck, 1998). In terms of extremity, praise can contain an extremely positive, even inflated, evaluation (*inflated praise,* e.g., "You did *incredibly* well") or a more modest, but still positive evaluation (*modest praise,* e.g., "You did well"; Brummelman, Thomaes, Orobio de Castro, Overbeek, & Bushman, 2014). Whether praise is inflated depends on its wording; inflated praise contains an adverb (e.g., *extremely, incredibly*) or adjective (e.g., *amazing, fantastic*) signaling a very positive evaluation.

When attempting to increase self-esteem or motivation, adults may be especially inclined to give person praise and inflated praise, as both are designed to make children feel as though they have high ability. Moreover, adults may be most likely to give such praise to children who seem to need it the most: those with low self-esteem, who do not have high appraisals of themselves or their ability to begin with. In a series of studies (Brummelman, Thomaes, Orobio de Castro et al., 2014; Brummelman, Thomaes, Overbeek et al., 2014), adults read scenarios involving children with high or low self-esteem (e.g., "Sarah is often unhappy with herself"), and then wrote down the praise they would give. Adults gave children with low self-esteem more person praise and more inflated praise than they gave children with high self-esteem.

Step 3: How do children respond to adults' praise?

Praise does more than just make children feel good in the moment. It can shape their understanding of themselves and their transactions with the world. Children are active meaning makers who readily use messages from their significant others, often their parents and teachers, to construct mental representations of themselves in relation to others and in relation to the tasks they perform in the world (Dweck, 2017). Praise may give children answers to such questions as: What does the adult think of me? What does the adult think caused my success? What does the adult expect from me in the future? What will the adult think of me if I don't do well in the future?

Person praise

When children are praised for their personal qualities (such as their intelligence) after a success, they may see the adult as telling them that their ability itself caused their success—not their particular strategies or efforts (Mueller & Dweck, 1998). They may also infer that the intelligence they are said to have is something important to adults and something that makes them special. As a result, children may become more concerned with how smart they are, and they may seek tasks that continue to prove their smartness and avoid tasks that could disprove it to themselves or others. When children later struggle or fail, they may attribute this to a *lack* of smartness, making them give up and feel down about themselves and their ability.

By contrast, when children are praised for the process they engaged in to bring about success (such as their effort or strategies), they may infer that future success or future ability development can be achieved by engaging in these processes (Mueller & Dweck, 1998). Consequently, children may become eager to take on challenges to improve themselves. When they struggle or fail, they may not attribute this to lack of smartness; rather, they may infer that they did not try hard enough or that they used suboptimal strategies, and may therefore be more likely to persist and improve.

A series of experimental studies have tested the effects of person and process praise (e.g., Cimpian, Arce, Markman, & Dweck, 2007; Haimovitz & Corpus, 2011; Kamins & Dweck, 1999; Mueller & Dweck, 1998; Skipper & Douglas, 2012; Zentall & Morris, 2012). In one series of studies (Mueller & Dweck, 1998), children succeeded on a task: "You got [number of problems] right. That's a really high score." Immediately after, children received person praise (e.g., "You must be smart at these problems"), process praise (e.g., "You must have worked hard at these problems"), or no praise. Children who received person praise not only endorsed more of a fixed mind-set (seeing intelligence as more fixed) but also were more likely to avoid challenges. Moreover, when they encountered a period of failure, they were more likely to denigrate their ability and to perform more poorly—and, later, to lie about the number of problems they had solved correctly. By contrast, children who received process praise not only endorsed more of a growth mind-set (viewing intelligence as something that could be developed) but also were more likely to embrace challenges and to be honest about their performance when it was poor. Moreover, when they failed, they were less likely to denigrate their ability; instead, they were more likely to persist and to perform well.

It seems that person praise, unlike process praise, makes children concerned about appearing smart. Consistent with this idea, in an experiment with 3- and 5-year-old children (Zhao, Heyman, Chen, & Lee, 2017), those who received person praise from the experimenter—"You are so smart!"—were more likely to cheat in a card-guessing game, probably in an attempt to uphold their reputation for being smart.

Longitudinal studies suggest that person and process praise may have long-term consequences in real-world settings. In one study (Pomerantz & Kempner, 2013), mothers completed a 10-day daily interview, reporting how often they gave their child person and process praise. Children who received more person praise were more likely to endorse a fixed mind-set and to avoid challenges 6 months later. In another study (Gunderson et al., 2018), parental praise was observed at home when children were 1, 2, or 3 years old. Children who received more process praise were more likely to endorse a growth mind-set 5 years later and, in turn, to achieve better math and reading scores 2 years after that in elementary school. Such motivational effects of process praise can already manifest at 18 months of age, when children comprehend process-focused words such as "try." In two observational studies (Lucca, Horton, & Sommerville, 2019), 18-month-old infants who received more process praise from their parents were more likely to persist at challenging tasks (e.g., engaging in a difficult stacking task).

Inflated praise

Like person praise, inflated praise may be intended to make children feel good and may sometimes do so. However, when children are praised in inflated ways, they may also feel pressure to live up to the implied expectations of them. Indeed, it has been argued that praise can convey an implicit demand for continued exceptional performance (Baumeister, Hutton, & Cairns, 1990; Ryan, 1982). When children are told that they performed incredibly well, they may infer that they should perform incredibly well all the time to keep the adult's high regard. Children, perhaps especially those who doubt their ability or are preoccupied with others' opinions of them, may then be afraid of not being able to live up to these standards. Everyone's life is full of struggles and setbacks, so children may eventually fall short of the standards set for them and feel down about themselves.

A series of experiments tested the effects of inflated praise. In one study (Brummelman, Thomaes, Orobio de Castro et al., 2014), children were asked to make a drawing, and their drawing was then shown to a professional painter. The painter gave them inflated praise ("You made an *incredibly* beautiful drawing!"), modest praise ("You made a beautiful drawing!"), or no praise. Children with low self-esteem who received inflated praise avoided subsequent challenging tasks, perhaps because they were afraid of not being able to live up to the standards set for them. In another study (Nikolić, Brummelman, Colonnesi, de Vente, & Bögels, 2018), children were invited to sing a song on stage, and their performance was evaluated by a professional singer. The singer gave children inflated praise ("You sang *incredibly* well!"), modest praise ("You sang well!"), or no praise. Socially anxious children who received inflated praise were likely to blush—often a hallmark of embarrassment, which may arise when children feel put on the spot to deserve or live up to the praise (Drummond & Su, 2012). Thus, inflated praise can make at-risk children concerned about living up to other people's expectations of them, potentially leading them to avoid challenges. Unlike inflated praise, modest praise did not have such effects; it led children with low self-esteem to embrace challenges, and did not cause socially anxious children to blush.

Even more directly relevant, in an observational-longitudinal study (Brummelman, Nelemans, Thomaes, & Orobio de Castro, 2017), parental praise was observed at home when children were ages 7–11. About 25% of all praise was inflated, and parents were more likely to give inflated praise to children with low self-esteem. However, the more inflated praise parents gave, the lower the children's self-esteem was 6, 12, and 18 months later—regardless of whether children started out with high or low self-esteem. That is, parents who respond to their children with inflated praise may inadvertently contribute to lower self-esteem in children over time (also see Lee, Kim, Kesebir, & Han, 2017).

In sum, although they are given with good intentions, person praise and inflated praise do not seem effective tools to raise or sustain children's self-confidence, challenge-seeking, and task persistence. Both forms of praise seem to make children focused on judgments of the self—judgments rendered by themselves or by others. The ability to see oneself as an object of judgment develops in early childhood (Burhans & Dweck, 1995). As we have noted, when children are praised for their personal abilities or in inflated ways, they may become concerned with upholding the positive evaluation. Especially in the face of setbacks, those who have received such praise may feel that they have to sacrifice learning and self-improvement for the sake of demonstrating their worth or ability—for example, by avoiding challenges, lying about their performance, or even cheating for purposes of "improving" their performance.

Step 4: How do children's responses to praise affect adults?

One might wonder: If person praise and inflated praise seem to backfire, why do adults continue to provide such praise? When adults give praise, children's initial response may most often be positive. From this initial response, adults may legitimately infer that children enjoy being praised, which fosters their continued use of praise. Person praise and inflated praise may backfire only later, after the initial flush of pleasure, and may do so particularly when children face challenges or setbacks. Adults may not recognize that these later effects can be consequences of the same pleasure-producing praise, because these effects run counter to their lay theories and may occur long after the praise has been delivered. In fact, as we have seen, children's lowered self-esteem and motivation may even motivate adults to continue to praise.

Summary and future directions

According to our model, then, adults hold lay theories that may encourage them to provide children with praise—including person praise and inflated praise—in an attempt to increase their self-esteem and motivation. However, these forms of praise can make children concerned about upholding the positive evaluation in their own eyes and in the eyes of others. In some cases, these concerns may lead children to avoid challenges, to give up or cheat when they struggle, and to feel bad about themselves in the face of setbacks. This lowered self-esteem and motivation may, in turn, encourage parents and teachers to provide even more praise, thus establishing a vicious cycle.

Several parts of our model deserve more research. First, our model assumes that adults' praise is driven by their lay theories about child-rearing, which hold that praise is key to children's self-esteem and motivation. These beliefs are historically situated and culturally specific; around the 1970s, they became a touchstone of Western child-rearing (Miller & Cho, 2018). What makes these beliefs appealing to Western parents and teachers? Can these beliefs explain why praise is more common in Western than in non-Western child-rearing? And could targeting these beliefs change the way parents and teachers praise children? We need more research to address these questions.

Second, our model suggests that some children may be more susceptible to the detrimental effects of praise than are others. We need more research to identify such individual differences. For example, are there children who gain motivation from extravagant praise and perform well, but who labor under great anxiety lest their performance fall and they are proven unworthy? In such cases, the praise may have seemed to work, but perhaps at great cost to children's well-being. These may not be children with low self-esteem but rather with high but "contingent" self-esteem.

Third, our model identifies ways to avoid adverse effects of praise. Some experts have suggested that parents and teachers should stop praising children altogether (Kohn, 2001). Yet it seems almost impossible for parents and teachers not to praise, and there are conditions under which praise can convey useful information about the utility of effort or strategies in learning. Instead, we suggest that interventions could teach the more useful forms of praise. In a randomized trial of a reading intervention (Andersen & Nielsen, 2016), parents were told about the malleability of their child's reading abilities (i.e., taught a growth mind-set) and how to support their child by praising his or her effort. The intervention increased children's reading and writing achievements at 2- and 7-month follow-up. We need more research to understand how best to use praise to benefit children's long-term outcomes. Praising effort alone may not always suffice, because children need successful strategies and effective help-seeking—not just effort—to learn and improve (Dweck, 2015). For example, would giving a variety of kinds of process praise (e.g., for using effective strategies, seeking advice, utilizing resources) be more effective than praise for just effort?

Conclusion

In their attempts to boost children's self-esteem and motivation, parents and teachers sometimes use forms of praise that can backfire. We have proposed a transactional model that sheds light on these paradoxical effects of praise. We hope that our model will encourage researchers to join forces in understanding how parents' and teachers' feedback can be optimized to help children seek challenges, enjoy learning, and achieve their potential.

Acknowledgments

The writing of this chapter was supported, in part, by funding from the European Union's Horizon 2020 research and innovation programme under the Marie Skłodowska-Curie grant agreement No 705217 to Eddie Brummelman.

References

Andersen, S. C., & Nielsen, H. S. (2016). Reading intervention with a growth mindset approach improves children's skills. *Proceedings of the National Academy of Sciences, USA, 113,* 12111–12113.

Baumeister, R. F., Hutton, D. G., & Cairns, K. J. (1990). Negative effects of praise on skilled performance. *Basic and Applied Social Psychology, 11,* 131–148.

Brummelman, E., Crocker, J., & Bushman, B. J. (2016). The praise paradox: When and why praise backfires in children with low self-esteem. *Child Development Perspectives, 10,* 111–115.

Brummelman, E., Nelemans, S. A., Thomaes, S., & Orobio de Castro, B. (2017). When parents' praise inflates, children's self-esteem deflates. *Child Development, 88,* 1799–1809.

Brummelman, E., & Thomaes, S. (2011). [Parents' beliefs about praise]. Unpublished raw data.

Brummelman, E., Thomaes, S., Orobio de Castro, B., Overbeek, G., & Bushman, B. J. (2014). "That's not just beautiful—that's incredibly beautiful!": The adverse impact of inflated praise on children with low self-esteem. *Psychological Science, 25*, 728–735.

Brummelman, E., Thomaes, S., Overbeek, G., Orobio de Castro, B., van den Hout, M. A., & Bushman, B. J. (2014). On feeding those hungry for praise: Person praise backfires in children with low self-esteem. *Journal of Experimental Psychology: General, 143*, 9–14.

Burhans, K. K., & Dweck, C. S. (1995). Helplessness in early childhood: The role of contingent worth. *Child Development, 66*, 1719–1738.

Cimpian, A., Arce, H.-M. C., Markman, E. M., & Dweck, C. S. (2007). Subtle linguistic cues affect children's motivation. *Psychological Science, 18*, 314–316.

Drummond, P. D., & Su, D. (2012). The relationship between blushing propensity, social anxiety and facial blood flow during embarrassment. *Cognition and Emotion, 26*, 561–567.

Dweck, C. S. (2015, September 22). Carol Dweck revisits the "growth mindset." *Education Week*. Retrieved from https://www.edweek.org/ew/articles/2015/09/23/carol-dweck-revisits-the-growth-mindset.html

Dweck, C. S. (2017). From needs to goals and representations: Foundations for a unified theory of motivation, personality, and development. *Psychological Review, 124*, 689–719.

Gunderson, E. A., Sorhagen, N. S., Gripshover, S. J., Dweck, C. S., Goldin-Meadow, S., & Levine, S. C. (2018). Parent praise to toddlers predicts fourth grade academic achievement via children's incremental mindsets. *Developmental Psychology, 54*, 397–409.

Haimovitz, K., & Corpus, J. H. (2011). Effects of person versus process praise on student motivation: Stability and change in emerging adulthood. *Educational Psychology, 31*, 595–609.

Haimovitz, K., & Dweck, C. S. (2017). The origins of children's growth and fixed mindsets: New research and a new proposal. *Child Development, 88*, 1849–1859.

Henderlong, J., & Lepper, M. R. (2002). The effects of praise on children's intrinsic motivation: A review and synthesis. *Psychological Bulletin, 128*, 774–795.

Kamins, M. L., & Dweck, C. S. (1999). Person versus process praise and criticism: Implications for contingent self-worth and coping. *Developmental Psychology, 35*, 835–847.

Kohn, A. (2001). Five reasons to stop saying "good job!" *Young Children, 56*, 24–30.

Lee, H. I., Kim, Y.-H., Kesebir, P., & Han, D. E. (2017). Understanding when parental praise leads to optimal child outcomes: Role of perceived praise accuracy. *Social Psychological and Personality Science, 8*, 679–688.

Lucca, K., Horton, R., & Sommerville, J. A. (2019). Keep trying!: Parental language predicts infants' persistence. *Cognition, 193*, 104025.

McKay, J. (1992). Building self-esteem in children. In M. McKay & P. Fanning (Eds.), *Self-esteem* (2nd ed., pp. 239–271). Oakland, CA: New Harbinger.

Miller, P. J., & Cho, G. E. (2018). *Self-esteem in time and place: How American families imagine, enact, and personalize a cultural ideal.* New York, NY: Oxford University Press.

Mueller, C. M., & Dweck, C. S. (1998). Praise for intelligence can undermine children's motivation and performance. *Journal of Personality and Social Psychology, 75*, 33–52.

Ng, F. F.-Y., Pomerantz, E. M., & Lam, S.-F. (2007). European American and Chinese parents' responses to children's success and failure: Implications for children's responses. *Developmental Psychology, 43*, 1239–1255.

Nikolić, M., Brummelman, E., Colonnesi, C., de Vente, W., & Bögels, S. M. (2018). When gushing leads to blushing: Inflated praise leads socially anxious children to blush. *Behaviour Research and Therapy, 106,* 1–7.

O'Mara, A. J., Marsh, H. W., Craven, R. G., & Debus, R. L. (2006). Do self-concept interventions make a difference? A synergistic blend of construct validation and meta-analysis. *Educational Psychologist, 41,* 181–206.

Plaks, J. E., Levy, S. R., & Dweck, C. S. (2009). Lay theories of personality: Cornerstones of meaning in social cognition. *Social and Personality Psychology Compass, 3,* 1069–1081.

Pomerantz, E. M., & Kempner, S. G. (2013). Mothers' daily person and process praise: Implications for children's theory of intelligence and motivation. *Developmental Psychology, 49,* 2040–2046.

Ryan, R. M. (1982). Control and information in the intrapersonal sphere: An extension of cognitive evaluation theory. *Journal of Personality and Social Psychology, 43,* 450–461.

Skipper, Y., & Douglas, K. (2012). Is no praise good praise? Effects of positive feedback on children's and university students' responses to subsequent failures. *British Journal of Educational Psychology, 82,* 327–339.

Zentall, S. R., & Morris, B. J. (2012). A critical eye: Praise directed toward traits increases children's eye fixations on errors and decreases motivation. *Psychonomic Bulletin and Review, 19,* 1073–1077.

Zhao, L., Heyman, G. D., Chen, L., & Lee, K. (2017). Praising young children for being smart promotes cheating. *Psychological Science, 28,* 1868–1870.

PART III
Self-perceptions

8

LEARNING ABOUT OTHERS TO LEARN ABOUT THE SELF

Early reasoning about the informativeness of others' praise

Mika Asaba and Hyowon Gweon

How do we learn about who we are? Learning about the self is an inherently interactive, social process; rather than relying solely on our own experiences with the external world, we learn about the self by interacting with others. We often receive others' opinions and evaluations about our performances, qualities, and even personality traits, and sometimes, we deliberately seek out feedback from others to learn about ourselves. The influence of others' feedback may be especially powerful early in life; as children begin to develop abstract, sophisticated self-concepts (Cimpian, Hammond, Mazza, & Corry, 2017), feedback from others can shape the ways children learn about the self, interact and communicate with others, and learn about the world.

Prior work has shown the power of specific kinds of praise, suggesting how different contents of praise can influence children's motivation and achievement, for better or for worse (e.g., *process vs. person praise*, Mueller & Dweck, 1998; *inflated praise*, Brummelman, Thomaes, Orobio de Castro, Overbeek, & Bushman, 2014; *generic praise*, Cimpian, Arce, Markman, & Dweck, 2007; for a review, see Henderlong & Lepper, 2002). This work has highlighted young children's early abilities to differentiate praise depending on its content, such as the target of evaluation (e.g., whether *effort* or *ability* is being evaluated; Mueller & Dweck, 1998). Importantly, praise may signal what qualities or traits are valued by others, thereby shaping what children themselves value. When they receive praise targeted at their effort, they may learn to value persistence and the process of trying hard in the face of a challenging task; when children receive praise targeted at their ability, however, they may be learning that their ability or performance is what really matters (Mueller & Dweck, 1998). Broadly, this literature has provided compelling evidence that the contents of praise can have both immediate and long-term consequences for young children's learning, motivation, and even self-evaluations (e.g., Cimpian et al., 2007).

As adults, however, we know that even the exact same praise can have very different meanings depending on the social context. Imagine that you just gave a presentation and someone told you, "That was a great talk!" If this praise came from a colleague who compliments everyone and everything (irrespective of quality), then you might discount the praise and remain uncertain about your performance. However, if you received the exact same praise from a colleague known for their stinginess in providing praise, then you might infer that your talk went quite well. Furthermore, the meaning of praise may also depend on the speaker's goal; one may praise others' work to provide honest feedback or to provide encouragements. Thus, the meaning of praise and its informativeness is modulated by who is providing it and why. The meaning of praise can also depend on cultural norms. In some societies, parents, caregivers, and educators routinely praise children's actions and performances and rarely provide criticisms, whereas in other cultures, children rarely receive praise. This might reflect cultural differences in beliefs about the functions of feedback and praise (i.e., whether they are considered as evaluations or encouragements) and their consequence (e.g., motivating vs. "spoiling").

The context-dependency in the meaning of praise can make it particularly challenging for young children to use others' feedback as a source of information for learning about the self. In order to use praise effectively to learn about the self, children must consider others' goals, standards, and even cultural norms to infer its meaning. This raises an important question: Do young children take all praise to be equally meaningful, or do they evaluate and interpret it flexibly depending on the context?

Parallels in learning about the world and learning about the self

Recent research suggests that young children engage in rich mental-state reasoning when deciding whom to trust (for a review, see Harris, Koenig, Corriveau, & Jaswal, 2018). Young children draw different inferences about the same content of testimony or instruction depending on a speaker's goals and knowledge (for a review, see Sobel & Kushnir, 2013). This work has characterized children as vigilant learners, selectively seeking out and trusting information from those who are more informative, rather than accepting all testimony at face value. However, this literature has focused on cases where children's primary goal is to learn from others about the external world (e.g., object labels, functions of objects).

Learning about the world, however, is often intertwined with learning about the self. Parents often provide information about the world ("That is a ball!") and the self ("You are good at kicking the ball!") in the same setting, allowing children to learn about both the referent of the word "ball" and their own competence for kicking. While it is possible that there are two distinct mechanisms that support learning about the world and learning about the self, perhaps a more parsimonious explanation exists: The ways in which children interpret and learn from others' feedback (e.g., praise) about the self may be akin to the processes by which children learn and interpret others' testimony about the world. Below we discuss the social-cognitive capacities that support reasoning about the informativeness of others' testimony (e.g., sensitivity to others' goals and epistemic states, as well as statistical patterns of data) and explore the possibility that these capacities may also support reasoning about the informativeness of others' feedback about the self.

Sensitivity to others' communicative goals

Understanding a speaker's goals is critical to interpreting their testimony. A speaker may not only have a goal to help a learner acquire accurate knowledge (i.e., an *epistemic* goal) but also have a goal to save the listener's face or prevent the learner from feeling bad (i.e., a *social* goal; Brown & Levinson, 1987). Recent computational work has formalized adults' inferences about others' feedback as inferences about the speaker's epistemic or social goals (Yoon, Tessler, Goodman, & Frank, 2016); if a speaker has a social goal to be nice and provides praise ("That is amazing!"), adults infer that the quality of the product is lower than if the speaker had an epistemic goal to be honest.

Prior work has shown that children draw strong inferences from demonstrations or testimony from people with epistemic goals, especially when children have uncertainty about the world. When an adult claims that she is knowledgeable and wants to show how a novel toy works, it is clear in the context that her goal is an epistemic one. For instance, when a teacher pedagogically demonstrates one function of a novel toy, children infer that it is the *only* function (Bonawitz et al., 2011; see Shneidman, Gweon, Schulz, & Woodward, 2016, for a cross-cultural replication in toddlers).

Importantly, when children are already knowledgeable about the world, they can also use others' testimony to learn about their informativeness. For instance, when two teachers provide different labels for a novel object, children endorse the testimony of a teacher who had previously provided correct labels of well-known objects over a teacher who had provided incorrect labels (e.g., Koenig, Clement, & Harris, 2004; see Harris et al., 2018, for a review). Children are also sensitive to more nuanced forms of misinformation, such as under-informative testimony. For instance, when a teacher demonstrates only one function of a toy of a four-function toy, children are sensitive to these omissions and penalize the teacher (Gweon & Asaba, 2018; Gweon, Pelton, Konopka, & Schulz, 2014). Collectively, this research suggests that children are sensitive to information communicated with an epistemic goal and use such information flexibly depending on their own knowledge, either for learning about the world or for learning about others' informativeness.

Just as children use others' testimony and demonstrations to go beyond the evidence and draw strong inferences about the world, children may also rely heavily on others' feedback to learn about their own performance or abilities, especially when they are uncertain about how well they did; for instance, if a child made two drawings, and a teacher praises one of the drawings by saying, "this one is great", children may infer that *only* that drawing is great and the other one is not great. On the other hand, when children are already certain about the quality of their own work, they might also recognize when people provide praise that they do not deserve. Interestingly, however, while someone who has an epistemic goal but provides inaccurate or incomplete testimony about the world is clearly unreliable as a teacher, someone who praises poor-quality work may not always be considered wrong; as shown in the work of Yoon et al. (2016), adults might infer that this person has a *social goal* to make the listener feel good, rather than an *epistemic goal* to tell the truth.

Indeed, prior work suggests that older children (7–11 year-olds) may be sensitive to others' social goals in evaluating their communicative actions. They evaluate white lies more positively (e.g., saying that one likes an undesirable gift) and blunt truths more negatively in politeness contexts (Heyman, Sweet, & Lee, 2009); furthermore, when asked to explain others' white lies, the majority of children referred to the potential benefits for the recipient (i.e., making the gift-giver feel good). Thus, one hypothesis is that just as they interpret others' white lies with respect to a social goal of being nice, children also understand that others' praise may stem from a social goal, especially when they are already certain about the quality of their work.

Sensitivity to others' epistemic states

Understanding the informativeness of testimony critically requires the ability to represent and reason about others' knowledge about the world. Prior work has suggested that children use others' knowledge to figure out whether to learn from them; for example, when a speaker has claimed knowledge about novel toys, children are more likely to endorse that speaker's labels for the toys than when the speaker has claimed ignorance (Sabbagh & Baldwin, 2001). Others' knowledge also guides who children approach for information; children appropriately choose whether to approach a doctor or a car mechanic depending on what they want to know (Danovitch & Keil, 2004). Furthermore, though children negatively evaluate a teacher whose demonstration was incomplete (Gweon & Asaba, 2018; Gweon et al., 2014), children exonerate these omissions when the teacher was ignorant to these other functions (i.e., they could not have been more informative; Bass, Bonawitz, & Gweon, 2017). Collectively, these studies suggest that others' knowledge guides whose information children endorse, who they seek out for information, and how they evaluate the speakers' informativeness.

The ways we endorse or dismiss others' praise may also critically depend on what we think others know. Just as children prefer testimony from knowledgeable informants, children may also value feedback when it comes from someone who is knowledgeable or skilled; for instance, when children receive praise about their drawing skills, they may take it more seriously if it came from an art teacher than one of their peers who is clearly a novice. Furthermore, just as children seek out information about the world from knowledgeable others, they may also do so for information about the self; if a child is uncertain about their drawing skills and wants to know how they are doing, they may seek out feedback from more knowledgeable and competent others.

Sensitivity to statistical patterns of evidence

Although knowing others' goals and knowledge helps us interpret their feedback, in many contexts, they are usually not explicitly stated and often left for the learners to infer. The ability to detect statistical regularities in the environment emerges early in life (Gweon & Schulz, 2011; Saffran, Aslin, & Newport, 1996), allowing children to draw these inferences even from minimal data. In prior work on epistemic trust (e.g., Harris et al., 2018), children learned about others' informativeness through observations of others' testimony or instruction; specifically, they were often provided with events that suggested a dependence between a teacher and the accuracy of their testimony (i.e., Teacher A provides accurate statements, Teacher B provides inaccurate statements). Remarkably, with even just a few observations of each teacher, they are able to use these data as strong evidence for their general informativeness and evaluate others' subsequent testimony in light of these inferences.

Children may also be able to draw inferences about the informativeness of praise from the patterns in a speaker's past praise and the quality of the work they observed. If their praise for drawings is contingent on higher quality work, children may infer that the speaker is knowledgeable and/or has the goal of being informative with respect to quality; however, when children observe a speaker whose praise is unrelated to quality of drawings, they may infer that the speaker is either ignorant (e.g., if praise is unrelated or inversely related to quality) and/ or that they have a social goal of "being nice" (e.g., if praise was provided indiscriminately). Thus, sensitivity to patterns of data may allow children to infer others' goals, epistemic states, and informativeness even when they are not explicitly provided in context.

Preliminary work

Drawing on work from early cognitive development and social learning, one recent study investigated whether children interpret others' feedback differently depending on their past informativeness (Asaba et al., 2018). Here, participants (4–5-year-olds; $N = 80$, preregistered) made two tracings that were put into envelopes (one tracing in each envelope). Then, they watched videos of teachers providing feedback on a student's six tracings (three clearly good tracings and three clearly bad tracings); Teacher Jane only praised the three good tracings, suggesting that her praise covaries with the quality of the tracings (Selective Teacher), whereas Teacher Susan praised all six tracings, suggesting she praises indiscriminately (Overpraise Teacher). Then, the experimenter said,

> Teacher Jane looked at one of your tracings and she said it was great. Teacher Susan looked at the other tracing and said it was great. Now you can bring back your best tracing to show your teacher! Which one do you think is the best?

Because their tracings were still in the envelopes, children had to rely on how these teachers had previously praised other tracings to respond.

Children were more likely to choose the tracing praised by the Selective Teacher (Selective vs. Overpraise: 72.5% vs. 27.5%, $p = .006$, Binomial). When asked which teacher was trying to be nice, however, they were more likely to choose the Overpraise Teacher (Selective vs. Overpraise: 17.5% vs. 82.5%, $p < .001$). A follow-up experiment provided additional evidence that children specifically trust praise that is contingent on higher quality work, rather than only valuing the frequency of praise. Thus, given the exact same praise, preschool-aged children can determine whose praise is more trustworthy based on their prior patterns of praise.

These findings provide initial support for the parallel between learning about the world and learning about the self. Just as children decide from whom to learn based on others' past informativeness, they also decide whose praise to endorse based on others' prior patterns of praise.

Challenges in learning about the self

So far, we have proposed that the process by which we learn about the world and learn about the self are rooted in the same cognitive capacities. However, there may be specific challenges and biases that come with learning about the self. When learning about the world, children are motivated to acquire *accurate* information; they want to acquire true, relevant, and complete information about the meanings of words, causal relations, and how things work. In learning about the self, however, children may be additionally motivated to acquire *desirable* (i.e., positive) information. Though information about the self can be both accurate and desirable, these dimensions may not always align with one another. Children may prefer receiving desirable information regardless of accuracy if they want to feel good about themselves, but preferentially seek out accurate information when they genuinely want to learn about their performance and figure out how to improve. Some prior work suggests children generally trust positively valenced information; children judge positive assessments of others' work as more accurate than negative assessments of others' work (Boseovski, Marble, & Hughes, 2017).

On the one hand, this suggests that the tendency to prefer desirable information might make it more difficult for young children to learn from others' feedback; they might discount criticisms or selectively endorse positive feedback. Critically however, in these past studies, children never saw the actual quality of the work, so they could not assess the informativeness of others' feedback; instead, they had to rely on the positivity of the speakers' feedback to evaluate their testimony. Additionally, the speakers' goals often remained ambiguous; if children assumed that the speaker had a social goal to be nice, then it would be reasonable to prefer someone who provides positive feedback. Thus, it remains an important question for future work to better understand the extent to which children's reasoning about praise and their learning about the self is colored by their preference for positive feedback.

Conclusion

As humans, we can acquire much knowledge about the self—our qualities, traits, and capacities—through our interactions with others. In particular, we do not simply take to heart the *content* of others' feedback; rather, we evaluate and interpret others' feedback about the self with respect to what we know about others and others' minds—their goals, beliefs, and knowledge. In turn, feedback from others about the self can also tell us a lot about others' goals, knowledge, and what they think of us. Our proposal is that the same inferential processes and representational capacities that allow children to effectively learn about the world from others may also help children learn about the self from others. We hope that future work bridges work in cognitive development and motivation to better understand the complex interactions of how children learn about others, learn about the self, and learn about the world.

References

Asaba, M., Hembacher, E., Qiu, H., Anderson, B., Frank, M., & Gweon, H. (2018). Young children use statistical evidence to infer the informativeness of praise. In C. Kalish, M. Rau, J. Zhu, & T. Rogers (Eds.), *Proceedings of the 40th annual conference of the Cognitive Science Society* (pp. 112–117). Austin, TX: Cognitive Science Society.

Bass, I., Bonawitz, L. B., & Gweon, H. (2017). Didn't know, or didn't show? Preschoolers consider epistemic state and degree of omission when evaluating teachers. In G. Gunzelmann, A. Howes, T. Tenbrink, & E. Davelaar, (Eds.), *Proceedings of the 39th annual conference of the Cognitive Science Society* (pp. 105–110). Austin, TX: Cognitive Science Society.

Bonawitz, E., Shafto, P., Gweon, H., Goodman, N. D., Spelke, E., & Schulz, L. (2011). The double-edged sword of pedagogy: Instruction limits spontaneous exploration and discovery. *Cognition, 120*, 322–330.

Boseovski, J. J., Marble, K. E., & Hughes, C. (2017). Role of expertise, consensus, and informational valence in children's performance judgments. *Social Development, 26*, 445–465.

Brown, P., & Levinson, S. C. (1987). *Politeness: Some universals in language usage* (Vol. 4). Cambridge, England: Cambridge University Press.

Brummelman, E., Thomaes, S., Orobio de Castro, B., Overbeek, G., & Bushman, B. J. (2014). "That's not just beautiful—that's incredibly beautiful!" The adverse impact of inflated praise on children with low self-esteem. *Psychological Science, 25*, 728–735.

Cimpian, A., Arce, H. M. C., Markman, E. M., & Dweck, C. S. (2007). Subtle linguistic cues affect children's motivation. *Psychological Science, 18*, 314–316.

Cimpian, A., Hammond, M. D., Mazza, G., & Corry, G. (2017). Young children's self-concepts include representations of abstract traits and the global self. *Child Development, 88*, 1786–1798.

Danovitch, J. H., & Keil, F. C. (2004). Should you ask a fisherman or a biologist? Developmental shifts in ways of clustering knowledge. *Child Development, 75*, 918–931.

Gweon, H., & Asaba, M. (2018). Order matters: Children's evaluation of underinformative teachers depends on context. *Child Development, 89*, e278–e292.

Gweon, H., Pelton, H., Konopka, J. A., & Schulz, L. E. (2014). Sins of omission: Children selectively explore when teachers are under-informative. *Cognition, 132*, 335–341.

Gweon, H., & Schulz, L. (2011, June 24). 16-month-olds rationally infer causes of failed actions. *Science, 332*, 1524–1524.

Harris, P. L., Koenig, M. A., Corriveau, K. H., & Jaswal, V. K. (2018). Cognitive foundations of learning from testimony. *Annual Review of Psychology, 69*, 251–273.

Henderlong, J., & Lepper, M. R. (2002). The effects of praise on children's intrinsic motivation: A review and synthesis. *Psychological Bulletin, 128*, 774–795.

Heyman, G. D., Sweet, M. A., & Lee, K. (2009). Children's reasoning about lie-telling and truth-telling in politeness contexts. *Social Development, 18*, 728–746.

Koenig, M. A., Clément, F., & Harris, P. L. (2004). Trust in testimony: Children's use of true and false statements. *Psychological Science, 15*, 694–698.

Mueller, C. M., & Dweck, C. S. (1998). Praise for intelligence can undermine children's motivation and performance. *Journal of Personality and Social Psychology, 75*, 33–52.

Sabbagh, M. A., & Baldwin, D. A. (2001). Learning words from knowledgeable versus ignorant speakers: Links between preschoolers' theory of mind and semantic development. *Child development, 72*(4), 1054–1070.

Saffran, J. R., Aslin, R. N., & Newport, E. L. (1996, December 13). Statistical learning by 8-month-old infants. *Science, 274*, 1926–1928.

Shneidman, L., Gweon, H., Schulz, L. E., & Woodward, A. L. (2016). Learning from others and spontaneous exploration: A cross-cultural investigation. *Child Development, 87*(3), 723–735.

Sobel, D. M., & Kushnir, T. (2013). Knowledge matters: How children evaluate the reliability of testimony as a process of rational inference. *Psychological Review, 120*, 779–797.

Yoon, E. J., Tessler, M. H., Goodman, N. D., & Frank, M. C. (2016). Talking with tact: Polite language as a balance between kindness and informativity. In A. Papafragou, D. Grodner, D. Mirman, & J. C. Trueswell (Eds.), *Proceedings of the 38th annual conference of the Cognitive Science Society* (pp. 2771–2776). Austin, TX: Cognitive Science Society.

9

"YOU'RE GOOD ENOUGH, YOU'RE SMART ENOUGH, AND DOGGONE IT, PEOPLE LIKE YOU"

Differing reactions to praise among people with higher and lower self-esteem

Linden R. Timoney and Joanne V. Wood

Self-esteem refers to one's self-worth (i.e., how much one likes and values oneself; Blascovich & Tomaka, 1991). People with lower self-esteem (LSEs) report experiencing less life satisfaction, happiness, and positive affect (DeNeve & Cooper, 1998; Diener & Diener, 1995), and less relationship satisfaction (Murray, Rose, Bellavia, Holmes, & Kusche, 2002) than people with higher self-esteem (HSEs).

How might self-esteem affect responses to praise? Two prominent theories from social psychology suggest different associations between self-esteem and praise: self-verification theory (Swann, 1983) and self-enhancement theory (Taylor & Brown, 1988). Self-verification theory (Swann, 1983; Swann & Read, 1981) posits that people seek out and prefer information that confirms their existing self-concept. That is, people with relatively positive views of themselves—such as HSEs—are more likely to favor feedback suggesting that others view them positively. Likewise, people with relatively negative self-views—such as LSEs—may prefer feedback suggesting that others see them relatively negatively. Conversely, self-enhancement theory suggests that people have a powerful motivation to seek positive information that enhances their self-views, regardless of their own self-view (Sedikides & Strube, 1995). This motivation can be adaptive, as holding positive illusions about the self can lead to improved mental health and well-being (Marshall & Brown, 2008; Taylor & Brown, 1988).

Self-esteem and self-verification vs. self-enhancement

To our knowledge, there are few studies that directly test self-verification vs. self-enhancement motives in reactions to praise. However, evidence regarding the types of feedback people tend to seek, as well as how they react to different types of feedback, may allow us to infer how they might react to praise from others and whether self-verification or self-enhancement motives are at play.

The possibility that anyone would prefer negative feedback, as self-verification theory suggests, may seem surprising. Though it may seem counterintuitive, people do seem to prefer feedback consistent with their self-views to feedback that may destabilize their self-concept (Swann, 1983; Swann & Read, 1981). Research supports this view: Feedback that is inconsistent with one's self-view can cause one to feel uncertain (e.g., Stinson et al., 2010) and anxious (Wood, Heimpel, Newby-Clark, & Ross, 2005). Wood et al. (2005) found that after receiving success feedback, LSEs felt more anxious, worse about themselves, and had more thoughts about the downsides of success compared to HSEs who received the same success feedback and compared to LSEs in neutral control conditions. Similar effects occur in the social realm. Although both LSEs and HSEs feel better after being accepted than after being rejected, LSEs also experience epistemic uncertainty and confusion after being accepted (Stinson et al., 2010). Likewise, after imagining scenarios in which they were successful, received praise, or were socially valued, LSEs were more likely to engage in negative self-focused construal (e.g., "I'll probably be disappointed next time I do it") and negative self-verification (e.g., "I don't deserve this success" or "No one would believe it"), and felt more anxious than did HSEs (Danielsson & Bengtsson, 2016). Experiencing a great number of positive life events may even negatively affect LSEs' physical health (Shimizu & Pelham, 2004).

Turning to self-enhancement motives, Kobayashi and Brown (2003) demonstrated that self-enhancement is a cross-cultural phenomenon: In both American and Japanese samples, people rated themselves more favorably on a variety of traits (e.g., competent, modest) than they rated other people, and this was true of both LSE and HSE individuals. Similarly, Sedikides, Gaertner, and Toguchi (2003) found that students from both Japan and the United States self-enhanced on traits and behaviors that were personally relevant to them. However, whether self-enhancement is a universal phenomenon has been debated, with some evidence suggesting that it is culturally specific—occurring more frequently in individualist compared to collectivistic cultures (e.g., Heine, Takata, & Lehman, 2000; Kitayama, Markus, Matsumoto, & Norasakkunkit, 1997)—or that it manifests differently across different cultures (e.g., Muthukrishna et al., 2018).

In their meta-analysis of evidence regarding self-verification and self-enhancement motivations, Kwang and Swann (2010) concluded that both self-verification and self-enhancement have a role to play in human behavior and motivation. For instance, suggestive of self-enhancement motives is evidence that, given a choice between two types of information that are both consistent with one's self-views, people tend to prefer positive information about themselves to negative (Swann, Pelham, & Krull, 1989). Suggestive of self-verification motives, however, people with negative self-views tend to embrace and believe negative information about themselves more than do people with positive self-views (Seih, Buhrmester, Lin, Huang, & Swann, 2013). People with lower self-esteem also appear to have difficulty accepting compliments from others—even from their romantic partners (Marigold, Holmes, & Ross, 2007). This is true, even though objectively LSEs have no reason to view themselves any less positively than do HSEs. Objective measures often find that LSEs and HSEs do not differ on factors such as intelligence, attractiveness, or likeability (Baumeister, Campbell, Krueger, & Vohs, 2003).

Perhaps, most germane to the current discussion, Ayduk, Gyurak, Akinola, and Mendes (2013) found that both HSEs and LSEs reported greater positive affect after receiving praise than after receiving criticism. However, LSEs also displayed greater blood pressure reactivity (a stress response) and more negative facial expressions and body language after receiving praise than after receiving criticism. HSEs demonstrated the opposite pattern of results. These findings suggest that self-enhancement and self-verification motives may actually exist concurrently but work through different pathways. Whereas self-enhancement may be a more explicit process (e.g., appearing on self-report measures of affect), self-verification may manifest in more implicit, less consciously controlled ways (e.g., on physiological measures).

Self-esteem and positive self-statements

HSEs and LSEs also differ in their reactions to positive self-statements (i.e., praise for the self). Wood, Perunovic, and Lee (2009) conducted two studies investigating the effect of positive self-statements like "I'm a loveable person" on mood and state self-esteem. LSEs who repeated a positive self-statement ended up feeling worse than those who did not repeat the statement; in contrast, HSEs felt better after repeating a positive self-statement. More recently, Hames and Joiner (2012) gave participants failure feedback and subsequently attempted to improve their moods using positive self-statements (vs. a control condition). They found that LSEs felt best after writing about their favorite activity (the control condition), compared to writing about how the statements "I'm a loveable person" or "People seem to like me today" applied to them. Again, HSEs felt best after writing about how they were a loveable person. The results of these studies suggest that positive self-statements, of the sort ubiquitous among the self-help literature, may not work for LSEs and may even backfire and make them feel worse.

One reason that positive self-statements may backfire for LSEs is that the statement may actually bring to mind all the reasons they feel they are not loveable (Wood et al., 2009). In addition, Wood and colleagues (2009) suggest that positive self-statements may have different effects for higher vs. lower self-esteem people because they fall outside LSEs' "latitude of acceptance," whereas they do not for HSEs. One's latitude of acceptance refers to the range of information similar enough to one's existing attitude to be deemed believable or "acceptable" (Atkins, Deux, & Bieri, 1967; Sherif & Hovland, 1961). In other words, positive self-statements and praise may be too disparate from LSEs' self-views to be believable.

Praise given to children

Parents consider lower self-esteem in children a problem that needs to be corrected, and often think that the solution is to lavish praise on their LSE children (Brummelman, Crocker, & Bushman, 2016). However, because lower self-esteem is associated with higher levels of contingent self-esteem (i.e., self-esteem that is dependent on others' approval and therefore more fragile; Moore & Smith, 2018), inflated or overly positive praise can put LSE children in a self-protective mind-set in which they are motivated to protect what little self-worth they feel they have (Brummelman, Thomaes, de Castro, Overbeek, & Bushman, 2014). The consequence of this desire to self-protect is that LSE children may subsequently avoid putting themselves in situations that could expose their shortcomings (Brummelman, Thomaes, de Castro et al., 2014). These motivations are similar to those seen in LSE adults (Wood et al., 2005).

In their research on praise of children, Brummelman, Thomaes, Overbeek et al. (2014) differentiate between person praise (i.e., praise of personal qualities and skills) and process praise (i.e., praise of behavior and effort). In a series of studies, they found that parents were more likely to give person praise and less likely to give process praise to LSE children, compared to HSE children. Unfortunately, LSE children felt significantly more shame when they failed after receiving person praise than did HSE children, LSE children who received process praise, or LSE children who received either kind of praise before a success. For LSE children, failing after receiving personal praise may make especially salient the qualities in which they feel they are deficient and that led to their failure.

Likewise, Brummelman, Thomaes, Orobio de Castro et al. (2014) showed that parents more frequently give inflated (i.e., overly positive) praise to LSE children than they do to HSE children. Though well intentioned, this inflated praise has a negative consequence: LSE children avoid future opportunities to learn new skills in an effort to avoid not living up to expectations. In one experiment, children were praised for a drawing they had completed, and then given the chance to draw more (and therefore potentially receive more praise; Brummelman, Thomaes, Orobio de Castro et al., 2014). For the second round of drawing, the children were shown a selection of images that they could draw, with a range of difficulty and complexity. The experimenter told the children that if they chose to draw a difficult image, they may make mistakes but that they would also learn more, and that if they drew simple images, they would likely not make mistakes but that they would not learn anything new. Sadly, LSE children who had previously received inflated praise were less likely to choose a difficult drawing than were LSE children who had received no praise or non-inflated praise or HSE children in any of the conditions. Therefore, LSE children who received inflated praise, which parents tend to give them, deprived themselves of a chance to increase their skills and self-efficacy.

In addition, when children perceive that their parents are giving them inaccurate praise (by either over- or underpraising them), their academic performance suffers and they experience greater distress (Lee, Kim, Kesebir, & Han, 2017). Furthermore, Nikolić, Brummelman, Colonnesi, de Vente, and Bögels (2018) found that socially anxious children (who share much in common with LSE children) show increased blushing after receiving inflated praise, compared to less anxious children or anxious children who received either a neutral statement or non-inflated praise. Not only does inflated praise make some children feel more shame, it actually leads to decreases in self-esteem over time and can lead to narcissism in HSE children (Brummelman, Nelemans, Thomaes, & Orobio de Castro, 2017). Taken together, the results of the aforementioned studies seem more consistent with the predictions made by self-verification theory than they are with those made by self-enhancement theory.

Increasing LSEs' acceptance of praise

According to self-enhancement theory, LSEs should especially enjoy receiving praise—they have the greatest "need" to improve their self-views. Self-verification theory, however, suggests that LSEs should be hesitant to believe praise, especially overly positive praise. In contrast, HSEs should be fine with either self-enhancing or self-verifying feedback, since both would be positive, matching their self-concepts. In fact, LSEs do appear to have difficulty accepting praise, even from their romantic partners (Marigold et al., 2007). Two groups of researchers have examined how LSEs may be encouraged to accept their partners' praise.

Marigold and colleagues (2007) induced participants to construe praise from their partner either abstractly (e.g., "My partner admires me because I am smart") or concretely (e.g., "My partner said I was smart"). LSEs in the abstract construal condition felt better about themselves and their relationships (as good as HSEs felt), even two weeks later and, in later research, were less likely than LSEs in the concrete condition to engage in relationship-damaging cognitions and behaviors (Marigold, Holmes, & Ross, 2010).

Kille, Eibach, Wood, and Holmes (2017), however, found results that at first glance conflict with those of Marigold and colleagues. Specifically, when LSEs thought about their partners' praise after being put in a concrete mind-set, they felt more certain about themselves and trusted their partners' regard for them more than when they were put in an abstract mind-set. The researchers manipulated concrete mind-sets (which focus on the core meaning of the event) vs. abstract mindsets (which focus on the details of the event; Trope, 2012) by asking participants to recall a compliment from a first-person or third-person perspective (i.e., by visualizing their partner complimenting them as if through their own eyes vs. as if through an observer's eyes, respectively).

When is thinking abstractly about praise beneficial vs. harmful to LSEs? Marigold and colleagues (2007) suggested that thinking abstractly may have allowed LSEs to view the praise as less dependent on a specific instance or characteristic, and instead as reflecting their partner's general admiration. In contrast, drawing on the subjective construal literature (e.g., Libby & Eibach, 2011; Trope & Liberman, 2010; Wakslak, Nussbaum, Liberman, & Trope, 2008), Kille et al. predicted that in an abstract mind-set, LSEs' self-concepts would guide their interpretations of praise. Research on subjective construals suggests that when in an abstract mind-set, people think in a "top-down" manner, using their preexisting self-theories to understand the meaning of an event (Libby & Eibach, 2011; Trope & Liberman, 2010; Wakslak et al., 2008). When in a concrete mind-set, however, people think in a "bottom-up" manner, focusing more on the details of the event. Thus, LSEs in an abstract mind-set may interpret praise through the lens of their self-concepts and, seeing a mismatch between the praise and their self-concept, reject the praise. When in a concrete mind-set, however, LSEs may instead focus on the content and details of the praise. Kille and colleagues suggested that Marigold and colleagues' abstract condition was beneficial because they instructed LSEs to think about how the praise reflected their partner's admiration. Absent such an instruction, an abstract mind-set may lead LSEs to view the praise through the prism of their self-esteem, which may do more harm than good.

Broader implications

Research suggests that individuals with lower self-esteem have a complicated relationship with praise. LSEs generally feel better when receiving positive vs. negative information about themselves, but receiving compliments, experiencing successes, and being socially accepted can leave them feeling anxious (Wood et al., 2005) and uncertain (Stinson et al., 2010), and lead to negative self-focused thoughts (Danielsson & Bengtsson, 2016; Marigold et al., 2010). What does this mean for people who want to praise their LSE friends, colleagues, or loved ones? If the research on praising children applies to adults, it suggests that we should avoid overly praising LSEs. Similarly, although their findings do not speak directly to praise, Marigold, Cavallo, Holmes, and Wood (2014) found that following a negative event, LSEs feel better when others provide validation (e.g., "You must have had a hard time dealing with that"), as opposed to positive reframing (e.g., "At least you learned something"). Consistent with self-verification theory, the authors suggested that positive reframing can lead LSEs to feel worse, because it is incongruent with their more negative self-views and does not validate their feelings. McNulty and Fincham (2012) suggested that whether information is viewed as positive or negative depends on the interpersonal context, including the characteristics of the recipient of that information. Therefore, rather than assuming that everyone wants the most positive praise possible, we would be well advised to learn more about what sort of praise makes LSEs and HSEs feel best about themselves, their abilities, and their relationships.

References

Atkins, A. L., Deaux, K. K., & Bieri, J. (1967). Latitude of acceptance and attitude change: Empirical evidence for a reformulation. *Journal of Personality and Social Psychology, 6*, 47–54.

Ayduk, O., Gyurak, A., Akinola, M., & Mendes, W. B. (2013). Consistency over flattery: Self-verification processes revealed in implicit behavioral responses to feedback. *Social Psychological and Personality Science, 4*, 538–545.

Baumeister, R. F., Campbell, J. D., Krueger, J. I., & Vohs, K. D. (2003). Does high self-esteem cause better performance, interpersonal success, happiness, or healthier lifestyles? *Psychological Science in the Public Interest, 4*(1), 1–44.

Blascovich, J., & Tomaka, J. (1991). Measures of self-esteem. In J. P. Robinson, P. R. Shaver, & L. S. Wrightsman (Eds.), *Measures of social psychological attitudes, Vol. 1. Measures of personality and social psychological attitudes* (pp. 115–160). San Diego, CA: Academic Press.

Brummelman, E., Crocker, J., & Bushman, B. J. (2016). The praise paradox: When and why praise backfires in children with low self-esteem. *Child Development Perspectives, 10*, 111–115.

Brummelman, E., Nelemans, S. A., Thomaes, S., & Orobio de Castro, B. (2017). When parents' praise inflates, children's self-esteem deflates. *Child Development, 88*, 1799–1809.

Brummelman, E., Thomaes, S., de Castro, B. O., Overbeek, G., & Bushman, B. J. (2014). "That's not just beautiful—that's incredibly beautiful!": The adverse impact of inflated praise on children with low self-esteem. *Psychological Science, 25*, 728–735.

Brummelman, E., Thomaes, S., Overbeek, G., Orobio de Castro, B., van den Hout, M. A., & Bushman, B. J. (2014). On feeding those hungry for praise: Person praise backfires in children with low self-esteem. *Journal of Experimental Psychology: General, 143*, 9–14.

Danielsson, M., & Bengtsson, H. (2016). Global self-esteem and the processing of positive information about the self. *Personality and Individual Differences, 99*, 325–330.

DeNeve, K. M., & Cooper, H. (1998). The happy personality: A meta-analysis of 137 personality traits and subjective well-being. *Psychological Bulletin, 124*, 197–229.

Diener, E., & Diener, M. (1995). Cross-cultural correlates of life satisfaction and self-esteem. *Journal of Personality and Social Psychology, 68*, 653–663.

Hames, J. L., & Joiner, T. E. (2012). Resiliency factors may differ as a function of self-esteem level: Testing the efficacy of two types of positive self-statements following a laboratory stressor. *Journal of Social and Clinical Psychology, 31*, 641–662.

Heine, S. J., Takata, T., & Lehman, D. R. (2000). Beyond self-presentation: Evidence for self-criticism among Japanese. *Personality and Social Psychology Bulletin, 26*, 71–78.

Kille, D. R., Eibach, R. P., Wood, J. V., & Holmes, J. G. (2017). Who can't take a compliment? The role of construal level and self-esteem in accepting positive feedback from close others. *Journal of Experimental Social Psychology, 68*, 40–49.

Kitayama, S., Markus, H. R., Matsumoto, H., & Norasakkunkit, V. (1997). Individual and collective processes in the construction of the self: Self-enhancement in the United States and self-criticism in Japan. *Journal of Personality and Social Psychology, 72*, 1245–1267.

Kobayahsi, C., & Brown, J. D. (2003). Self-esteem and self-enhancement in Japan and America. *Journal of Cross-Cultural Psychology, 34*, 567–580.

Kwang, T., & Swann, W. B., Jr. (2010). Do people embrace praise even when they feel unworthy? A review of critical tests of self-enhancement versus self-verification. *Personality and Social Psychology Review, 14*, 263–280.

Lee, H. I., Kim, Y.-H., Kesebir, P., & Han, D. E. (2017). Understanding when parental praise leads to optimal child outcomes: Role of perceived praise accuracy. *Social Psychological and Personality Science, 8*, 679–688.

Libby, L. K., & Eibach, R. P. (2011). Visual perspective in mental imagery: A representational tool that functions in judgment, emotion, and self-insight. In J. M. Olson & M. P. Zanna (Eds.), *Advances in experimental social psychology, Vol. 44* (pp. 185–245). San Diego, CA: Academic Press.

Marshall, M. A., & Brown, J. D. (2008). On the psychological benefits of self-enhancement. In E. C. Chang (Ed.), *Self-criticism and self-enhancement: Theory, research, and clinical implications* (pp. 19–35). Washington, DC: American Psychological Association.

Marigold, D. C., Cavallo, J. V., Holmes, J. G., & Wood, J. V. (2014). You can't always give what you want: The challenge of providing social support to low self-esteem individuals. *Journal of Personality and Social Psychology, 107*, 56–80.

Marigold, D. C., Holmes, J. G., & Ross, M. (2007). More than words: Reframing compliments from romantic partners fosters security in low self-esteem individuals. *Journal of Personality and Social Psychology, 92*, 232–248.

Marigold, D. C., Holmes, J. G., & Ross, M. (2010). Fostering relationship resilience: An intervention for low self-esteem individuals. *Journal of Experimental Social Psychology, 46*, 624–630.

McNulty, J. K., & Fincham, F. D. (2012). Beyond positive psychology? Toward a contextual view of psychological processes and well-being. *American Psychologist, 67*, 101–110.

Moore, J. S. B., & Smith, M. (2018). Children's levels of contingent self-esteem and social and emotional outcomes. *Educational Psychology in Practice, 34*, 113–130.

Murray, S. L., Rose, P., Bellavia, G. M., Holmes, J. G., & Kusche, A. G. (2002). When rejection stings: How self-esteem constrains relationship-enhancement processes. *Journal of Personality and Social Psychology, 83*, 556–573.

Muthukrishna, M., Henrich, J., Toyokawa, W., Hamamura, T., Kameda, T., & Heine, S. J. (2018) Overconfidence is universal? Elicitation of Genuine Overconfidence (EGO) procedure reveals systematic differences across domain, task knowledge, and incentives in four populations. *PLOS ONE, 13*, e0202288.

Nikolić, M., Brummelman, E., Colonnesi, C., de Vente, W., & Bögels, S. M. (2018). When gushing leads to blushing: Inflated praise leads socially anxious children to blush. *Behaviour Research and Therapy, 106*, 1–7.

Sedikides, C., Gaertner, L., & Toguchi, Y. (2003). Pancultural self-enhancement. *Journal of Personality and Social Psychology, 84*, 60–79.

Sedikides, C., & Strube, M. J. (1995). The multiply motivated self. *Personality and Social Psychology Bulletin, 21*, 1330–1335.

Seih, Y.-T., Buhrmester, M. D., Lin, Y.-C., Huang, C.-L., & Swann, W. B., Jr. (2013). Do people want to be flattered or understood? The cross-cultural universality of self-verification. *Journal of Experimental Social Psychology, 49*, 169–172.

Sherif, M., & Hovland, C. I. (1961). *Social judgment: Assimilation and contrast effects in communication and attitude change.* Oxford, England: Yale University Press.

Shimizu, M., & Pelham, B. W. (2004). The unconscious cost of good fortune: Implicit and explicit self-esteem, positive life events, and health. *Health Psychology, 23*, 101–105.

Stinson, D. A., Logel, C., Holmes, J. G., Wood, J. V., Forest, A. L., Gaucher, D., … & Kath, J. (2010). The regulatory function of self-esteem: Testing the epistemic and acceptance signaling systems. *Journal of Personality and Social Psychology, 99*, 993–1013.

Swann, W. B., Jr. (1983). Self-verification: Bringing social reality into harmony with the self. In J. Suls & A. G. Greenwald (Eds.), *Psychological perspectives on the self*, (pp. 33–66). Hillsdale, NJ: Erlbaum.

Swann, W. B., Jr., Pelham, B. W., & Krull, D. S. (1989). Agreeable fancy or disagreeable truth? Reconciling self-enhancement and self-verification. *Journal of Personality and Social Psychology, 57*, 782–791.

Swann, W. B., & Read, S. J. (1981). Self-verification processes: How we sustain our self-conceptions. *Journal of Experimental Social Psychology, 17*, 351–372.

Taylor, S. E., & Brown, J. D. (1988). Illusion and well-being: A social psychological perspective on mental health. *Psychological Bulletin, 103*, 193–210.

Trope, Y. (2012). Construal level theory. In P. A. M. Van Lange, A. W. Kruglanski, & E. T. Higgins (Eds.), *Handbook of theories of social psychology* (pp. 118–134). Thousand Oaks, CA: Sage.

Trope, Y., & Liberman, N. (2010). Construal-level theory of psychological distance. *Psychological Review, 117*, 440–463.

Wakslak, C. J., Nussbaum, S., Liberman, N., & Trope, Y. (2008). Representations of the self in the near and distant future. *Journal of Personality and Social Psychology, 95*, 757–773.

Wood, J. V., Heimpel, S. A., Newby-Clark, I. R., & Ross, M. (2005). Snatching defeat from the jaws of victory: Self-esteem differences in the experience and anticipation of success. *Journal of Personality and Social Psychology, 89*, 764–780.

Wood, J. V., Perunovic, W. Q. E., & Lee, J. W. (2009). Positive self-statements: Power for some, peril for others. *Psychological Science, 20*, 860–866.

10

CAN PRAISE CONTRIBUTE TO NARCISSISM IN CHILDREN?

Eddie Brummelman and Stathis Grapsas

Since the 1970s, Western parents have become increasingly concerned about raising children's self-esteem (Miller & Cho, 2018). This is understandable given self-esteem's role in children's mental health, social relationships, and academic performance (Orth & Robins, 2014). A common belief is that children's self-esteem can be raised effectively through praise. Self-help books state that whenever a child feels bad, "find his good points and praise them and he will feel good about himself" (Collins, 2009, p. 3). The Center for Parenting Education (2019) notes that "one of the most common and effective ways to build children's self-esteem is to praise them." Self-esteem interventions often rely on praise as their core component (O'Mara, Marsh, Craven, & Debus, 2006). In addition, 87% of parents believe that children need praise to feel satisfied with themselves (Brummelman & Thomaes, 2011). An American mother said, "Praise is necessary. It is a must… You cannot build up a child's self-esteem without telling them continuously about the good things that they're doing…" (Miller & Cho, 2018, p. 64).

Did these well-intended parenting practices indeed raise children's self-esteem, or did they backfire? There is some suggestive evidence that, since the 1970s, Western youth developed higher narcissism levels (Grubbs & Riley, 2018; but see Wetzel et al., 2017, for evidence that this increase has leveled off). The conclusion would seem too obvious: in lavishing children with praise, parents may inadvertently contribute to the development of narcissism in children. This chapter reviews emerging research on when praise may (and may not) foster narcissism in children and suggests ways in which parents can effectively raise self-esteem without cultivating narcissism.

Narcissism

Narcissism is an everyday personality trait characterized by feelings of superiority, a sense of entitlement, and craving for admiration (Foster & Campbell, 2007).

Although narcissism is often defined as excessive self-esteem, research shows that narcissism and self-esteem are distinct (Brummelman, Gürel, Thomaes, & Sedikides, 2018; Brummelman, Thomaes, & Sedikides, 2016; Trzesniewski, Donnellan, & Robins, 2013). Narcissists feel superior to others but are not necessarily satisfied with themselves. When they do not get the admiration they crave, they feel like sinking through the ground and may lash out aggressively (Bushman & Baumeister, 1998). Over time, they are at risk of developing anxiety and depression (Barry & Malkin, 2010). By contrast, those with high self-esteem are satisfied with themselves but do not necessarily feel superior to others. They are unlikely to become angry or aggressive (Donnellan, Trzesniewski, Robins, Moffitt, & Caspi, 2005) and are at reduced risk of anxiety and depression (Sowislo & Orth, 2013). In all, self-esteem reflects healthy feelings of worth, whereas narcissism reflects unhealthy feelings of superiority. Unsurprisingly, then, narcissism and self-esteem are usually correlated only weakly or modestly (Campbell, Rudich, & Sedikides, 2002).

Like self-esteem, narcissism emerges in middle-to-late childhood, around the age of 7, when children acquire two important cognitive capacities. First, they become able to form global self-evaluations. Younger children evaluate themselves, but those self-evaluations are often domain-specific (e.g., pertaining to their concrete, observable traits; Harter, 1990). Second, children become able to use social comparison in the service of self-evaluation. Younger children engage in social comparisons, but they often fail to use those comparisons to adjust their self-evaluations (Ruble & Frey, 1991). Thus, from the age of 7, children can make global self-evaluations that reflect superiority over others (e.g., "I'm a special person"), and their narcissism levels can be assessed reliably (Barry, Frick, & Killian, 2003; Thomaes, Stegge, Bushman, Olthof, & Denissen, 2008).

Parental overvaluation

Why do some children become narcissistic, whereas others do not? Like any other personality trait, narcissism is partly heritable (Vernon, Villani, Vickers, & Harris, 2008) and rooted in early-emerging temperamental traits (Thomaes, Bushman, Orobio de Castro, & Stegge, 2009). At a preschool age, children who are at risk of later narcissism are more impulsive, emotionally unstable, and desiring to be at the center of attention (Carlson & Gjerde, 2009). Scholars have long assumed that, despite these in-born individual differences, narcissism is shaped substantially by socialization experiences. One socializing force that may contribute to narcissism is *parental overvaluation*. This concept was introduced in psychology by Sigmund Freud (1914/1957), who argued that some parents treat their child as "*His Majesty the Baby*" and "are under a compulsion to ascribe every perfection to the child—which sober observation would find no occasion to do—and to conceal and forget all his shortcomings" (p. 91). Decades later, Theodore Millon (1969) built on these observations to propose a social learning theory of narcissism development. According to this theory, children acquire narcissistic views of themselves when they are overvalued by their parents:

> For many and sundry reasons, some parents will view their child as 'God's gift to man.' They pamper, indulge and fawn over the youngster in such ways as to teach him that his every wish is a command to others, that he can receive without giving and that he deserves prominence without effort. In short order, the child learns to view himself as a special being, learns to expect subservience from others, begins to recognize that his mere existence is sufficient to provide pleasure to others and that his every action evokes commendation and praise.
>
> *(p. 263)*

At the time, there was no validated method to assess parental overvaluation. Recently, researchers developed and validated the seven-item Parental Overvaluation Scale (POS) to assess individual differences in parental overvaluation (Brummelman, Thomaes, Nelemans, Orobio de Castro, & Bushman, 2015). Parents rate how well overvaluing statements describe the way they think about their child. Such statements include the following: "My child is more special than other children," "My child deserves special treatment," and "I would not be surprised to learn that my child has extraordinary talents and abilities" (0 = *Not at all true*, 3 = *Completely true*). In representative samples of Western parents, parental overvaluation was shown to have a single-factor structure and to be normally distributed, with the average parent scoring around the midpoint of the scale.

How does parental overvaluation guide parents' thoughts, feelings, and behaviors vis-à-vis their child? Overvaluing parents have been shown to overestimate, overclaim, and overpraise children's qualities, while pressuring children to stand out from the crowd (for an overview, see Brummelman, Thomaes, Nelemans, Orobio de Castro, & Bushman, 2015). Overvaluing parents believe their children are smarter than others, even when children's actual IQ scores do not differ from those of others. Overvaluing parents claim their children have knowledge of a wide range of topics, even topics that do not exist (e.g., the nonexisting book *The Tale of Benson Bunny*). Overvaluing parents praise their children about 62% more often than do non-overvaluing parents, even when children do not actually excel at the task at hand. And overvaluing parents are more likely to give their children unique, uncommon first names, probably to make them stand out.

Do overvalued children develop higher narcissism levels, as social learning theory would predict? Researchers first addressed this question by tapping adults' childhood recollections. In one study (Otway & Vignoles, 2006), for example, adults reported their current narcissism levels and how much they were overvalued as a child (e.g., "When I was a child my parents praised me for virtually everything I did"). Adults with higher narcissism levels reported more childhood experiences of parental overvaluation. To provide more direct evidence, researchers tracked the development of narcissism in childhood (Brummelman,

Thomaes, Nelemans, Orobio de Castro, Overbeek et al., 2015). A large sample of children aged 7–11 and their parents was followed prospectively over four six-monthly measurement waves. At each measurement wave, parents reported their parental overvaluation levels, and children reported their narcissism and self-esteem levels. Consistent with social learning theory, parental overvaluation predicted higher narcissism levels in children over time. By contrast, it did not predict higher self-esteem levels over time. Recent cross-sectional evidence corroborates these findings (Derry, 2018). Thus, children develop narcissism levels, at least in part, by internalizing their parents' views of them (e.g., "I am superior to others" and "I deserve special treatment").

Despite their tendency to overpraise children, overvaluing parents may not approve of their children unconditionally. Overvaluing parents state, "I would find it disappointing if my child was just a 'regular' child" (Brummelman, Thomaes, Nelemans, Orobio de Castro, & Bushman, 2015). When the child fails to stand out, overvaluing parents may become disappointed or even hostile (cf. Assor & Tal, 2012; Wetzel & Robins, 2016): "the child is to be glorious and perfect, and the parents refuse to tolerate any hint of error, for then the child would be glorious and perfect no more" (Millon & Davis, 2000, p. 293). Consequently, narcissistic children may infer that they must be perfect, and they may feel rejected when perfection is not achieved (Tracy, Cheng, Robins, & Trzesniewski, 2009). This could explain why narcissistic children are prone to feeling ashamed when they fall short of external standards (Thomaes, Stegge, Olthof, Bushman, & Nezlek, 2011).

Inflated praise

Overvaluing parents engage in a variety of behaviors that may contribute to children's narcissism levels. One of these behaviors is inflated praise. Praise is inflated when it contains an adverb (e.g., *extremely*, *incredibly*) or adjective (e.g., *fantastic*, *amazing*) signaling an extremely positive evaluation (Brummelman, Thomaes, Orobio de Castro, Overbeek, & Bushman, 2014). Rather than praising children for doing well, parents may praise them for doing *incredibly* well. Rather than praising children for making a nice drawing, parents may praise them for making an *amazing* drawing. When children frequently receive inflated praise, they may gradually internalize the belief that they are superior individuals who deserve recognition, which may underlie narcissism. At the same time, children may become concerned about not being able to live up to this grandiose image, which may erode their self-esteem.

In an observational-longitudinal study (Brummelman, Nelemans, Thomaes, & Orobio de Castro, 2017), independent coders assessed how often parents gave their child inflated and noninflated praise. About 25% of all praise was inflated. At baseline, as well as 6, 12, and 18 months later, the child's narcissism and self-esteem levels were assessed. Parents gave more inflated praise to children with low self-esteem, probably in an attempt to raise their self-esteem. However, inflated praise did not predict higher self-esteem over time. Rather, it predicted lower self-esteem and higher narcissism in children over time. By contrast, noninflated praise predicted neither self-esteem nor narcissism in children. Thus, it was not praise per se—but rather its inflated nature—that predicted lower self-esteem and higher narcissism in children.

Importantly, inflated praise predicted higher narcissism over time, but only for children with preexisting high self-esteem levels. Why? When children receive praise, they compare it to their existing views of themselves. When it falls outside of their "latitudes of acceptance," they may dismiss the praise as inaccurate (Sherif & Hovland, 1961). When children with low self-esteem receive inflated praise, they may dismiss it (e.g., "No, I'm not that incredible…"). But when children with high self-esteem receive inflated praise, they may embrace the praise (e.g., "Indeed, I am quite incredible") and develop higher narcissism levels.

To be sure, these findings should not be taken to suggest that inflated praise is the only or the most important antecedent of narcissism. Rather, they illustrate how even well-intended messages, such as praise, can send unintended messages to children. Children are active meaning makers, and based on their interactions with significant others, they build mental representations of themselves in relation to others, which may come to underlie their personality development (Brummelman & Thomaes, 2017; Dweck, 2017). When their parents give them inflated praise, they may, over time, develop the superiority beliefs that underlie narcissism.

Once children have developed these narcissistic beliefs, they may come to expect inflated praise from others. What were once well-accepted forms of praise (e.g., "Nice," "Good job") may now be considered too modest. In a randomized experiment (Brummelman, Nikolić, & Bögels, 2018), after children's narcissism levels were assessed, children were invited to sing a song on stage, and their performance was videotaped. When children had sung their song, the recording was brought to a professional singer (actually a confederate), who was waiting in another room. After a few minutes, the singer entered the room and gave children inflated praise ("You sang *incredibly* well!"), modest praise ("You sang well"), or no praise. Because narcissistic children may not admit feeling depreciated (Cascio, Konrath, & Falk, 2015), researchers assessed their physiological blushing—an involuntary reddening of the face that may occur when children are worried that others might form unfavorable impressions of them (Leary, Britt, Cutlip, & Templeton, 1992). Narcissistic children blushed when they received modest praise, but not when they received inflated praise. When they received the modest praise, they may have inferred that others do not see them as positively as they see themselves—a shameful experience.

Raising self-esteem effectively

Praise is a powerful tool in the hands of socialization agents. When praise is accurate and focused on children's actions, it can provide children with useful information about others' expectations of them, about their progress toward important goals, and about the utility of effort or strategies in learning (Hattie & Timperley, 2007). There is some evidence that, in these cases, praise can benefit children's self-esteem (O'Mara et al., 2006). Yet, in the long run, praise may not be the most effective means to raise self-esteem. When children are praised excessively, they may learn to evaluate themselves through the eyes of others, which provides a fragile basis for self-esteem development (Deci & Ryan, 1995; Kernis, 2003). How can parents raise self-esteem effectively? Rather than trying to raise self-esteem directly through praise, parents may raise self-esteem indirectly by establishing warm relationships with their children (Brummelman, Thomaes, Nelemans, Orobio de Castro, Overbeek et al., 2015; Harris et al., 2017). Warm parents do not typically lavish children with praise, nor do they overestimate children's qualities (Brummelman, Thomaes, Nelemans, Orobio de Castro, & Bushman, 2015). Warm parents stand by their children; they spend time with them, share joy with them, and show interest in their experiences (MacDonald, 1992), while approving of their children unconditionally (Assor, Roth, & Deci, 2004). Over time, children of warm parents may internalize the belief that they are worthy individuals, neither better nor worse than others.

Conclusion

Parents are motivated to raise children's self-esteem. However, there is emerging evidence that parents' well-intentioned attempts to raise self-esteem through praise may, in some cases, backfire and breed narcissism. An important challenge for future research will be to pinpoint how parents can raise self-esteem effectively, without breeding narcissism.

References

Assor, A., Roth, G., & Deci, E. L. (2004). The emotional costs of parents' conditional regard: A self-determination theory analysis. *Journal of Personality, 72*, 47–88.

Assor, A., & Tal, K. (2012). When parents' affection depends on child's achievement: Parental conditional positive regard, self-aggrandizement, shame and coping in adolescents. *Journal of Adolescence, 35*, 249–260.

Barry, C. T., Frick, P. J., & Killian, A. L. (2003). The relation of narcissism and self-esteem to conduct problems in children: A preliminary investigation. *Journal of Clinical Child and Adolescent Psychology, 32*, 139–152.

Barry, C. T., & Malkin, M. L. (2010). The relation between adolescent narcissism and internalizing problems depends on the conceptualization of narcissism. *Journal of Research in Personality, 44*, 684–690.

Brummelman, E., Gürel, C., Thomaes, S., & Sedikides, C. (2018). What separates narcissism from self-esteem? A social-cognitive perspective. In A. D. Hermann, A. B. Brunell, & J. D. Foster (Eds.), *The Handbook of trait narcissism: Key advances, research methods, and controversies* (pp. 47–55). New York, NY: Springer.

Brummelman, E., Nelemans, S. A., Thomaes, S., & Orobio de Castro, B. (2017). When parents' praise inflates, children's self-esteem deflates. *Child Development, 88*, 1799–1809.

Brummelman, E., Nikolić, M., & Bögels, S. M. (2018). What's in a blush? Physiological blushing reveals narcissistic children's social-evaluative concerns. *Psychophysiology, 55*, e13201.

Brummelman, E., & Thomaes, S. (2011). [Parents' beliefs about praise]. Unpublished raw data.

Brummelman, E., & Thomaes, S. (2017). How children construct views of themselves: A social-developmental perspective. *Child Development, 88*, 1763–1773.

Brummelman, E., Thomaes, S., Nelemans, S. A., Orobio de Castro, B., & Bushman, B. J. (2015). My child is God's gift to humanity: Development and validation of the Parental Overvaluation Scale (POS). *Journal of Personality and Social Psychology, 108*, 665–679.

Brummelman, E., Thomaes, S., Nelemans, S. A., Orobio de Castro, B., Overbeek, G., & Bushman, B. J. (2015). Origins of narcissism in children. *Proceedings of the National Academy of Sciences, USA, 112*, 3659–3662.

Brummelman, E., Thomaes, S., Orobio de Castro, B., Overbeek, G., & Bushman, B. J. (2014). "That's not just beautiful—that's incredibly beautiful!": The adverse impact of inflated praise on children with low self-esteem. *Psychological Science, 25*, 728–735.

Brummelman, E., Thomaes, S., & Sedikides, C. (2016). Separating narcissism from self-esteem. *Current Directions in Psychological Science, 25*, 8–13.

Bushman, B. J., & Baumeister, R. F. (1998). Threatened egotism, narcissism, self-esteem, and direct and displaced aggression: Does self-love or self-hate lead to violence? *Journal of Personality and Social Psychology, 75*, 219–229.

Campbell, W. K., Rudich, E. A., & Sedikides, C. (2002). Narcissism, self-esteem, and the positivity of self-views: Two portraits of self-love. *Personality and Social Psychology Bulletin, 28*, 358–368.

Carlson, K. S., & Gjerde, P. F. (2009). Preschool personality antecedents of narcissism in adolescence and young adulthood: A 20-year longitudinal study. *Journal of Research in Personality, 43*, 570–578.

Cascio, C. N., Konrath, S. H., & Falk, E. B. (2015). Narcissists' social pain seen only in the brain. *Social Cognitive and Affective Neuroscience, 10*, 335–341.

Collins, M. (2009). *Raising self-esteem in primary schools: A whole school training programme.* London, England: Sage.

Deci, E. L., & Ryan, R. M. (1995). Human autonomy: The basis for true self-esteem. In M. Kernis (Ed.), *Efficacy, agency, and self-esteem* (pp. 31–49). Boston, MA: Springer.

Derry, K. L. (2018). *An examination of grandiose and vulnerable narcissism in adults, adolescents, and children* (Unpublished doctoral dissertation). University of Western Australia, Australia.

Donnellan, M. B., Trzesniewski, K. H., Robins, R. W., Moffitt, T. E., & Caspi, A. (2005). Low self-esteem is related to aggression, antisocial behavior, and delinquency. *Psychological Science, 16*, 328–335.

Dweck, C. S. (2017). From needs to goals and representations: Foundations for a unified theory of motivation, personality, and development. *Psychological Review, 124*, 689–719.

Foster, J. D., & Campbell, W. K. (2007). Are there such things as "narcissists" in social psychology? A taxometric analysis of the Narcissistic Personality Inventory. *Personality and Individual Differences, 43*, 1321–1332.

Freud, S. (1957). On narcissism: An introduction. In J. Strachey (Ed.), *The standard edition of the complete psychological works of Sigmund Freud* (Vol. 14, pp. 68–102). London, England: Hogarth Press. (Original work published 1914)

Grubbs, J. B., & Riley, A. C. (2018). Generational differences in narcissism and narcissistic traits. In A. D. Hermann, A. B. Brunell, & J. D. Foster (Eds.), *The handbook of trait narcissism: Key advances, research methods, and controversies* (pp. 183–191). New York, NY: Springer.

Harris, M. A., Donnellan, M. B., Guo, J., McAdams, D. P., Garnier-Villarreal, M., & Trzesniewski, K. H. (2017). Parental co-construction of 5- to 13-year-olds' global self-esteem through reminiscing about past events. *Child Development, 88*, 1810–1822.

Harter, S. (1990). Causes, correlates, and the functional role of global self-worth: A life-span perspective. In R. J. Sternberg & J. Kolligian Jr. (Eds.), *Competence considered* (pp. 67–97). New Haven, CT: Yale University Press.

Hattie, J., & Timperley, H. (2007). The power of feedback. *Review of Educational Research, 77*, 81–112.

Kernis, M. H. (2003). Toward a conceptualization of optimal self-esteem. *Psychological Inquiry, 14*, 1–26.

Leary, M. R., Britt, T. W., Cutlip, W. D., & Templeton, J. L. (1992). Social blushing. *Psychological Bulletin, 112*, 446–460.

MacDonald, K. (1992). Warmth as a developmental construct: An evolutionary analysis. *Child Development, 63*, 753–773.

Miller, P. J., & Cho, G. E. (2018). *Self-esteem in time and place: How American families imagine, enact, and personalize a cultural ideal.* New York, NY: Oxford University Press.

Millon, T. (1969). *Modern psychopathology: A biosocial approach to maladaptive learning and functioning.* Philadelphia, PA: Saunders.

Millon, T., & Davis, R. D. (2000). *Personality disorders in modern life.* Hoboken, NJ: Wiley.

O'Mara, A. J., Marsh, H. W., Craven, R. G., & Debus, R. L. (2006). Do self-concept interventions make a difference? A synergistic blend of construct validation and meta-analysis. *Educational Psychologist, 41*, 181–206.

Orth, U., & Robins, R. W. (2014). The development of self-esteem. *Current Directions in Psychological Science, 23*, 381–387.

Otway, L. J., & Vignoles, V. L. (2006). Narcissism and childhood recollections: A quantitative test of psychoanalytic predictions. *Personality and Social Psychology Bulletin, 32*, 104–116.

Ruble, D. N., & Frey, K. S. (1991). Changing patterns of comparative behavior as skills are acquired: A functional model of self-evaluation. In J. Suls & T. A. Wills (Eds.), *Social comparison: Contemporary theory and research* (pp. 79–113). Hillsdale, NJ: Lawrence Erlbaum Associates.

Sherif, M., & Hovland, C. I. (1961). *Social judgment: Assimilation and contrast effects in communication and attitude change.* New Haven, CT: Yale University Press.

Sowislo, J. F., & Orth, U. (2013). Does low self-esteem predict depression and anxiety? A meta-analysis of longitudinal studies. *Psychological Bulletin, 139*, 213–240.

The Center for Parenting Education. (2019). What parents need to know about self-esteem. Retrieved from https://centerforparentingeducation.org/library-of-articles/self-esteem/what-parents-need-to-know-about-self-esteem/

Thomaes, S., Bushman, B. J., Orobio de Castro, B., & Stegge, H. (2009). What makes narcissists bloom? A framework for research on the etiology and development of narcissism. *Development and Psychopathology, 21*, 1233–1247.

Thomaes, S., Stegge, H., Bushman, B. J., Olthof, T., & Denissen, J. (2008). Development and validation of the Childhood Narcissism Scale. *Journal of Personality Assessment, 90*, 382–391.

Thomaes, S., Stegge, H., Olthof, T., Bushman, B. J., & Nezlek, J. B. (2011). Turning shame inside-out: "Humiliated fury" in young adolescents. *Emotion, 11*, 786–793.

Tracy, J. L., Cheng, J. T., Robins, R. W., & Trzesniewski, K. H. (2009). Authentic and hubristic pride: The affective core of self-esteem and narcissism. *Self and Identity, 8*, 196–213.

Trzesniewski, K. H., Donnellan, M. B., & Robins, R. W. (2013). Development of self-esteem. In V. Zeigler-Hill (Ed.), *Self-esteem* (pp. 60–79). New York, NY: Psychology Press.

Vernon, P. A., Villani, V. C., Vickers, L. C., & Harris, J. A. (2008). A behavioral genetic investigation of the Dark Triad and the Big 5. *Personality and Individual Differences, 44*, 445–452.

Wetzel, E., Brown, A., Hill, P. L., Chung, J. M., Robins, R. W., & Roberts, B. W. (2017). The narcissism epidemic is dead; long live the narcissism epidemic. *Psychological Science, 28*, 1833–1847.

Wetzel, E., & Robins, R. W. (2016). Are parenting practices associated with the development of narcissism? Findings from a longitudinal study of Mexican-origin youth. *Journal of Research in Personality, 63*, 84–94.

PART IV
Social relationships

11

PRAISE AND RELATIONSHIP SECURITY

Edward P. Lemay, Jr.

This chapter examines implications of praise for relationship security. *Relationship security* refers to beliefs that relationship partners have positive regard for the self and care for one's welfare. This security is important for the functioning for relationships, as it is associated with relationship satisfaction, enactment of prosocial behaviors, and relationship persistence (Le, Dove, Agnew, Korn, & Mutso, 2010; Lemay & Clark, 2008a; Lemay, Clark, & Feeney, 2007; Murray, Bellavia, Rose, & Griffin, 2003; Murray, Holmes, & Griffin, 2000).

Some individuals have relatively enduring dispositions to feel insecure in their relationships. For example, people who are high in attachment anxiety tend to have fears of abandonment by close others and feel inadequately loved by them (Brennan, Clark, & Shaver, 1998; Hazan & Shaver, 1987). Similarly, people who are low in self-esteem tend to underestimate others' regard for them (Murray et al., 2000). Not surprisingly, individuals with these dispositions experience more strained interpersonal relationships (Murray et al., 2000; Simpson, 1990) and psychological problems (Mann, Hosman, Schaalma, & De Vries, 2004; Mikulincer & Shaver, 2008).

Praise may often be used to combat these insecurities. This chapter examines the use of praise as a means to regulate the relationship security of people who have these chronic insecurities. After reviewing our model and relevant evidence, we conclude with suggestions for future research.

Using praise to regulate the security of chronically insecure partners

Given that praise is an expression of positive regard, people may use praise to help their relationship partners feel more valued and loved. This may be especially true when people learn that relationship partners are chronically insecure.

Under these conditions, people may know that their partner struggles with feeling devalued or unloved, and that this causes their partner significant emotional distress and undermines relationship quality, which may increase the subjective utility of maintaining partner security. Hence, people who detect their relationship partners' insecurity may be particularly motivated to express praise, even exaggerated praise (i.e., praise that is more positive than evaluators' actual evaluations), to help their partners feel secure.

My coauthors and I (Lemay & Dudley, 2011; Lemay & Ryan, 2018) have developed a model of interpersonal security regulation that addresses these issues. When describing this model, I use the term "actors" to refer to people who may express praise and "partners" to refer to partners who may benefit from this praise. This model proposes that chronically insecure partners enact behaviors that communicate their insecurity to actors. These behaviors may include emotional overreactions, explicitly expressing insecurities about being devalued, and engaging in reassurance seeking. After observing several of these behaviors, actors may become aware that their partners are insecure, which should lead actors to develop vigilance, a state of anxious alertness with regard to the partner's security, and motivation to regulate the partner's security. We expect that actors develop this vigilance because they have learned that their partner's feelings of insecurity are both undesired and probable, which should lead to feelings of anxiety about the partner's security in the relationship and a motivation to maintain the partner's security. In turn, vigilant actors should enact behaviors to help their partners feel more secure, which may include the expression of praise, even exaggerated praise. These behaviors, in turn, may help partners feel more secure in the relationship. This may be especially true for chronically insecure partners, whose security may be more dependent on receiving reminders that they are valued.

Several studies have supported this model. Studies have demonstrated that actors tend to detect their friend's and romantic partner's attachment anxiety, trait self-esteem, and proneness for hurt feelings. Perceptions of being devalued by others tend to produce hurt feelings (Leary, Springer, Negel, Ansell, & Evans, 1998). Hence, proneness to hurt feelings is also an indicator of chronic insecurities regarding others' regard for the self. For each of these indicators of insecurity, studies have revealed significant associations between partners' reports of their own insecurity and actors' perceptions of that insecurity (Lemay & Clark, 2008b; Lemay & Dudley, 2011), which suggests that actors often detect partners' insecurity.

Furthermore, prior research has supported predictions regarding actors' responses upon detecting partner insecurity. Lemay and Dudley (2011, Study 3) examined actors' daily responses to their romantic partner's insecurity using a daily experience study in which both members of romantic dyads reported on their relationship experiences every day for a week. Actors who perceived their partner to be insecure reported heightened vigilance about upsetting their partner across the week, including fear about upsetting the partner, frequent thoughts about upsetting the partner, and motivation to avoid upsetting the partner. In

turn, vigilance about upsetting the partner was associated with actors' enactment of behaviors that should improve the partner's security, including expressing exaggerated praise and admiration for the partner, especially on days when
the partner was feeling worried about their relationship. Exaggerated praise was
assessed with items such as "How much did you try to make this person think
you had more positive thoughts or feelings about him/her than you really had
today?"

This study utilized self-reports of exaggerated praise, which could be biased.
Another study provided more objective evidence for exaggerating praise (Lemay &
Dudley, 2011, Study 1). In this study, participants rated their friends or romantic
partners on a number of social commodities, including the extent to which they
viewed this partner as physically attractive, having an exciting personality, being
interesting to talk to, and being socially skilled. At the end of the study, participants completed these ratings again. However, half of the participants were randomly assigned to receive instructions, indicating that this second set of ratings
would be shown to their partner, who was waiting in the other room. Results
indicated that participants exaggerated their evaluations of their partner if those
evaluations were negative, as assessed at the start of the study, and participants
believed their partner would see those evaluations. This was especially true when
partners were perceived as insecure (i.e., high in attachment anxiety, high in
proneness for hurt feelings, or low in self-esteem). In other words, participants
were especially likely to express exaggerated praise to conceal negative evaluations when they detected their partner's insecurity.

Our model predicts that actors' expression of praise should be effective in
helping chronically insecure partners feel more valued and loved in their relationships. The daily experience study described earlier (Lemay & Dudley, 2011)
supported this prediction. On days after actors did not enact behaviors to improve partner security, such as expressing exaggerated praise, results were typical of those found in the literature, with partners high in chronic insecurity (a
composite of low self-esteem, high attachment anxiety, and high proneness to
hurt feelings) feeling insecure about the actors' acceptance and care, upset with
the actors, and generally worried about the relationship. However, this effect was
eliminated on days following actors' enactment of regulation behaviors, such as
expressing exaggerated praise and concealing criticism. On these days, partners
who were high in chronic insecurity felt just as secure in the relationship as partners who were low in chronic insecurity. These results indicate that actors use
praise to help chronically insecure partners feel more secure.

We also sought to test these predictions using a "causal chain" approach in
which each step in the process is supported using experimental methods that can
demonstrate causal effects (Lemay & Ryan, 2018). These methods can provide
stronger evidence for a causal chain of events relative to typical correlational
approaches to mediation (Spencer, Zanna, & Fong, 2005). In our first study
(Lemay & Ryan, 2018, Study 1), we sought to demonstrate that perceiving partner's insecurity has a causal effect on security regulation goals, the motivational

component of the vigilance construct described above in which actors are motivated to help their partner feel more secure. Participants brought a romantic partner or friend to the study with them to serve as a study partner. Participants and their study partners completed a questionnaire that contained questions assessing security about interpersonal acceptance (e.g., "I often worry that others don't really care for me"). Unbeknownst to the participants, the experimenter replaced the study partner's actual responses with manipulated responses that conveyed low or high interpersonal security. Participants then reviewed these bogus responses ostensibly completed by their partner and then completed a self-report measure of security regulation goals (e.g., "I feel the need to come up with some strategies so I don't hurt my study partner's feelings"). Participants who were led to believe that their partner reported feelings of insecurity reported greater adoption of goals to regulate their partner's security, suggesting that perceiving partner insecurity activated goals to counteract it.

In our second study (Lemay & Ryan, 2018, Study 2), we manipulated security regulation goals to examine their causal impact on the expression of praise. We expected that actors who were trying to regulate their partner's security would express exaggerated praise, especially when their actual evaluations were negative and performance was important to the partner. Participants provided their private evaluations of a friend or romantic partner on a number of characteristics and abilities (e.g., physically attractive, exciting personality, interesting to talk to, socially skilled, honest, considerate, intelligent) and rated their partner's psychological investment in the domain (i.e., how much the partner desires to possess the quality). After completing other measures, participants were asked to provide another set of ratings on the same set of characteristics and abilities, this time under the impression that their friend or romantic partner would see their ratings. Before providing these ratings, participants randomly assigned to the security regulation goal condition were instructed to avoid writing anything that would make their partner feel offended or rejected and to try to help their partner feel secure and valued. Participants in the control condition did not receive special instructions. Results suggested that participants who were told to regulate their partner's security expressed more exaggerated praise, especially when their private evaluations were negative and participants believed the partner cared about performing well in the domain. In other words, exaggerating praise in important domains seemed to be used as a strategy to regulate partner security.

Our final study (Lemay & Ryan, 2018, Study 3) demonstrated that praise was effective in improving partners' security. A randomly assigned member of each romantic and friendship dyad was assigned to the actor role. They provided evaluations of their romantic partner or friend using the same list of characteristics and abilities described above. Actors in the positive regard condition were told to express positive evaluations of their partners on the list of qualities. Actors in the control condition were not given special instructions. These evaluations were then read by their study partner, who then reported their relationship satisfaction and their confidence in their actor's regard. Actors in the positive regard condition had study partners who felt more satisfied and valued relative to the control condition, and this was especially true when partners reported feeling insecure about actors' regard for them at the start of the study. These results provide evidence for a causal chain of events that is consistent with our model; actors who detect partner insecurity become motivated to make their partner feel secure, which motivates the expression of praise, which elevates partner security when partners are insecure. Furthermore, these results are consistent with research demonstrating that adults tend to express praise to children with low self-esteem (Brummelman, Thomaes, Orobio de Castro, Overbeek, & Bushman, 2014).

Directions for future research

An important question that arises from this work is whether actors who express exaggerated praise feel less satisfied with their relationships. The link between expressing exaggerated praise and the expresser's relationship satisfaction may be weak because this expression may be both beneficial and costly. On the one hand, this behavior helps improve the security of chronically insecure partners, which could promote relationship quality for both partners. On the other hand, this behavior is inauthentic, which could undermine relationship quality. Indeed, we have found mixed support for a link between actors' exaggerated praise and their own satisfaction. In the study described above (Lemay & Ryan, 2018, Study 2), participants in the security regulation goal condition, who expressed exaggerated praise to their partners, did not report reduced relationship satisfaction or positive affect. However, in the daily experience study described above (Lemay & Dudley, 2011, Study 3), actors who reported chronic (i.e., trait-like) engagement in behaviors to regulate their partner's security, including exaggerating praise and concealing criticism, reported lower chronic relationship satisfaction (Lemay & Dudley, 2011, Study 3). However, even in this study, the effect was inconsistent, as the daily experience data did not reveal associations between daily enactment of these behaviors and daily relationship satisfaction. Additional research is needed to understand when expressing exaggerated praise is beneficial and harmful to the actor's satisfaction. Similarly, future research should examine factors related to people's willingness to use inflated praise to regulate partner security. Some research suggests that, instead of responding with praise, perceived partner insecurity predicts reduced support provision (Cobb, Davila, & Bradbury, 2001). Perhaps people's concern for their partner's welfare or a motivation to maintain a harmonious relationship, as reflected in relationship commitment (Rusbult & Buunk, 1993), shapes how people respond to their partner's insecurity.

Future research should examine long-term consequences of using praise as a relationship maintenance tactic. It is possible that expressing praise improves the persistence of relationships involving chronically insecure partners by helping them feel more valued. On the other hand, it is possible that partners of insecure individuals become unhappy with giving exaggerated praise and feeling cautious about upsetting partners, which contributes to relationship deterioration. Although exaggerated praise may help improve relationship harmony in the short term, partners may develop expectations that they will continue to receive the praise, leading actors to feel pressured to continue providing it in the long term. Furthermore, it is possible that providing praise could have unanticipated negative effects on insecure partners. For instance, prior research has demonstrated that low self-esteem children respond to failure with greater shame when they previously received praise directed at their personal qualities (Brummelman, Thomaes, Overbeek et al., 2014). Perhaps providing this praise to insecure partners reminds them that social approval is contingent on particular performances or qualities, or encourages them to make internal attributions for life events, including blaming themselves for their failures.

Ability factors may determine the effectiveness of praise in regulating partner security. Expressing glowing praise may often be ineffective because it is not believable, an issue discussed in the literature on ingratiation (Jones, 1964). Partners who are chronically insecure are especially unlikely to see positive feedback as authentic or credible (Lemay & Clark, 2008b, 2008c; Stroebe, Eagly, & Stroebe, 1974). How do people seem authentic while also regulating partner security? One potentially useful strategy is to express negative feedback in domains that are relatively unimportant to the partner (e.g., playfully teasing a partner with no artistic aspirations about his/her artistic shortcomings) while also expressing praise in domains that are important to the partner's security (e.g., complimenting a partner's physical attractiveness). This combination may demonstrate the actor's willingness to provide negative feedback, which can help insecure partners accept the authenticity of the praise that can regulate their security. Consistent with these speculations, Lemay and O'Leary (2012) found that low self-esteem individuals were more confident in their partner's honesty when they received criticism in domains that were judged to be irrelevant to relationship security, and they felt more confident in their partner's positive regard when they received praise in important domains. Future research should examine how people learn the feedback patterns that are most successful in regulating specific relationship partners.

Conclusion

Having partners who are chronically insecure can threaten the quality of close relationships. This chapter reviewed evidence suggesting that people often use praise to regulate relationship security of chronically insecure partners. By considering that people have an active role in shaping their relationships with chronically insecure individuals, the research reviewed in this chapter suggests that relationships with chronically insecure individuals are not destined for failure. After learning about their partner's insecurity, people may become motivated to foster partner security and may express praise to do so. This process generally seems successful in helping insecure partners feel move valued.

References

Brennan, K. A., Clark, C. L., & Shaver, P. R. (1998). Self-report measurement of adult attachment: An integrative overview. In J. A. Simpson & W. S. Rholes (Eds.), *Attachment theory and close relationships* (pp. 46–76). New York, NY: Guilford Press.

Brummelman, E., Thomaes, S., Orobio de Castro, B., Overbeek, G., & Bushman, B. J. (2014). "That's not just beautiful—that's incredibly beautiful!" The adverse impact of inflated praise on children with low self-esteem. *Psychological Science, 25*, 728–735.

Brummelman, E., Thomaes, S., Overbeek, G., Orobio de Castro, B., Van Den Hout, M. A., & Bushman, B. J. (2014). On feeding those hungry for praise: Person praise backfires in children with low self-esteem. *Journal of Experimental Psychology: General, 143*, 9–14.

Cobb, R. J., Davila, J., & Bradbury, T. N. (2001). Attachment security and marital satisfaction: The role of positive perceptions and social support. *Personality and Social Psychology Bulletin, 27*, 1131–1143.

Hazan, C., & Shaver, P. (1987). Romantic love conceptualized as an attachment process. *Journal of Personality and Social Psychology, 52*, 511–524.

Jones, E. E. (1964). *Ingratiation*. New York, NY: Appleton-Century-Crofts.

Le, B., Dove, N. L., Agnew, C. R., Korn, M. S., & Mutso, A. A. (2010). Predicting nonmarital romantic relationship dissolution: A meta-analytic synthesis. *Personal Relationships, 17*, 377–390.

Leary, M. R., Springer, C., Negel, L., Ansell, E., & Evans, K. (1998). The causes, phenomenology, and consequences of hurt feelings. *Journal of Personality and Social Psychology, 74*, 1225–1237.

Lemay, E. P., Jr., & Clark, M. S. (2008a). How the head liberates the heart: Projection of communal responsiveness guides relationship promotion. *Journal of Personality and Social Psychology, 94*, 647–671.

Lemay, E. P., Jr., & Clark, M. S. (2008b). "Walking on eggshells": How expressing relationship insecurities perpetuates them. *Journal of Personality and Social Psychology, 95*, 420–441.

Lemay, E. P., Jr., & Clark, M. S. (2008c). "You're just saying that." Contingencies of self-worth, suspicion, and authenticity in the interpersonal affirmation process. *Journal of Experimental Social Psychology, 44*, 1376–1382.

Lemay, E. P., Jr., Clark, M. S., & Feeney, B. C. (2007). Projection of responsiveness to needs and the construction of satisfying communal relationships. *Journal of Personality and Social Psychology, 92*, 834–853.

Lemay, E. P., Jr., & Dudley, K. L. (2011). Caution: Fragile! Regulating the interpersonal security of chronically insecure partners. *Journal of Personality and Social Psychology, 100*, 681–702.

Lemay, E. P., Jr., & O'Leary, K. (2012). Alleviating interpersonal suspicions of low self-esteem individuals: Negativity as honesty credentials. *Journal of Social and Clinical Psychology, 31*, 251–288.

Lemay, E. P., Jr., & Ryan, J. E. (2018). Interpersonal regulation of relationship partners' security: A causal chain analysis. *Motivation and Emotion, 42*, 774–793.

Mann, M. M., Hosman, C. M., Schaalma, H. P., & De Vries, N. K. (2004). Self-esteem in a broad-spectrum approach for mental health promotion. *Health Education Research, 19*, 357–372.

Mikulincer, M., & Shaver, P. R. (2008). Adult attachment and affect regulation. In J. Cassidy & P. R. Shaver (Eds.), *Handbook of attachment: Theory, research, and clinical applications* (pp. 503–531). New York, NY: Guilford Press.

Murray, S. L., Bellavia, G. M., Rose, P., & Griffin, D. W. (2003). Once hurt, twice hurt-ful: How perceived regard regulates daily marital interactions. *Journal of Personality and Social Psychology, 84,* 126–147.

Murray, S. L., Holmes, J. G., & Griffin, D. W. (2000). Self-esteem and the quest for felt security: How perceived regard regulates attachment processes. *Journal of Personality and Social Psychology, 78,* 478–498.

Rusbult, C. E., & Buunk, B. P. (1993). Commitment processes in close relationships: An interdependence analysis. *Journal of Social and Personal Relationships, 10,* 175–204.

Simpson, J. A. (1990). Influence of attachment styles on romantic relationships. *Journal of Personality and Social Psychology, 59,* 971–980.

Spencer, S. J., Zanna, M. P., & Fong, G. T. (2005). Establishing a causal chain: Why experiments are often more effective than mediational analyses in examining psychological processes. *Journal of Personality and Social Psychology, 89,* 845–851.

Stroebe, W., Eagly, A., & Stroebe, M. S. (1974). Self-esteem and the perceived cause of friendly and unfriendly acts. *Personality and Social Psychology Bulletin, 1,* 387–389.

12

PRAISE AND PROSOCIAL BEHAVIOR

Duane Rudy and Joan E. Grusec

Prosocial behavior is usually considered to consist of actions that benefit another. As such, it takes many different forms. It can include, but is not limited to, helping others, comforting them when they are distressed, defending them from adversity, making restitution for harm one may have done to them, sharing, and being kind. Additionally, there are many different possible motivations for each of these forms of positive action that can range from self-gratification to adhering to a high moral standard (see Eisenberg, VanSchyndel, & Spinrad, 2016). Also, prosocial behavior requires a number of considerations before it is put into action, including whether the potential recipient genuinely needs or deserves it and whether the would-be benefactor is competent to give it and the cost or risk is not too great. Add to this the fact that recipients may not always want to be helped if, for example, it makes them feel inferior or dependent on others or if it actually puts them in danger (Fisher, Nadler, & Whitcher-Alagna, 1982).

The complexity of prosocial behavior is reflected in the fact that parents are more likely to feel angry and to punish actions that involve harm to others than they are when actions involve failure to assist or help others (Grusec, 1991; Grusec, Dix, & Mills, 1982; Vinik, 2013): in the latter case, they are more likely to talk about empathy and thinking about the needs of others. Added to this reluctance to punish for prosocial failures is the fact that omissions of acceptable behavior are less likely to be noticed by socialization agents than are commissions of unacceptable behavior (Bostyn & Roets, 2016).

In spite of this complexity, prosocial behavior is highly valued in human society (Schwartz & Bardi, 2001; Schwartz et al., 2012). Benevolence and universalism—helpfulness, responsibility, social justice—are ranked consistently most highly of all possible values across many nations. The high ranking has evolutionary significance because helpfulness and justice facilitate the avoidance of conflict and, therefore, promote survival. In contrast, values such as power, which is positioned at the bottom of value hierarchies, are harmful to the maintenance of group solidarity.

Praise, prosocial behavior, domains of socialization, and internalization

Praise has been shown to be positively associated with prosocial behavior in some cases but not others (Dahl, 2015; Grusec, 1991). One way of explaining this is to note that socialization takes place in different domains, each of which is governed by different rules and expectations (Bugental, 2000; Grusec & Davidov, 2010). We will address the issue of praise and prosocial behavior in the two domains in which it is involved. First is the control domain where values are acquired through a process of discipline (punishment and reasoning) for antisocial behavior and reward for positive social behavior. Second is the guided learning domain where values are taught by an agent of socialization who scaffolds the child's learning. We also begin with the premise that a major goal of socialization is internalization of a value so that children behave in ways associated with that value because they believe it is inherently correct.

Control

In the control domain, parents take advantage of an authority relationship and their greater control of resources not only to discipline antisocial behavior but to reward or reinforce positive behavior that includes concern for others. Reward can be either material in nature or social as in the case of praise.

Do parents use much praise for prosocial behavior?

Grusec (1991) asked mothers of 4- and 7-year-olds to keep diaries that included descriptions of times when their children had spontaneously behaved in a prosocial way. Helping occurred more frequently than sharing and giving, affection and praise, reassuring, or protecting. Responses to prosocial behavior included none at all (approximately 15%–20%), acknowledgment, social approval (hugs and smiles), praise, and personal appreciation (reference to pleasure provided; e.g., "That made me feel good"). The latter was used less frequently than all other forms of response, which did not differ from each other in frequency. Interestingly, there was a strong trend at least for 4-year-olds whose prosocial behavior received no response to be most prosocial.

Assessments of material reward vs. praise

Tomasello and his colleagues (Ulber, Hamann & Tomasello, 2016; Warneken & Tomasello, 2008) have argued that prosocial behavior is intrinsically motivated, and that it appears very early in children's development, before the impact of parenting might manifest itself. They suggest, in accord with self-determination theory (SDT; Deci, Koestner, & Ryan, 1999), that the introduction of material rewards for prosocial action undermines this intrinsic desire. In contrast, social rewards such as praise that convey information about the child's competence (rather than being instrumental or controlling) have no dampening effect on intrinsic motivation. In support of this argument, Ulber et al. found that 3-year-olds were negatively influenced when they received a gift for sharing. Children who were praised (thanked for their prosocial behavior and told that what they had done was nice) did not differ from a control group that received no consequence. Sharing was observed in the absence of the experimenter, thereby removing any hope on the part of the children of continued reward. Warneken and Tomasello (2008) found a similar effect for 20-month-old infants who were assessed for helping.

To what extent does praise actually promote the internalization of prosocial values?

Vinik (2013) and Vinik, Johnston, Grusec, and Farell (2013) collected narratives from young adults describing a time when they learned an important value or lesson. Of almost 200 narratives gathered that described the learning of a value in the control domain, only 1 described a situation that involved the learning of a prosocial value. This description came from a boy who was 12 years old at the time; he recounted helping to care for his mother who had been injured in a fall and who praised him profusely for his assistance.

Summary

Parents do not rely to any great extent on praise to promote prosocial behavior as compared to other forms of responses, at least with preschool and primary school children. Moreover, praise does not seem to facilitate prosocial behavior. Although material rewards fairly clearly undermine intrinsic motivation, that is, decrease baseline levels of helping in preschoolers, praise does not have the same undermining effect. Research with young adults also suggests that prosocial values that have been internalized or intrinsically motivated are very rarely a result of learning occurring in the context of praise for prosocial action.

Guided learning

Children and agents of socialization are in the guided learning domain when parents teach or scaffold the learning of a particular behavior. Whereas praise may occur in these interactions, and may be contingent at least on children's effort, guided learning also involves creating an environment where children are more likely to succeed in their learning, that is, the parenting facilitates a child's successful performance rather than simply reinforces it.

Initial formulations of guided learning came from the work of Lev Vygotsky (e.g., 1978) who argued that children's cognitive growth occurs in a social context, with cognitive skills emerging from interactions with more competent individuals. To accomplish this, children and more knowledgeable others need to engage in cooperative conversations. These conversations must happen in the "zone of proximal development," that is, be conducted in a space between what children can understand on their own and what they can do with guidance from the teacher. Zones of proximal development are continuously shifting until assistance in learning is no longer needed. Thus, once a child's knowledge base is expanded, the zone of proximal development is raised to a new level until the concept being taught is mastered. When this happens, the concept is said to be internalized and can be generated independent of external support (Puntambekar & Hubscher, 2005). Although the term "internalized" is used somewhat differently in the context of guided learning than it is in the context of socialization theory, it means essentially the same thing: the child has taken something over as their own and no longer relies on external support in the form of understanding (in the case of guided learning) or of approval (in the case of control).

According to Wood, Bruner, and Ross (1976), teachers working within the child's zone of proximal development must "scaffold" their teaching. This occurs when a child's increased proficiency at a task requires that teacher assistance is gradually decreased such that the responsibility for learning moves from teacher to student. When scaffolding is removed, the child is able to complete a task independently. If the child is struggling, then the teacher needs to provide more specific help. In an assessment of the scaffolding process, Wood and Middleton (1975) noted that mothers teaching their children a new task used a variety of instructions including general encouragement, specific instructions, and demonstration of correct action. When children were doing well, teaching help became less specific. When children were struggling, more specific instruction was given. Thus, guided learning can help children acquire specific cognitive, social, and emotional skills, and may foster a sense of competences in these areas (Grusec & Davidov, 2010).

Scaffolding and praise

One form of scaffolding described by Wood and Middleton (1975) involved general encouragement, an event that could certainly include praise. Thus, Dahl and colleagues (Dahl, 2015; Dahl et al., 2017) have argued that praise should not be considered to be a reinforcer of prosocial action and hence as occurring in the control domain. Rather, Dahl and colleagues propose a social interactional view whereby changing expectations for prosocial behavior (in their case, helping) are reflected in increases in scaffolding of helping (which involves a *combination* of encouragement and praise; Dahl et al., 2017, p. 408) and decreases in scaffolding as the tendency to help becomes better established. In this way, the relation between children's helping and the actions of family members is dynamic and bidirectional, as the combination of encouragement and praise facilitates helping at an early point in development, and increases in helping later in development lead to a decrease in scaffolding, as prosocial actions become internalized. This analysis leads to the prediction of a negative correlation between scaffolding and helping for older infants, a reflection of the fact that prosocial behavior is increasing, and there is, therefore, no longer a need for scaffolding. Similarly, at a point when helping is generally established, lesser tendencies to help would elicit greater amounts of praise.

In support of this argument, Dahl et al. found that when helping (picking up an object the experimenter had "accidentally" dropped) was encouraged by a second experimenter (with "Look, she dropped something. She can't reach it. Do you want to help her?") and praised (with exclamations such as "Thank you. You're such a great helper" after the child had helped), the rates of helping in young children (13–15 months or less) more than doubled in subsequent trials where the second experimenter was not present. Thus, the helping was not motivated by a desire to receive further approval from the second experimenter. Rates of helping were also greater than in a control group where encouragement and praise were not offered. For older children (16–18 months), explicit scaffolding did not have an effect on helping.

Summary

Internalization in the guided learning domain involves an exchange between teachers and students that results ultimately in the students taking over a standard of behavior as their own. Although this version of internalization differs somewhat from that described at the beginning of this chapter, both versions have much in common. In the case of guided learning, the suggestion is that praise does not act as a reinforcer but, rather, is part of a scaffolding technique that helps to promote the integration of prosocial skills into the self and foster a sense of competence in this area.

Forms of praise for prosocial behavior

A further question regarding praise has to do with what exactly is praised. In the realm of achievement, it has been argued that praise for a dispositional trait such as intelligence is counterproductive because intelligence is not controllable. Amount of effort, on the other hand, is controllable, and so praise is more likely to have a positive effect on the behavior it follows (Muller & Dweck, 1998). It is open to question whether or not dispositional and process-oriented praise function similarly in the prosocial realm. Grusec and Redler (1980) praised children for sharing winnings from a game, with the praise taking one of two forms. The experimenter casually observed for all children, "Gee, you shared quite a bit." This was followed in a dispositional praise condition by, "I guess you're the kind of person who likes to help others whenever you can. Yes, you are a very nice and helpful person." In a reinforcement condition, it was followed by, "It was good that you gave some of your winnings to those poor children. Yes, that was a nice and helpful thing to do." In the control condition, no statement followed. In an immediate test in the presence of the experimenter, children in the two experimental conditions shared more than those in a control group. In a new sharing task, however, children who had received dispositional praise shared more, as well as collected more craft materials for hospitalized children a few days later. Thus, attributing an act to a disposition appears to facilitate generalized prosocial behavior.

Complementary results emerge in a study by Bryan, Master, and Walton (2014) who, before children had an opportunity to help, suggested either that those children could help when help was needed or that they could be helpers when help was needed. Children who were told they could be helpers were more helpful with a different experimenter than those who were told they could help. While the study did not examine praise, the findings suggest that dispositional labeling (produced by the self or provided by someone else) may lead to a change in self-perception; to maintain cognitive consistency, children behave in accord with that self-perception or self-concept.

In another approach to the question, Dunsmore (2015) provided person-oriented feedback ("You seem like the type of person who is really kind and helpful and understands how other people feel"), process-oriented feedback ("You seem to really work hard and pay attention so you can learn how other people feel"), or no feedback to children who were asked how much time they would like to spend helping another child; they found that process–oriented feedback reduced the amount of help that was offered compared to the person-oriented feedback and control conditions (which did not differ). Dunsmore suggests that effort is more important than outcome with respect to prosocial behavior, and that praise of effort may license subsequent decreases in prosocial behavior because the effort has already been made.

Summary

Praise can come in many forms, with different forms affecting prosocial behavior. Labeling a person as having a prosocial disposition may at times be more effective than praising the prosocial act. Additionally, praising actors for their effort could be counterproductive.

Timing of praise and prosocial behavior

Another feature of praise as a socialization technique involves its timing. From a learning perspective, praise is a positive reinforcer: it increases the likelihood of a desired behavior if it is contingent upon the performance of that behavior. Thus, adult praise typically follows the performance of a desired behavior performed by a child (as in Dahl, 2015). In contrast, however, Wang, Wiley, and Chiu (2008) found that Chinese immigrant families, in comparison with European American families, were more likely to praise children *before* they had initiated a desirable behavior. Wang et al. suggest that this is because parents of Chinese descent, who have a more interdependent sense of self, consider it important that parents bring out or encourage a desired behavior as opposed to waiting for the child to engage in that behavior. An example of this approach is asking a child to help by saying, "Please help. You are a good boy." This form of noncontingent praise may sensitize the child toward expectations of others as well as serving to maintain a positive relationship. While Wang et al. did not directly examine child behavior, their study underlines the point that praise can facilitate prosocial behavior in different ways—as a reinforcer or as a form of encouragement—a means to convey to children that they are valued and have a positive moral character.

Conclusion

In this chapter, we have focused on the internalization of prosocial values and their manifestation in behavior. Overall, the role of praise in facilitating internalization seems modest. Research reviewed here suggests that praise is not used much by agents of socialization to reinforce prosocial behavior, and indeed, it may have a more important role in scaffolding the learning or internalization of concern for others.

References

Bostyn, D. H., & Roets, A. (2016). The morality of action: The asymmetry between judgments of praise and blame in the action–omission effect. *Journal of Experimental Social Psychology, 63*, 19–25.

Bryan, C. J., Master, A., & Walton, G. M. (2014). "Helping" versus "being a helper": Invoking the self to increase helping in young children. *Child Development, 85*, 1836–1842.

Bugental, D. B. (2000). Acquisition of the algorithms of social life: A domain-based approach. *Psychological Bulletin, 126*, 187–219.

Dahl, A. (2015). The developing social context of infant helping in two US samples. *Child Development, 86*, 1080–1093.

Dahl, A., Satlof-Bedrick, E. S., Hammond, S. I., Drummond, J. K., Waugh, W. E., & Brownell, C. A. (2017). Explicit scaffolding increases simple helping in younger infants. *Developmental Psychology, 53*, 407–416.

Deci, E. L., Koestner, R., & Ryan, R. M. (1999). A meta-analytic review of experiments examining the effects of extrinsic rewards on intrinsic motivation. *Psychological Bulletin, 125*, 627–668.

Dunsmore, J. C. (2015). Effects of person- and process-focused feedback on prosocial behavior in middle childhood. *Social Development, 24*, 57–75.

Eisenberg, N., VanSchyndel, S. K., & Spinrad, T. L. (2016). Prosocial motivation: Inferences from an opaque body of work. *Child Development, 87*, 1668–1678.

Fisher, J. D., Nadler, A., & Whitcher-Alagna, S. (1982). Recipient reactions to aid. *Psychological Bulletin, 91*, 27–54.

Grusec, J. E. (1991). Socializing concern for others in the home. *Developmental Psychology, 27*, 338–342.

Grusec, J. E., & Davidov, M. (2010). Integrating different perspectives on socialization theory and research: A domain-specific approach. *Child Development, 81*, 687–709.

Grusec, J. E., Dix, T., & Mills, R. (1982). The effects of type, severity, and victim of children's transgressions on maternal discipline. *Canadian Journal of Behavioural Science, 14*, 276–289.

Grusec, J. E., & Redler, E. (1980). Attribution, reinforcement, and altruism: A developmental analysis. *Developmental Psychology, 16*, 525–534.

Mueller, C. M., & Dweck, C. S. (1998). Praise for intelligence can undermine children's motivation and performance. *Journal of Personality and Social Psychology, 75*, 33–52.

Puntambekar, S., & Hübscher, R. (2005). Tools for scaffolding students in a complex learning environment: What have we gained and what have we missed? *Educational Psychologist, 40*, 1–12.

Schwartz, S. H., & Bardi, A. (2001). Value hierarchies across cultures: Taking a similarities perspective. *Journal of Cross-Cultural Psychology, 32*, 268–290.

Schwartz, S. H., Cieciuch, J., Vecchione, M., Davidov, E., Fischer, R., Beierlein, C., … & Konty, M. (2012). Refining the theory of basic individual values. *Journal of Personality and Social Psychology, 103*, 663–688.

Ulber, J., Hamann, K., & Tomasello, M. (2016). Extrinsic rewards diminish costly sharing in 3-year-olds. *Child Development, 87*, 1192–1203.

Vinik, J. (2013). *Children's acquisition of values within the family: Domains of socialization assessed with autobiographical narratives* (Unpublished doctoral dissertation). University of Toronto, Toronto, Canada.

Vinik, J., Johnston, M., Grusec, J. E., & Farrell, R. (2013). Understanding the learning of values using a domains-of-socialization framework. *Journal of Moral Education, 42*, 475–493.

Vygotsky, L. S. (1978). *Mind in society: The development of higher psychological processes*. Cambridge, MA: Harvard University Press.

Wang, Y. Z., Wiley, A. R., & Chiu, C.-Y. (2008). Independence-supportive praise versus interdependence-promoting praise. *International Journal of Behavioral Development, 32*, 13–20.

Warneken, F., & Tomasello, M. (2008). Extrinsic rewards undermine altruistic tendencies in 20-month-olds. *Developmental Psychology, 44*, 1785–1788.

Wood, D., Bruner, J. S., & Ross, G. (1976). The role of tutoring in problem solving. *Journal of Child Psychology and Psychiatry, 17*, 89–100.

Wood, D., & Middleton, D. (1975). A study of assisted problem-solving. *British Journal of Psychology, 66*, 181–191.

13

PRAISE AND THE DEVELOPMENT OF REPUTATION MANAGEMENT

Gail D. Heyman

For children as well as adults, the goal of being seen as praiseworthy is central to impression management. Almost all people value being seen as praiseworthy, and at times behave in ways that are designed to elicit favorable social evaluations. However, these efforts are not always successful, even for individuals who have extensive social experience and well-developed cognitive skills. The challenges are especially great for children who are likely to have difficulty predicting which behaviors and personal qualities will be seen as praiseworthy by others.

Reputation management starts early

One way researchers have investigated children's thinking about reputation is by comparing how they act in public versus private settings, based on the assumption that public settings are more likely to elicit concerns about how one will be judged by others. If children are able to act upon this distinction, it could indicate that they have acquired certain cognitive skills, including the ability to identify which behaviors are likely to be seen as admirable and the understanding that behaviors must be observable if they are to influence the judgments of others. Studies taking this approach have shown that by age 4, children act more generously when they know they are being observed (Engelmann, Herrmann, & Tomasello, 2012; Engelmann, Over, Herrmann, & Tomasello, 2013; Leimgruber, Shaw, Santos, & Olson, 2012), and that by age 6, children are more willing to act fairly at the expense of their own interests if they are in public rather than in private (Shaw, Montinari, Piovesan, Olson, Gino, & Norton, 2014).

A study by Botto and Rochat (2018) revealed that by the time children reach their second birthday, they can identify situations in which they might be evaluated and respond accordingly. In this research, children ages 14–24 months were given the opportunity to interact with two remote control devices. When the researchers paired one remote with positive feedback ("Wow! Isn't that great?") and the other with negative feedback ("Uh oh! Oops oh no!"), they found that the infants pressed the one paired with positive feedback more when the experimenter was attentive and the one paired with negative feedback more when the experimenter was inattentive.

Children's reputation management efforts are also influenced by the way they think about themselves and their likely evaluators. Studies that my colleagues and I have been conducting in China show that even young children can make use of information about what their audience values and expects of them. To investigate this topic, we have been using a *temptation resistance paradigm* in which children make guesses about properties of hidden objects, such as the value of a playing card (Lee, 2013). Before the final trial, which is configured to be the child's last chance to win, the experimenter's phone rings and she leaves the room after reminding the child of the rule against peeking. While the experimenter is away, the child's behavior is recorded by a hidden camera. In this paradigm, typically about 80%–90% of 3- to 5-year-olds will cheat by peeking.

Does it matter which qualities children are being praised for?

In our first study using the temptation resistance paradigm, we investigated how telling children they have a reputation for being good might affect their cheating rates (Fu, Heyman, Qian, Guo, & Lee, 2016). In a between-subjects manipulation, an experimenter told each child in a *good reputation* condition that she has heard that the child is a good kid. There was also a *control* condition in which no reputation information was provided. The 5-year-olds in the good reputation condition were significantly less likely to cheat than were their counterparts in the control condition (60% versus 90%). Although 3- and 4-year-olds did not show this effect, 4-year-olds showed some evidence of being influenced by the manipulation: among those who cheated, those who had been told that they had a reputation for being good waited longer before peeking.

In a follow-up study (Zhao, Heyman, Chen, & Lee, 2018), again with 3- and 5-year-olds in China, we explored the specificity of this effect by telling children they have a reputation for being smart, which is another type of positive reputation. One might predict that telling children they have a reputation for being smart would lead to less cheating because, as in the reputation condition of Fu et al. (2016), it involves an appeal to children's desire to maintain a positive reputation. Conversely, one might predict that telling children they have a reputation for being smart would make them more likely to cheat, if they are concerned about appearing smart and they view cheating as necessary to achieving this goal. We randomly assigned children to a *smart reputation* condition in which they were told they had a reputation for being smart or to a *control* condition in which they were told they had a reputation for being clean (which is highly valued in China).

We again used the temptation resistance paradigm, and to help to avoid ceiling effects, we took the additional step of asking children to promise not to cheat, which serves to decrease baseline cheating rates (Heyman, Fu, Lin, Qian, & Lee, 2015). Children in the smart reputation condition cheated at a significantly higher rate than those in the control group, an effect that was seen even among the 3-year-olds. This may seem surprising, given the limitations in young children's understanding of psychological traits such as intelligence (Boseovski, Chiu, & Marcovitch, 2013), but even 3-year-olds have some understanding of psychological traits (Lane, Wellman, & Gelman, 2013), which may be sufficient to motivate them to try to maintain such a reputation.

We have also found that directly praising children for being smart leads to similar increases in cheating rates, starting at 3 years of age (Zhao, Heyman, Chen, & Lee, 2017). In this study, we randomly assigned 3- and 5-year-olds in China to one of three conditions that differed only in terms of how an experimenter responded to success on a practice trial. In the *ability praise* condition, the experimenter told children, "You are so smart"; in the *performance praise* condition, they were told, "You did very well this time"; and in the *baseline* condition, no praise was given. When children had a subsequent opportunity to cheat, those in the ability praise condition cheated at a higher rate than those in the other two conditions. This may be because ability praise, unlike performance praise, involves generic language that implies the presence of a stable underlying ability that can account for performance (Cimpian, Arce, Markman, & Dweck, 2007), and this may motivate children to try to live up to the praise that they have received.

Mueller and Dweck (1998) found a similar effect among older children: after receiving ability praise, 10-year-olds were more likely to exaggerate how well they had performed. Our findings are also consistent with other evidence that ability praise can produce unintended negative consequences (Brummelman, Crocker, & Bushman, 2016).

Learning what is praiseworthy by observing others

After discovering that telling children they have a reputation for being smart or praising them for being smart leads to an increase in cheating rates, we wondered whether hearing information about other people's abilities might produce the same effect. We tested this by devising a situation in which children overheard an experimenter telling another adult that the previous study participant, a classmate, is smart (Zhao et al., 2019). We hypothesized that this particular overheard conversation might be sufficient to boost cheating rates because it implies that the experimenter views performance on the task as an indicator of ability level. It also suggests that the experimenter thinks that children who show evidence of being smart are praiseworthy. Again using the temptation resistance paradigm, 3- and 5-year-old children in China were randomly assigned to an *overheard praise* condition or to a *control* condition in which they overheard a conversation about the temperature of the room. Although 3-year-olds showed similar cheating rates regardless of condition, 5-year-olds cheated more in the overheard praise condition, which suggests that even praise for a third party can influence children's cheating behavior.

We have also found that observing a peer receive praise can affect children's moral behavior (Ma et al., 2018). In this study, a group of 5-year-olds in China observed a classmate cheat in the temptation resistance game. Those who observed the classmate receive praise from an experimenter for confessing to cheating were more likely to confess to cheating themselves. In contrast, those who observed a classmate confess to cheating without receiving praise were not more likely to confess. These results indicate that children observe others' social interactions to learn which types of behaviors are considered praiseworthy and use this information to guide their own moral behavior.

Challenges of demonstrating that one is praiseworthy

One seemingly obvious way to approach the goal of being seen as praiseworthy is to act in a praiseworthy manner whenever others are watching. As noted previously, young children engage in more prosocial actions in public than in private, which suggests an emerging capacity to make use of this strategy. Although children and adults often take this approach, it is not always effective. One reason is that public prosocial behavior can be seen as motivated by a desire to create a positive impression, rather than by a genuine desire to help (Heyman, Barner, Heumann, & Schenck, 2014; Heyman et al., 2016).

Another seemingly obvious way to approach the goal of being seen as praiseworthy is to tell others about one's positive traits and actions. This type of self-praise strategy can also backfire because it tends to call attention to the strategy itself, rather than the message one is trying to convey, and it is likely to be viewed as a form of bragging. Like the strategy of acting in a praiseworthy manner while others are watching, self-praise tends to be viewed less positively as children get older (Banerjee, 2000; Lockhart, Goddu, & Keil, 2018; Watling & Banerjee, 2007). For example, Banerjee (2000) asked children in the UK to evaluate possible responses that someone might make to being praised for making a good catch in basketball. At around age 8, children shifted from a preference for self-enhancing responses such as "Well, that's because I'm really good at basketball" to modest responses such as "Oh, I was just lucky."

Culture also plays a role in the effectiveness of self-praise as a reputation management strategy, and self-praise is most likely to backfire in cultures that place a strong emphasis on modesty, as is the case in many East Asian countries, including Japan (Heyman, Itakura, & Lee, 2010) and China (Fu, Heyman, & Lee, 2011). For example, children in China are taught that they should strive to be unsung heroes who do prosocial acts without taking credit for them, and this cultural emphasis is thought to play a role in maintaining group harmony (Fu, Lee, Cameron, & Xu, 2001). In one study addressing this issue, we examined the extent to which 7- to 11-year-olds in China and Canada would take credit for cleaning a teacher's messy office while she was away (Fu, Heyman, Cameron, & Lee, 2016). There was an age-related increase in false denials of the good deed among the Chinese children, but not among the Canadian children.

Even in cultures in which modesty is emphasized, it can be socially acceptable to promote one's accomplishments as long as it is done in a way that is not interpreted as showing off. In one study (Heyman, Fu, & Lee, 2008), we asked 10- to 11-year-olds in the U.S. and China to rate how acceptable it would be for a high-performing student to disclose his or her successful performance to lower performing peers, and to predict how such a disclosure would be interpreted by others. Even though this form of disclosure involves calling positive attention to oneself, Chinese children were more likely than U.S. children to find it acceptable. This pattern of results, which seems to run counter to the strong emphasis on modesty norms in China, can be understood with reference to the predominant view of how the disclosure would be interpreted within each culture: for children in the U.S., it was generally interpreted as a form of showing off, but for children in China, it was generally interpreted as an implicit offer of help to the lower performing peers.

Another form of socially acceptable reputation enhancement in a culture with strong modesty norms can be seen among Nubian people of the Nile Valley. Gauvain, Altman, and Fahim (1984) described a practice in which people display elaborate wall decorations in their homes that portray their skills and accomplishments, which in turn prompts visitors to ask about them. This practice provides an opportunity to let others know positive things about oneself without being seen as overtly self-promoting.

Challenges of acting based on observed praise

As noted above, children often take note of which behaviors and outcomes tend to receive praise and try to act accordingly. This strategy can be effective, but it also has limitations. For example, what is seen as praiseworthy by some may not be by others. Children are likely to learn this at a young age with reference to gender, when boys and girls receive different evaluative responses to the disclosure of the same information, such as an interest in playing with dolls (Gee & Heyman, 2007). There are other ways in which children may observe the same action leading to different evaluative responses depending on who is doing it. For example, an adult family member might be praised for cutting a toddler's hair, whereas a 4-year-old would likely be scolded for it.

Another problem with using observed praise to inform behavior is that the implications of praise can sometimes be unclear. For example, when someone praises a student's effort, it could mean that effort is valued and that it offers a pathway to improving one's abilities, but it could also imply that the student must work extra hard because he or she lacks innate ability (Amemiya & Wang, 2018).

Praise can be insincere, which makes it a false signal about what others value. Even young children sometimes mention this possibility. In a study in which children were asked how their parents would respond if they made a small mistake, a 5-year-old replied, "My parents would say 'great job' but they wouldn't really mean it" (Heyman, Dweck, & Cain, 1992). Insincere praise can emerge from a variety of different motives, including a desire to protect someone's feelings (Heyman, Sweet, & Lee, 2009) or to be ingratiating (Bennett & Yeeles, 1990). Once children come to understand that praise can be insincere, the way they judge the sincerity of a specific instance of praise is likely to depend on how much they want to believe it, as well as what it means within their cultural context (Heyman, Fu, & Lee, 2013).

Conclusion

Taken as a whole, research on praise and reputation management suggests that even young children value being seen as praiseworthy, and that they act strategically based on what they think others know about them and expect of them. As they develop, children learn which behaviors and traits are considered praiseworthy within their culture based on their own experiences and social observations. Along the way children must navigate many pitfalls, such as the possibility that overt attempts to call positive attention to oneself will fail or even backfire, and that observable instances of praise may not be reliable indicators of what others value.

References

Amemiya, J., & Wang, M. T. (2018). Why effort praise can backfire in adolescence. *Child Development Perspectives, 12*, 199–203.

Banerjee, R. (2000). The development of an understanding of modesty. *British Journal of Developmental Psychology, 18*, 499–517.

Bennett, M., & Yeeles, C. (1990). Children's understanding of showing off. *The Journal of Social Psychology, 130*, 591–596.

Boseovski, J. J., Chiu, K., & Marcovitch, S. (2013). Integration of behavioral frequency and intention information in young children's trait attributions. *Social Development, 22*, 38–57.

Botto, S. V., & Rochat, P. (2018). Sensitivity to the evaluation of others emerges by 24 months. *Developmental Psychology, 54*, 1723–1734.

Brummelman, E., Crocker, J., & Bushman, B. J. (2016). The praise paradox: When and why praise backfires in children with low self-esteem. *Child Development Perspectives, 10*, 111–115.

Cimpian, A., Arce, H. M. C., Markman, E. M., & Dweck, C. S. (2007). Subtle linguistic cues affect children's motivation. *Psychological Science, 18*, 314–316.

Engelmann, J. M., Herrmann, E., & Tomasello, M. (2012). Five-year-olds, but not chimpanzees, attempt to manage their reputations. *PLOS ONE, 7*, e48433.

Engelmann, J. M., Over, H., Herrmann, E., & Tomasello, M. (2013). Young children care more about their reputation with ingroup members and potential reciprocators. *Developmental Science, 16*, 952–958.

Fu, G., Heyman, G. D., Cameron, C. A., & Lee, K. (2016). Learning to be unsung heroes: Development of reputation management in two cultures. *Child Development, 87*, 689–699.

Fu, G., Heyman, G. D., & Lee, K. (2011). Reasoning about modesty among adolescents and adults in China and the U.S. *Journal of Adolescence, 34*, 599–608.

Fu, G., Heyman, G. D., Qian, M., Guo, T., & Lee, K. (2016). Young children with a positive reputation to maintain are less likely to cheat. *Developmental Science, 19*, 275–283.

Fu, G., Lee, K., Cameron, C. A., & Xu, F. (2001). Chinese and Canadian adults' categorization and evaluation of lie- and truth-telling about prosocial and antisocial behaviors. *Journal of Cross-Cultural Psychology, 32*, 720–727.

Gauvain, M., Altman, I., & Fahim, H. (1984). Homes and social change: A case study of the impact of resettlement. In K. Gergen & M. Gergen (Eds.), *Historical social psychology* (pp. 211–235). Hillsdale, NJ: Erlbaum.

Gee, C. L., & Heyman, G. D. (2007). Children's evaluation of other people's self-descriptions. *Social Development, 16*, 800–810.

Heyman, G. D., Barner, D., Heumann, J., & Schenck, L. (2014). Children's sensitivity to ulterior motives when evaluating prosocial behavior. *Cognitive Science, 38*, 683–700.

Heyman, G. D., Dweck, C. S. & Cain, K. M. (1992). Young children's vulnerability to self-blame and helplessness: Relationship to beliefs about goodness. *Child Development, 63*, 401–415.

Heyman, G. D., Fu, G., Barner, D., Zhishan, H., Zhou, L., & Lee, K. (2016). Children's evaluation of public and private generosity and its relation to behavior: Evidence from China. *Journal of Experimental Child Psychology, 150*, 16–30.

Heyman, G. D., Fu, G., & Lee, K. (2008). Reasoning about the disclosure of success and failure to friends among children in the U.S. and China. *Developmental Psychology, 44*, 908–918.

Heyman, G. D., Fu, G., & Lee, K. (2013). Selective skepticism: American and Chinese children's reasoning about evaluative academic feedback. *Developmental Psychology, 49*, 543–553.

Heyman, G. D., Fu, G., Lin, J., Qian, M. K., & Lee, K. (2015). Eliciting promises from children reduces cheating. *Journal of Experimental Child Psychology, 139*, 242–248.

Heyman, G. D., Itakura, S., & Lee, K. (2011). Japanese and American children's reasoning about accepting credit for prosocial behavior. *Social Development, 20*, 171–184.

Heyman, G. D., Sweet, M. A., & Lee, K. (2009). Children's reasoning about lie-telling and truth-telling in politeness contexts. *Social Development, 18*, 728–746.

Lane, J. D., Wellman, H. M., & Gelman, S. A. (2013). Informants' traits weigh heavily in young children's trust in testimony and in their epistemic inferences. *Child Development, 84*, 1253–1268.

Leimgruber, K. L., Shaw, A., Santos, L. R., & Olson, K. R. (2012). Young children are more generous when others are aware of their actions. *PLOS ONE, 7*, e48292.

Lee, K. (2013). Little liars: Development of verbal deception in children. *Child Development Perspectives, 7*, 91–96.

Lockhart, K. L., Goddu, M. K., & Keil, F. C. (2018). When saying "I'm best" is benign: Developmental shifts in perceptions of boasting. *Developmental Psychology, 54*, 521–535.

Ma, F., Heyman, G. D., Jing, C., Fu, Y., Compton, B. J., Xu, F., & Lee, K. (2018). Promoting honesty in young children through observational learning. *Journal of Experimental Child Psychology, 167*, 234–245.

Mueller, C. M., & Dweck, C. S. (1998). Praise for intelligence can undermine children's motivation and performance. *Journal of Personality and Social Psychology, 75*, 33–52.

Shaw, A., Montinari, N., Piovesan, M., Olson, K. R., Gino, F., & Norton, M. I. (2014). Children develop a veil of fairness. *Journal of Experimental Psychology: General, 143*, 363–375.

Watling, D., & Banerjee, R. (2007). Children's understanding of modesty in front of peer and adult audiences. *Infant and Child Development, 16*, 227–236.

Zhao, L., Chen, L., Sun, W., Compton, B. J., Lee, K., & Heyman, G. D. (2019). Young children are more likely to cheat after overhearing that a classmate is smart. *Developmental Science,* e12930.

Zhao, L., Heyman, G. D., Chen, L., & Lee, K. (2017). Praising young children for being smart promotes cheating. *Psychological Science, 28*, 1868–1870.

Zhao, L., Heyman, G. D., Chen, L., & Lee, K. (2018). Telling young children they have a reputation for being smart promotes cheating. *Developmental Science, 21*, e12585.

14

EVALUATIVE FEEDBACK EXPRESSES AND REINFORCES CULTURAL STEREOTYPES

Andrea C. Vial and Andrei Cimpian

When used appropriately, evaluative feedback (i.e., praise and criticism) is a powerful motivator (Yeager et al., 2014). Often, however, feedback fails to shape behavior as intended (Brophy, 1981) or even causes harm (Brummelman, Thomaes, Orobio de Castro, Overbeek, & Bushman, 2014). Here, we describe the harm that emerges when feedback intersects with stereotypes: By giving voice to what society expects of the members of various groups, feedback ultimately reinforces group stereotypes and contributes to the maintenance of group disparities. We first describe how stereotypes influence the feedback provided to stereotyped individuals. Our review focuses on stereotypes about gender and race because most of the research does as well. We then describe how stereotyped feedback shapes stereotyped individuals' self-perceptions and ability to succeed in counter-stereotypical fields.

The effects of stereotypes on evaluative feedback

To clarify, we use the terms *feedback*, *praise*, and *criticism* to refer to an overt evaluation of a behavior; in our terminology, an *evaluation* is a private judgment or attitude (e.g., X approves of Y's behavior) that is made public by the act of providing feedback (e.g., X says to Y, "That was great!"). At a first pass, we might use two dimensions to predict the type of feedback that an individual will receive for a behavior. The first dimension is the *valence* of the attribute that is illustrated by the behavior (the *x*-axis in Figure 14.1A). For instance, donating to charity illustrates a positively valenced attribute (namely, generosity), whereas punching someone illustrates a negatively valenced attribute (namely, aggression). The second dimension is the *level* or degree to which the behavior illustrates the relevant attribute (the *y*-axis). For instance, donating $100 illustrates higher levels

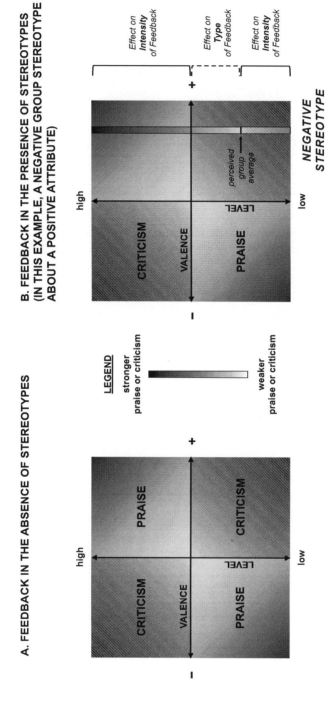

FIGURE 14.1   Evaluative feedback for a behavior as a function of the valence of the attribute illustrated by the behavior (x-axis) and the level or degree to which the behavior demonstrates that attribute (y-axis). Praise is depicted by the solid areas, criticism by the hatched areas. Feedback intensity is depicted via shading (darker shades = more intense feedback). Panel A illustrates feedback in the absence of stereotypes. Panel B provides a specific example of the effects of a negative stereotype on feedback (see "Negative stereotype" column); the brackets and labels on the right side of Panel B map onto this specific example.

of generosity than donating $1. The midpoint on this dimension represents the average perceived level of an attribute in the population.

On this simple analysis, behaviors that demonstrate high levels of a positively valenced attribute (e.g., generosity) will result in praise, whereas behaviors that demonstrate low levels of the same attribute will result in criticism. This relation is reversed for negatively valenced attributes (e.g., aggression). The *intensity* of the feedback for a behavior (e.g., whether a person receives lukewarm vs. effusive praise) depends on both the level and the valence of the attribute displayed: The more extreme a behavior is on either dimension, the more intense the feedback (as illustrated by darker shading in Figure 14.1A). For instance, a person will receive more effusive praise for displaying a level of math skill *far* above the perceived average than *just* above average.

Effects of stereotypes on whether a behavior is evaluated positively vs. negatively

A stereotype is a generic belief about a social group (Bian & Cimpian, 2017; Hammond & Cimpian, 2017). Most stereotypes assign a certain level (high or low) of an attribute (positive or negative) to a certain group. For example, common stereotypes are that women are bad at math (i.e., this group has low average levels of a positive attribute) or that Black people are athletic (i.e., this group has high average levels of a positive attribute). By informing people's perceptions of the average level of an attribute for a group (see the "perceived group average" line in Figure 14.1B), stereotypes set the standard relative to which evaluative feedback is provided for individuals in that group (Biernat & Kobrynowicz, 1997). In turn, reliance on these stereotype-based standards affects both the *intensity* and the *type* of feedback provided to stereotyped individuals.

#1. Stereotype effects on the intensity of feedback. Stereotypes affect the intensity of the feedback provided to members of stereotyped groups. To illustrate, as a member of a group that is negatively stereotyped in the domain of math, a woman who displays strong mathematical skill—above both the perceived population average and the stereotype of her group—is likely to receive more effusive praise than other individuals at the same skill level (see Figure 14.1B). This is because her skill is more extreme relative to the (low) standard by which she is judged than would be the case for a man. Similarly, this low stereotyped standard means that she might also receive milder criticism for poor performance in math.

Several studies provide evidence for the effect of stereotypes on feedback intensity. For example, negative stereotypes that men are unlikely to be altruistic lead individual men to receive more effusive praise than women for behaving altruistically in the workplace (Heilman & Chen, 2005; Kobrynowicz & Biernat, 1997). Other studies have found similar intensification effects in contexts where women are negatively stereotyped, such as sports (Biernat & Vescio, 2002). Stereotypes about racial groups intensify evaluative feedback as well

(Biernat & Kobrynowicz, 1997; Biernat & Manis, 1994). For example, lower stereotype-based standards lead participants to judge the standardized test performance of a Black student to be "better" than the same performance by a White student (Biernat, Collins, Katzarska-Miller, & Thompson, 2009). (To clarify, the fact that members of negatively stereotyped groups sometimes receive inflated praise does not mean that observers' evaluation of the underlying attribute is inflated as well. Despite the effusive praise, negatively stereotyped individuals are often assumed to display lower levels of the underlying attribute than non-stereotyped individuals [Biernat & Vescio, 2002].) Comparable findings emerge for positive group stereotypes: People who endorse positive stereotypes of athleticism for Black people tend to evaluate Black individuals' athleticism less positively, especially when the standard of comparison is the stereotypic average for this group (Biernat & Manis, 1994; see Heilman & Chen, 2005, for a gender-relevant example).

#2. **Stereotype effects on the type of feedback.** Stereotypes can affect the type of feedback (praise vs. criticism) received by an individual (see Figure 14.1B). For instance, as a member of a group that is negatively stereotyped in the domain of math, a woman who performs better than would be expected given the stereotypes of her gender may receive praise even if her performance is *below* the perceived population average (which includes men). Thus, a behavior that might have been criticized in others is now met with praise. Similarly, members of negatively stereotyped groups are sometimes spared criticism for poor performance compared to other groups—and may even receive praise: White students showed a positivity bias when giving feedback on a poor-quality essay ostensibly written by a Black (vs. White) student (Harber, 1998), as did White teachers when giving feedback on Black and Latinx (vs. White) students' essays (Harber et al., 2012).

Effects of stereotypes on evaluative feedback: beyond positivity vs. negativity

The two effects described above address only how stereotypes influence the degree to which a behavior is evaluated positively or negatively. But stereotypes also affect (#3) causal attributions for behavior and, in some cases, (#4) global evaluations of the feedback recipient, as well as (#5) the frequency of feedback in a stereotyped domain. We describe each of these effects below.

#3. **Stereotype effects on causal attributions.** Feedback can convey information about how observers *explained* the behavior under evaluation (Cimpian, Arce, Markman, & Dweck, 2007; Mueller & Dweck, 1998), and stereotypes have systematic effects on this aspect of feedback: Whether a group is stereotyped positively or negatively, feedback for an individual's stereotype-*consistent* behavior (e.g., a Black person's excellent athletic performance) is more likely to reference the individual's inherent traits or properties as an explanation, in part because stereotypes are generally understood as describing the inherent attributes of group members (Cimpian & Salomon, 2014; Hammond & Cimpian, 2017). In contrast, feedback for an individual's stereotype-*inconsistent* behavior (e.g., a woman's excellent math performance) is more likely to explain that behavior in ways that reconcile it with the stereotype and portray the individual or the circumstances as unusual (e.g., "she worked really hard," "she got lucky"; see Richards & Hewstone, 2001). Indeed, teachers praise boys more often than they praise girls for the intellectual quality of their work (Dweck, Davidson, Nelson, & Enna, 1978), which is as expected given that high-level intellectual ability is a male-stereotypic trait (Bian, Leslie, & Cimpian, 2018; Gálvez, Tiffenberg, & Altszyler, 2019; Leslie, Cimpian, Meyer, & Freeland, 2015). Conversely, teachers systematically attribute girls' good performance to hard work (J. Cimpian, Lubienski, Timmer, Makowski, & Miller, 2016).

#4. Stereotype effects on global impressions of the person. Many stereotypes are *descriptive* beliefs about the members of a group. When people believe that women are bad at math or that Black people are athletic, they are endorsing descriptive stereotypes. They do not typically think that women *should* be bad at math or that Black people *should* be athletic. However, some stereotypes— particularly about gender—have a normative element as well, dictating what people in a group *should be* like; these are known as *prescriptive* stereotypes (Burgess & Borgida, 1999). When people believe that it is desirable for women in particular to be modest or for men in particular to be ambitious, they are endorsing prescriptive stereotypes (Smith & Huntoon, 2014). Beyond influencing feedback intensity/type for specific behaviors (as described above), prescriptive stereotypes also affect an observer's *global* evaluation of the *person*. For example, several studies have shown negative global evaluations of successful female targets, who are often perceived to violate gender prescriptions when they project ambition and confidence (Heilman & Okimoto, 2007; Phelan, Moss-Racusin, & Rudman, 2008). When a woman brags about her accomplishments or fails to act in altruistic ways, criticism of her behavior is often tinged with dislike for her as a person (Heilman, 2001). Similarly, male targets who violate gender prescriptions by being modest about their accomplishments often elicit negative global feedback (Moss-Racusin, Phelan, & Rudman, 2010).

#5. Stereotype effects on the frequency of feedback. The value-laden layer of prescriptive stereotypes has another important effect: *It makes feedback more likely to be provided in the first place.* Individuals are more likely to be praised or criticized for behaviors that conform or fail to conform, respectively, to a prescriptive stereotype than a merely descriptive stereotypic standard. This is likely because observers care more about prescriptive stereotypic standards and may also assume that individuals being evaluated care more about these standards as well and would thus benefit from the feedback. Illustrating this phenomenon, women are more likely to be praised or complimented for their appearance than men (Eckert & McConnell-Ginet, 2003), whereas men are more frequently praised for their skills and abilities (Holmes, 1988; Parisi & Wogan, 2006; Rees-Miller, 2011).

The effects of stereotyped evaluative feedback

Evaluative feedback that is influenced by stereotypes contributes to the mainte-nance of the societal status quo, (re)producing inequality in several ways, as we describe next. Due in part to their effects on praise and criticism, stereotypes are ultimately self-reinforcing—they bring about, and maintain, the version of reality they project.

Stereotyped feedback shapes self-concepts

Stereotyped feedback reinforces the status quo by shaping stereotyped individ-uals' self-concepts (i.e., what they value, what they think they are good at) from a young age (Block, Gonzalez, Schmader, & Baron, 2018). A child who is often praised (or criticized) for displaying (or failing to display) an attribute stereotyp-ically associated with their group might over time begin to value that attribute themselves—to incorporate it as part of their self-concept. This effect follows from general principles of operant conditioning (Domjan, 2000): There are few reinforcers as powerful as the perception that others approve of us and few pun-ishers as effective as the prospect of social disapproval (Tomasello, 2014; though see Brummelman, 2018). Differentially reinforcing (with praise) and punishing (with criticism) the behavior of certain groups (e.g., girls) with respect to certain attributes (e.g., being altruistic) is likely to modulate the behaviors and attitudes associated with those attributes. Ultimately, these developmental processes can be observed in the way that adults sort themselves into stereotype-congruent ca-reers (e.g., women choose more communally oriented careers; Diekman, Brown, Johnston, & Clark, 2010). The fact that self-selection among adults occurs seem-ingly free from external influence—people choose the careers they *want*—is in part a function of prior shaping of an individual's desires by stereotype-driven evaluations from parents, teachers, and peers (Sullivan, Moss-Racusin, Lopez, & Williams, 2018; Thomas & Blakemore, 2013).

Stereotyped praise and criticism shape not just what individuals want but also *what they believe they can achieve*, another key facet of the self-concept. For exam-ple, praising the success of negatively stereotyped groups (e.g., girls doing well in math) in terms of their effort, while potentially beneficial in some respects (Mueller & Dweck, 1998), might also lead members of these groups—as well as observers—to infer that their effort compensates for a lack of ability (Amemiya & Wang, 2018; Meyer, 1992). In turn, this inference is likely to trigger concerns about belonging and undermine persistence in members of stigmatized groups (Graham & Taylor, 2014; Smith, Lewis, Hawthorne, & Hodges, 2013).

Stereotyped feedback creates obstacles

Stereotyped feedback reinforces the status quo not just by changing how mem-bers of stigmatized groups think about themselves but also by creating exter-nal barriers that keep individuals out of domains that are not stereotypically associated with their group (Gaddis, 2015; Heilman, 2001). Some of these effects are direct and obvious: Evaluating individuals through the lens of their group membership carries the risk of failing to appropriately recognize and reward their good performance. For example, women who excel in a male-typed career are often viewed as highly competent but "cold," which is a violation of gender prescriptions. As a result, women who are successful in male-typed domains often receive fewer organizational rewards than comparable men (Heilman, Wallen, Fuchs, & Tamkins, 2004). More generally, there is evidence that the stereotyped expectations and evaluations of those in positions of authority deprive individuals from stigmatized groups of opportunities to show their abilities and further their careers (Bian, Leslie, & Cimpian, 2018; Biernat & Vescio, 2002; Moss-Racusin, Dovidio, Brescoll, Graham, & Handelsman, 2012).

Beyond the direct effects that stereotyped feedback can have on the opportunities afforded to stigmatized groups, stereotyped feedback can—more indirectly and subtly—undermine their motivation and success. An individual who perceives that others are evaluating them in light of a certain stereotype is likely to experience a sense of psychological threat even if they *reject* that stereotype (Schmader, Johns, & Forbes, 2008; Steele, 2011). As a result of this threat, the individual may experience uncertainty about whether they belong in that context, decreased trust, and other psychological states that are not conducive to success (Bian, Leslie, Murphy, & Cimpian, 2018; Emerson & Murphy, 2015; Walton & Cohen, 2007). Thus, stereotyped feedback can set into motion a host of processes within the recipient that ultimately limit their success in a counter-stereotypical domain, thereby reinforcing the status quo.

Conclusion

Whether we are aware of it or not, the feedback we give to others is not just a function of their behavior (i.e., the objective stimulus). Critically, others' perceived social identities influence the standards we use to evaluate their behavior and, as a result, the feedback we give them. The evidence reviewed here suggests that stereotypes affect multiple aspects of feedback, from its positivity and frequency to the factors that we think explain the person's behavior, and these effects are themselves consequential. Much like a self-fulfilling prophecy, the recipients of stereotyped feedback often end up conforming to society's perceptions of their groups, thereby "validating" these biased perceptions and perpetuating social inequality.

Acknowledgments

The writing of this chapter was supported in part by the Dream Gap Postdoctoral Fellowship awarded to Andrea Vial and by National Science Foundation grant BCS-1733897 awarded to Andrei Cimpian. We are grateful to Eddie Brummelman and the members of the Cognitive Development Lab at New York University for their helpful comments on previous drafts of this chapter.

References

Amemiya, J., & Wang, M. T. (2018). Why effort praise can backfire in adolescence. *Child Development Perspectives, 12*, 199–203.

Bian, L., & Cimpian, A. (2017). Are stereotypes accurate? A perspective from the cognitive science of concepts. *Behavioral and Brain Sciences, 40*, e3.

Bian, L., Leslie, S. J., & Cimpian, A. (2018). Evidence of bias against girls and women in contexts that emphasize intellectual ability. *American Psychologist, 73*, 1139–1153.

Bian, L., Leslie, S. J., Murphy, M. C., & Cimpian, A. (2018). Messages about brilliance undermine women's interest in educational and professional opportunities. *Journal of Experimental Social Psychology, 76*, 404–420.

Biernat, M., Collins, E. C., Katzarska-Miller, I., & Thompson, E. R. (2009). Race-based shifting standards and racial discrimination. *Personality and Social Psychology Bulletin, 35*, 16–28.

Biernat, M., & Kobrynowicz, D. (1997). Gender- and race-based standards of competence: Lower minimum standards but higher ability standards for devalued groups. *Journal of Personality and Social Psychology, 72*, 544–557.

Biernat, M., & Manis, M. (1994). Shifting standards and stereotype-based judgments. *Journal of Personality and Social Psychology, 66*, 5–20.

Biernat, M., & Vescio, T. K. (2002). She swings, she hits, she's great, she's benched: Implications of gender-based shifting standards for judgment and behavior. *Personality and Social Psychology Bulletin, 28*, 66–77.

Block, K., Gonzalez, A. M., Schmader, T., & Baron, A. S. (2018). Early gender differences in core values predict anticipated family versus career orientation. *Psychological Science, 29*, 1540–1547.

Brophy, J. (1981). Teacher praise: A functional analysis. *Review of Educational Research, 51*, 5–32.

Brummelman, E. (2018). Praise. In M. H. Bornstein (Ed.), *The Sage encyclopedia of lifespan human development* (pp. 1708–1709). Thousand Oaks, CA: Sage.

Brummelman, E., Thomaes, S., Orobio de Castro, B., Overbeek, G., & Bushman, B. J. (2014). "That's not just beautiful—that's incredibly beautiful!": The adverse impact of inflated praise on children with low self-esteem. *Psychological Science, 25*, 728–735.

Burgess, D., & Borgida, E. (1999). Who women are, who women should be: Descriptive and prescriptive gender stereotyping in sex discrimination. *Psychology, Public Policy, and Law, 5*, 665–692.

Cimpian, A., Arce, H. M. C., Markman, E. M., & Dweck, C. S. (2007). Subtle linguistic cues affect children's motivation. *Psychological Science, 18*, 314–316.

Cimpian, A., & Salomon, E. (2014). The inherence heuristic: An intuitive means of making sense of the world, and a potential precursor to psychological essentialism. *Behavioral and Brain Sciences, 37*, 461–480.

Cimpian, J. R., Lubienski, S. T., Timmer, J. D., Makowski, M. B., & Miller, E. K. (2016). Have gender gaps in math closed? Achievement, teacher perceptions, and learning behaviors across two ECLS-K cohorts. *AERA Open, 2*, 1–19.

Diekman, A. B., Brown, E. R., Johnston, A. M., & Clark, E. K. (2010). Seeking congruity between goals and roles: A new look at why women opt out of science, technology, engineering, and mathematics careers. *Psychological Science, 21*, 1051–1057.

Domjan, M. (2000). *The essentials of conditioning and learning*. Belmont, CA: Wadsworth-Thomson Learning.

Dweck, C. S., Davidson, W., Nelson, S., & Enna, B. (1978). Sex differences in learned helplessness: II. The contingencies of evaluative feedback in the classroom and III. An experimental analysis. *Developmental Psychology, 14*, 268–276.

Eckert, P., & McConnell-Ginet, S. (2013). *Language and gender.* New York, NY: Cambridge University Press.

Emerson, K. T., & Murphy, M. C. (2015). A company I can trust? Organizational lay theories moderate stereotype threat for women. *Personality and Social Psychology Bulletin, 41*, 295–307.

Gaddis, S. M. (2015). Discrimination in the credential society: An audit study of race and college selectivity in the labor market. *Social Forces, 93*, 1451–1479.

Gálvez, R. H., Tiffenberg, V., & Altszyler, E. (2019). Half a century of stereotyping associations between gender and intellectual ability in films. *Sex Roles, 81*, 643–654.

Graham, S., & Taylor, A. Z. (2014). An attributional approach to emotional life in the classroom. In R. Pekrun & L. Linnenbrink-Garcia (Eds.), *International handbook of emotions in education* (pp. 96–119). New York, NY: Routledge.

Hammond, M. D., & Cimpian, A. (2017). Investigating the cognitive structure of stereotypes: Generic beliefs about groups predict social judgments better than statistical beliefs. *Journal of Experimental Psychology: General, 146*, 607–614.

Harber, K. D. (1998). Feedback to minorities: Evidence of a positive bias. *Journal of Personality and Social Psychology, 74*, 622–628.

Harber, K. D., Gorman, J. L., Gengaro, F. P., Butisingh, S., Tsang, W., & Ouellette, R. (2012). Students' race and teachers' social support affect the positive feedback bias in public schools. *Journal of Educational Psychology, 104*, 1149–1161.

Heilman, M. E. (2001). Description and prescription: How gender stereotypes prevent women's ascent up the organizational ladder. *Journal of Social Issues, 57*, 657–674.

Heilman, M. E., & Chen, J. J. (2005). Same behavior, different consequences: Reactions to men's and women's altruistic citizenship behavior. *Journal of Applied Psychology, 90*, 431–441.

Heilman, M. E., & Okimoto, T. G. (2007). Why are women penalized for success at male tasks? The implied communality deficit. *Journal of Applied Psychology, 92*, 81–92.

Heilman, M. E., Wallen, A. S., Fuchs, D., & Tamkins, M. M. (2004). Penalties for success: Reactions to women who succeed at male gender-typed tasks. *Journal of Applied Psychology, 89*, 416–427.

Holmes, J. (1988). Paying compliments: A sex-preferential politeness strategy. *Journal of Pragmatics, 12*, 445–465.

Kobrynowicz, D., & Biernat, M. (1997). Decoding subjective evaluations: How stereotypes provide shifting standards. *Journal of Experimental Social Psychology, 33*, 579–601.

Leslie, S. J., Cimpian, A., Meyer, M., & Freeland, E. (2015, January 16). Expectations of brilliance underlie gender distributions across academic disciplines. *Science, 347*, 262–265.

Meyer, W-U. (1992) Paradoxical effects of praise and criticism on perceived ability. *European Review of Social Psychology, 3*, 259–283.

Moss-Racusin, C. A., Dovidio, J. F., Brescoll, V. L., Graham, M. J., & Handelsman, J. (2012). Science faculty's subtle gender biases favor male students. *Proceedings of the National Academy of Sciences, USA, 109*, 16474–16479.

Moss-Racusin, C. A., Phelan, J. E., & Rudman, L. A. (2010). When men break the gender rules: Status incongruity and backlash against modest men. *Psychology of Men and Masculinity, 11*, 140–151.

Muller, C., & Dweck, C. (1998). Praise for intelligence can undermine children's motivation and performance. *Journal of Personality and Social Psychology, 75*, 33–52.

Parisi, C., & Wogan, P. (2006). Compliment topics and gender. *Women and Language, 29*, 21–28.

Phelan, J. E., Moss-Racusin, C. A., & Rudman, L. A. (2008). Competent yet out in the cold: Shifting criteria for hiring reflect backlash toward agentic women. *Psychology of Women Quarterly, 32,* 406–413.

Rees-Miller, J. (2011). Compliments revisited: Contemporary compliments and gender. *Journal of Pragmatics, 43,* 2673–2688.

Richards, Z., & Hewstone, M. (2001). Subtyping and subgrouping: Processes for the prevention and promotion of stereotype change. *Personality and Social Psychology Review, 5,* 52–73.

Schmader, T., Johns, M., & Forbes, C. (2008). An integrated process model of stereotype threat effects on performance. *Psychological Review, 115,* 336–356.

Smith, J. L., & Huntoon, M. (2014). Women's bragging rights: Overcoming modesty norms to facilitate women's self-promotion. *Psychology of Women Quarterly, 38,* 447–459.

Smith, J. L., Lewis, K. L., Hawthorne, L., & Hodges, S. D. (2013). When trying hard isn't natural: Women's belonging with and motivation for male-dominated STEM fields as a function of effort expenditure concerns. *Personality and Social Psychology Bulletin, 39,* 131–143.

Steele, C. M. (2011). *Whistling Vivaldi: How stereotypes affect us and what we can do.* New York, NY: WW Norton.

Sullivan, J., Moss-Racusin, C., Lopez, M., & Williams, K. (2018). Backlash against gender stereotype-violating preschool children. *PLOS ONE, 13,* e0195503.

Thomas, R. N., & Blakemore, J. E. O. (2013). Adults' attitudes about gender nonconformity in childhood. *Archives of Sexual Behavior, 42,* 399–412.

Tomasello, M. (2014). The ultra-social animal. *European Journal of Social Psychology, 44,* 187–194.

Walton, G. M., & Cohen, G. L. (2007). A question of belonging: Race, social fit, and achievement. *Journal of Personality and Social Psychology, 92,* 82–96.

Yeager, D. S., Purdie-Vaughns, V., Garcia, J., Apfel, N., Brzustoski, P., Master, A., ... & Cohen, G. L. (2014). Breaking the cycle of mistrust: Wise interventions to provide critical feedback across the racial divide. *Journal of Experimental Psychology: General, 143,* 804–824.

PART V

Development and culture

15

DEVELOPMENTAL PSYCHOLOGY OF PRAISE

Sander Thomaes and Patty Leijten

From the first stages of life, children are often positively evaluated, or praised, by other people. In fact, even from well before they are able to grasp the contents of what others say, many children are frequently exposed to phrases such as "look at you, you're so cute!" Such positive evaluations remain common when children grow up—such as in school, where they are frequently praised for their performances or efforts.

Praise can be a powerful tool for parents, educators, therapists, and others to influence young people's development. Still little is known, though, about how the consequences of praise may depend on age. Does a simple phrase such as "good job!" have similar consequences for an infant who just managed to stand upright for the first time, a kindergartener who comes back home from the first school day, a 9-year-old who just gave a talk in class, or a teenager who just finished her first driving lesson? And do apparently subtle differences in type of praise—i.e., how praise is phrased—affect children of different ages differentially? The goal of this chapter is to provide an overview of current knowledge of developmental differences in the consequences of praise for young people's adjustment and list priorities for future work.

Infancy

One may wonder whether praise can have any effects on infants, who are not yet able to truly understand verbal content. Research suggests that—in some contexts and for some behaviors—it can. For example, one study found that 10-month-old infants are more likely to imitate the play behaviors modeled by their mothers when they are praised for doing so (e.g., "way to go, baby"; Poulson & Kymissis, 1988). Similarly, research has found that 12- to 20-month-old infants engage more in modeled vocalizations, accept more bites in feeding episodes, and (especially younger infants) show more helping behaviors, when they are praised or verbally encouraged (Dahl et al., 2017; Dearden et al., 2009; Poulson, Kymissis, Reeve, Andreatos, & Reeve, 1991).

These studies illustrate how praise does not necessarily require understanding of verbal content on the receiver's part to be consequential. Infants discriminate and process the intonation or vocal affect of praise, or the facial expressions or postural changes that go along with it, which can then impact their behavior. In one particularly insightful study (Fernald, 1993), 5-month-old American infants were exposed to praise (i.e., the equivalents of "you're so good") versus disapproval (the equivalents of "you're so naughty") in several languages that were unfamiliar to them. This way, the researcher insured that children would not understand any of its content. Infants showed positive affect, as indexed by their smiling, when they heard praise in German and Italian (i.e., affectively expressive languages), but not Japanese (i.e., a less affectively expressive language). Thus, from at least as young as 5 months of age, infants can process praise from its affective tone.

Early childhood

Somewhat later in development, in early childhood—a time of exploration and rapidly increasing verbal understanding—praise can shape children's learning behavior. For example, research has found that praise provides an effective strategy for preschool teachers to help socialize effective learning behavior in their pupils. One study (Fullerton, Conroy, & Correa, 2009) showed that when preschool teachers are trained to use *labeled* praise in their classrooms—praise that makes explicit what behavior a child is praised for ("Good job washing your hands," also called *specific* praise)—2- to 4-year-old children show increased compliance (i.e., observed adherence to teacher instruction) and engagement (i.e., observed appropriate participation or interaction) in class. Importantly, all participants in this study had been identified by their teachers as showing problem behaviors that interfered with classroom engagement: Teacher praise can benefit the behavior of preschoolers who particularly need it.

Furthermore, from the time when children have developed a rudimentary verbal understanding, it already matters *how* praise is phrased. Sometimes, even apparently subtle differences in how praise is phrased matter. Consider the distinction between generic praise and nongeneric praise (Gelman & Heyman, 1999). Generic praise implies that a particular behavior that a child is praised for stems from an inherent and stable trait or skill; by contrast, nongeneric praise implies situation specificity of the behavior. In one study (Cimpian, Arce, Markman, & Dweck, 2007), 4-year-olds who had initial success on a drawing task (that they enacted with a hand puppet) were either told, "You're a good drawer" (i.e., generic praise) or "You did a good job drawing" (nongeneric praise). When they subsequently received criticism on the task, those who had received generic praise reacted more negatively—they denigrated their skill and disengaged from the task. Presumably, they inferred from the generic praise that their performance on the task signals their inherent ability. When they received criticism, they took this to imply that they lacked ability, and they felt and behaved accordingly.

Another study (Zhao, Heyman, Chen, & Lee, 2017), involving 3- to 5-year-olds, found that generic praise impacts children's moral behavior and can promote cheating. In the first stages of a guessing game, children were either told "You are so smart" (i.e., generic praise) or "You did very well this time" (i.e., nongeneric praise). Children who had received generic praise were more likely to cheat later on in the game—they were observed to peek more, even if they had promised not to do so, when the experimenter left the room. They likely did so in an attempt to maintain their reputation for being smart. Together, results such as these illustrate how, already from young age, apparently small differences in how praise is phrased may actually be psychologically salient and meaningful, and influence children's learning and achievement behaviors accordingly.

Middle and late childhood

One significant change as children move from early into middle childhood is that individual differences in social adjustment (e.g., the quality of relations with peers) become increasingly stable and consequential (Nelson, Rubin, & Fox, 2005). Research suggests that teachers can influence children's social adjustment at school by creating socially safe school environments—and it is their use of praise that can play a major role in this process. For example, in one study (Spilt, Leflot, Onghena, & Colpin, 2016), second graders (i.e., mostly 7-year-olds) from 30 Belgian classrooms took part in a teacher-mediated preventive intervention, called the *Good Behavior Game*. The intervention seeks to broadly promote pupils' positive social and on-task behavior through teachers' behavior management. The intervention led to increases in the frequency with which teachers praised pupils for positive, compliant behavior. This increase in teacher praise, in turn, drove decreases in pupils' preferences to be alone and avoid contact with peers—as assessed from the beginning to the end of the school year, according to both teachers and children themselves. Thus, by adequately praising their pupils, teachers can help foster a social climate in their classrooms that helps withdrawn children improve relationships with peers.

Similarly, when parents are trained to use praise when interacting with their children, this can help to promote child compliance and reduce child disruptive behavior. In one experiment (Leijten, Thomaes, Orobio de Castro, Dishion, & Matthys, 2016), parents of children (mostly 4- to 8-year-olds) who were at risk for disruptive behavior problems were first requested to praise their child (or not) for compliant behavior. Next, parents asked their children to clean up a game that they were playing with. Children who had been praised were subsequently more compliant and needed less time to finish the cleaning-up. Next, these same parents were trained to use praise in their day-to-day interaction with their child for a two-week period. By the end of the period, they reported reductions in their children's disruptive behavior (as compared to baseline), more than did parents who were not trained to use praise.

Children's responsiveness to how praise is phrased, which originates in early childhood, continues in middle and late childhood. For example, primary school-aged children who receive generic, ability-focused praise (also called *person* praise, e.g., "you're so smart") tend to show helpless responses in the face of challenge or setbacks. They shy away from challenge or give up easily, and when confronted with failure or criticism, they may engage in self-blame or experience shame. Children who receive nongeneric, effort-focused, or strategy-focused praise (also called *process* praise, e.g., "you worked so hard") are less likely to show such helpless responses (Brummelman, Thomaes, Overbeek et al., 2014; Kamins & Dweck, 1999; Mueller & Dweck, 1998). What is more, the consequences of praise in school-aged children depend on whether or not praise involves social comparison (e.g., "You did better than other kids!"; Corpus, Ogle, & Love-Geiger, 2006), is inflated (contains an adverb or adjective that magnifies its positivity, e.g., "You're *extremely* good"; Brummelman, Thomaes, Orobio de Castro, Overbeek, & Bushman, 2014), or is perceived to be inaccurate (Lee, Kim, Kesebir, & Han, 2017).

Importantly, research in middle and late childhood also shows that the type of praise that adults use may depend on child characteristics—in particular, children's level of self-esteem (or at least, adults' *estimation* of children's level of self-esteem). In one series of studies, parents read scenarios involving children with high self-esteem versus low self-esteem who performed some act (e.g., played the piano), and they wrote down how they would praise the child. Parents gave more generic (i.e., *person*) and inflated praise to children with high (vs. low) self-esteem (Brummelman, Thomaes, Overbeek et al., 2014; Brummelman, Thomaes, Orobio de Castro et al., 2014). Similarly, in an observational study, parents administered mathematics problems to their own children. They were observed to give more inflated praise to the extent that their children had lower self-esteem (Brummelman, Thomaes, Orobio de Castro et al., 2014).

This tendency for parents to attune their praise to their children's level of self-esteem makes intuitive sense—parents may think that praise that directly contradicts children's habitual self-views may help them overcome their insecurities. Unfortunately, the consequences of such intuitive (i.e., generic and inflated) praise for children with low self-esteem are not what one would hope. They trigger in children with low self-esteem a tendency to validate their worth as a person—to prove they are as competent and worthy as the praise that they receive suggests they are. As a consequence, they tend to avoid challenge and feel down on themselves in the face of failure (Brummelman, Crocker, & Bushman, 2016).

Adolescence and emerging adulthood

Around the time children enter adolescence, their perceptions of praise—and thus, the potential consequences of praise—tend to change. For example, compared to younger children, adolescents are more likely to believe that the praise that they receive from others is reflective of how those others perceive their ability (Meyer, 1992; Möller, 2005).

This development is consequential, especially with regard to the consequences of effort praise. Throughout childhood, effort praise facilitates intrinsic motivation by instilling in children the belief that effort improves ability. In adolescence, however, effort praise can actually *compromise* motivation (Amemiya & Wang, 2018). Why is this the case? As compared to younger children, adolescents increasingly come to believe that effort and ability are inversely related (a belief that is common among adults as well; Barker & Graham, 1987). This belief holds that, for example, smart people do not need to work hard, and vice versa, that is, working hard implies that one may not be smart. For adolescents, receiving effort praise may therefore implicitly convey the message that they lack ability (or at least, that the person providing praise thinks they do). In a study that addressed this explanation (Lam, Yim, & Ng, 2008), it was shown that effort praise (i.e., praise for invested effort) is indeed less motivating to adolescents to the extent that they have more firmly adopted the belief that effort and ability are inversely related. Moreover, when the researchers experimentally made salient the "inverse relation" belief (i.e., by having participants read an article that endorsed this idea), effort praise hampered their task perseverance.

In secondary school, teachers tend to place more emphasis on students' performance as compared to their learning trajectory (Eccles & Roeser, 2013; Midgley, Anderman, & Hicks, 1995). This may be one factor contributing to adolescents' belief that effort and ability are inversely related: Adolescents notice that teachers approach high- and low-achieving students differently, and tend to praise lower achieving students for effort in an attempt to encourage them (Butler, 1994). For adolescents, effort praise may therefore come with the connotation of low ability.

Unfortunately, still relatively little is known about the consequences of praise beyond adolescence. That said, a few interesting studies have been timed in the developmental stage of emerging adulthood. This work, which involved college students as participants, has shown that praise continues to have motivational potential in academic and performance settings. For example, one study found that college students who, throughout a course, were verbally praised by their professor for the time they had spent on their homework, performed better at the final course examination, and also reported more motivation to learn than those who were not praised (Hancock, 2002).

There is some debate as to whether the potential undermining impact of effort praise found in adolescents continues into emerging adulthood. One experiment suggested that this might be the case (Koestner, Zuckerman, & Koestner, 1987). College students who worked on a series of puzzles and received effort praise experienced less intrinsic motivation and chose less challenging puzzles to work on than did those who received person praise—in some cases even less than those who received no praise at all. Later research, however, showed that (depending on students' level of seniority) effort praise actually can enhance college students' intrinsic task motivation, but such effects specifically surfaced in the face of a failure experience (Haimovitz & Henderlong Corpus, 2011). The psychological impact of effort praise in older youth and young adults is complex, and its motivational benefits seem less straightforward than in children.

Research priorities

The most direct, and arguably most informative, approach to investigate whether and how the consequences of praise may depend on children's age is longitudinal. As it stands, our understanding of age dependencies in the consequences of praise is limited to comparisons of studies that use somewhat similar designs across different age groups. A more precise understanding could be gained from longitudinal research that assesses the child outcomes associated with praise (e.g., parents' or teachers' habits in praising children) across development. For example, such research could establish more conclusively at what age children begin to perceive and be responsive to how praise is phrased; at what age children's behavior and learning outcomes are most potently shaped by praise; and at what age adolescents come to conceive of (effort) praise as potentially signaling low ability.

To be sure, some longitudinal work into the consequences of praise does exist. For example, research has found that the tendency for parents to spontaneously praise their young children (14–38 months) for effort foretells relevant child outcomes years later: When children were ages 7–8, those who received more praise for effort at young age were more likely to view intelligence as a malleable trait (Gunderson et al., 2013). Again 1–2 years later, these children performed better in mathematics and reading comprehension, an effect that was driven by the belief that intelligence is malleable (Gunderson et al., 2018). Notwithstanding these longitudinal findings, a priority for future work is to help understand whether, how, and why the consequences of praise change over the course of development.

A second priority for future work will be to better understand cultural differences in the consequences of praise. Cultural context shapes how adults communicate with children about their desirable behavior, ability, successes, and failures (Fu & Markus, 2014; Ng, Pomerantz, Lam, 2007; Wang, Wiley, & Chiu, 2008). For example, there are cultural differences in the extent to which adults' praise primarily serves to foster children's independence (i.e., their feelings of autonomy and competence, by meeting performance standards) versus their interdependence (i.e., their feelings of relatedness, by meeting the desires and expectations of others; Wang et al., 2008). Accordingly, the consequences of praise (and different types of praise, such as the types discussed in this chapter) for child adjustment are likely to differ across culture.

It is unfortunate, then, that our current understanding of praise and its consequences stems mostly from research in Western (i.e., North American, European) samples; generalization to youth growing up in other cultures is problematic. A priority for future work is to build an understanding of the consequences of praise that is not only developmentally but also culturally informed—an understanding of how the consequences of praise may vary both over the course of development and across culture.

Coda

From young age, receiving praise is psychologically powerful. Indeed, praise can be a potent source of young people's motivation, learning, well-being, and behavioral adjustment. And yet, in some cases, praise can have unintended, more disadvantageous consequences as well, such as when it pressures receivers to live up to high expectations. This chapter has reviewed the developmental psychology of praise: current knowledge of how the consequences of praise—and different *types* of praise—may vary across age, from infancy into emerging adulthood. Throughout development, young people care about being praised, but how they construe and react to being praised differs substantially across age.

References

Amemiya, J., & Wang, M. T. (2018). Why effort praise can backfire in adolescence. *Child Development Perspectives, 12*, 199–203.

Barker, G. P., & Graham, S. (1987). Developmental study of praise and blame as attributional cues. *Journal of Educational Psychology, 79*, 62–66.

Brummelman, E., Crocker, J., & Bushman, B. J. (2016). The praise paradox: When and why praise backfires in children with low self-esteem. *Child Development Perspectives, 10*, 111–115.

Brummelman, E., Thomaes, S., Orobio de Castro, B., Overbeek, G., & Bushman, B. J. (2014). "That's not just beautiful—that's incredibly beautiful!" The adverse impact of inflated praise on children with low self-esteem. *Psychological Science, 25*, 728–735.

Brummelman, E., Thomaes, S., Overbeek, G., Orobio de Castro, B., Van den Hout, M., & Bushman, B. J. (2014). On feeding those hungry for praise: Person praise backfires in children with low self-esteem. *Journal of Experimental Psychology: General, 143*, 9–14.

Butler, R. (1994). Teacher communications and student interpretations: Effects of teacher responses to failing students on attributional inferences in two age groups. *British Journal of Educational Psychology, 64*, 277–294.

Cimpian, A., Arce, H. M. C., Markman, E. M., & Dweck, C. S. (2007). Subtle linguistic cues affect children's motivation. *Psychological Science, 18*, 314–316.

Corpus, J. H., Ogle, C. M., & Love-Geiger, K. E. (2006). The effects of social-comparison versus mastery praise on children's intrinsic motivation. *Motivation and Emotion, 30*, 335–345.

Dahl, A., Satlof-Bedrick, E. S., Hammond, S. I., Drummond, J. K., Waugh, W. E., & Brownell, C. A. (2017). Explicit scaffolding increases simple helping in younger infants. *Developmental Psychology, 53*, 407–416.

Dearden, K. A., Hilton, S., Bentley, M. E., Caulfield, L. E., Wilde, C., Ha, P. B., & Marsh, D. (2009). Caregiver verbal encouragement increases food acceptance among Vietnamese toddlers. *The Journal of Nutrition, 139*, 1387–1392.

Eccles, J. S., & Roeser, R. W. (2013). Schools, academic motivation, and stage-environment fit. In R. M. Lerner & L. Steinberg (Eds.), *Handbook of adolescent psychology* (2nd ed., pp. 125–153). Hoboken, NJ: Wiley.

Fernald, A. (1993). Approval and disapproval: Infant responsiveness to vocal affect in familiar and unfamiliar languages. *Child Development, 64*, 657–674.

Fu, A. S., & Markus, H. R. (2014). My mother and me: Why tiger mothers motivate Asian Americans but not European Americans. *Personality and Social Psychology Bulletin, 40*, 739–749.

Fullerton, E. K., Conroy, M. A., & Correa, V. I. (2009). Early childhood teachers' use of specific praise statements with young children at risk for behavioral disorders. *Behavioral Disorders, 34*, 118–135.

Gelman, S. A., & Heyman, G. D. (1999). Carrot-eaters and creature-believers: The effects of lexicalization on children's inferences about social categories. *Psychological Science, 10*, 489–493.

Gunderson, E. A., Gripshover, S. J., Romero, C., Dweck, C. S., Goldin-Meadow, S., & Levine, S. C. (2013). Parent praise to 1-to 3-year-olds predicts children's motivational frameworks 5 years later. *Child Development, 84*, 1526–1541.

Gunderson, E. A., Sorhagen, N. S., Gripshover, S. J., Dweck, C. S., Goldin-Meadow, S., & Levine, S. C. (2018). Parent praise to toddlers predicts fourth grade academic achievement via children's incremental mindsets. *Developmental Psychology, 54*, 397–409.

Haimovitz, K., & Henderlong Corpus, J. (2011). Effects of person versus process praise on student motivation: Stability and change in emerging adulthood. *Educational Psychology, 31*, 595–609.

Hancock, D. R. (2002). Influencing graduate students' classroom achievement, homework habits and motivation to learn with verbal praise. *Educational Research, 44*, 83–95.

Kamins, M. L., & Dweck, C. S. (1999). Person versus process praise and criticism: Implications for contingent self-worth and coping. *Developmental psychology, 35*, 835–847.

Koestner, R., Zuckerman, M., & Koestner, J. (1987). Praise, involvement, and intrinsic motivation. *Journal of Personality and Social Psychology, 53*, 383–390.

Lam, S. F., Yim, P. S., & Ng, Y. L. (2008). Is effort praise motivational? The role of beliefs in the effort-ability relationship. *Contemporary Educational Psychology, 33*, 694–710.

Lee, H. I., Kim, Y. H., Kesebir, P., & Han, D. E. (2017). Understanding when parental praise leads to optimal child outcomes: Role of perceived praise accuracy. *Social Psychological and Personality Science, 8*, 679–688.

Leijten, P., Thomaes, S., Orobio de Castro, B., Dishion, T., & Matthys, W. (2016). What good is labeling what's good? A field experimental investigation of parental labeled praise and child compliance. *Behaviour Research and Therapy, 87*, 134–141.

Meyer, W. U. (1992). Paradoxical effects of praise and criticism on perceived ability. *European Review of Social Psychology, 3*, 259–283.

Midgley, C., Anderman, E., & Hicks, L. (1995). Differences between elementary and middle school teachers and students: A goal theory approach. *The Journal of Early Adolescence, 15*, 90–113.

Möller, J. (2005). Paradoxical effects of praise and criticism: Social, dimensional and temporal comparisons. *British Journal of Educational Psychology, 75*, 275–295.

Mueller, C. M., & Dweck, C. S. (1998). Praise for intelligence can undermine children's motivation and performance. *Journal of Personality and Social Psychology, 75*, 33–52.

Nelson, L. J., Rubin, K. H., & Fox, N. A. (2005). Social withdrawal, observed peer acceptance, and the development of self-perceptions in children ages 4 to 7 years. *Early Childhood Research Quarterly, 20*, 185–200.

Ng, F. F. Y., Pomerantz, E. M., & Lam, S. F. (2007). European American and Chinese parents' responses to children's success and failure: Implications for children's responses. *Developmental Psychology, 43,* 1239–1255.

Poulson, C. L., & Kymissis, E. (1988). Generalized imitation in infants. *Journal of Experimental Child Psychology, 46,* 324–336.

Poulson, C. L., Kymissis, E., Reeve, K. F., Andreatos, M., & Reeve, L. (1991). Generalized vocal imitation in infants. *Journal of Experimental Child Psychology, 51,* 267–279.

Spilt, J. L., Leflot, G., Onghena, P., & Colpin, H. (2016). Use of praise and reprimands as critical ingredients of teacher behavior management: Effects on children's development in the context of a teacher-mediated classroom intervention. *Prevention Science, 17,* 732–742.

Wang, Y. Z., Wiley, A. R., & Chiu, C. Y. (2008). Independence-supportive praise versus interdependence-promoting praise. *International Journal of Behavioral Development, 32,* 13–20.

Zhao, L., Heyman, G. D., Chen, L., & Lee, K. (2017). Praising young children for being smart promotes cheating. *Psychological Science, 28,* 1868–1870.

16

THE ROLE OF CULTURE IN PARENTS' RESPONSES TO CHILDREN'S PERFORMANCE

The case of the West and East Asia

Eva M. Pomerantz, Janice Ng, and Florrie Fei-Yin Ng

Beginning early in their lives, individuals are shaped by the culture in which they reside (for a review, see Greenfield, Keller, Fuligni, & Maynard, 2003). In most cultures, parents are a central channel of cultural transmission as they are not only considered responsible for children's development but also looked to by children for guidance. Moreover, as adults, parents are knowledgeable about the norms and values of their culture. Thus, parents often adopt goals for children that support children in developing the characteristics to thrive in their culture (e.g., Lamm et al., 2018). Such goals may influence how parents respond to children's behavior (Ng, Xiong et al., 2019), which has long been considered a key mechanism by which parents shape children's development (e.g., Gunderson et al., 2013; Hoffman & Salzstein, 1967). Parents' responses may ultimately place children on trajectories of development in line with the priorities of their culture (Pomerantz, Ng, Cheung, & Qu, 2014).

We delineate a model of cultural socialization in which parents' responses to children's performance—including parents' praise—play a central role in children's emotional and academic adjustment (see Figure 16.1). We focus on the West and East Asia given differences in cultural orientation that may shape parents' responses via their goals for children. The societal structure (e.g., the educational system) of the two regions differs as well, which we briefly point out may also be influential. Our discussion of the conceptualization of the model and empirical evidence supporting it centers on the United States and China where most of the research to date has been conducted. Our major concern is with how parents' responses to children's performance maintain cultural priorities by fostering adjustment among children consistent with such priorities. However, we also discuss how parents' responses may contribute to cultural change.

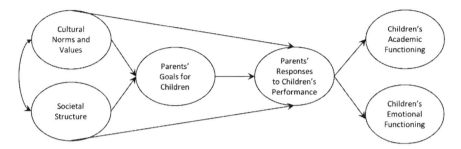

FIGURE 16.1   Cultural socialization model.

Although cultural socialization models such as the one we propose focus on the process by which variation develops *between* cultures, they can also provide insight into the process by which variation develops *within* cultures. For example, although cultural norms and values may play a large role in the goals parents adopt for children, parents may vary in the extent to which they embrace such norms and values, leading to variability within cultures in the goals parents adopt for children and the parenting that ensues. Notably, the evidence to date, which comes almost exclusively from the United States and China, is generally consistent with the idea that the pathways in the model we propose (i.e., from parents' goals to their responses and from their responses to children's adjustment) operate similarly in the West and East Asia (Ng, Pomerantz, & Lam, 2007; Ng, Xiong et al., 2019). Thus, the model is relevant to understanding both between- and within-culture socialization. Both are important, but our focus is on between-culture socialization.

A cultural socialization model of parents' responses to children's performance

Responses to performance can vary on a variety of dimensions (for a review, see Henderlong & Lepper, 2002). At the heart of the model we propose is the extent to which responses are success-oriented versus failure-oriented. The essence of *success-oriented* responses to children's performance is a focus on the positive, which often involves praise. For example, when children succeed, parents make a big deal out of it, highlighting children's effort or ability. When children struggle, parents emphasize what they did well (e.g., go over the strategies children used for each problem they solved correctly). In contrast, *failure-oriented* responses center around children's difficulties. When children do well, this may involve concentrating on children's only mistake; when children do poorly, it may mean making a big deal of it, including criticizing children for a lack of effort or ability and going over what they missed.

The role of culture in parents' goals for children

Western countries such as the United States are oriented toward independence in that emphasis is placed on the individual as distinct from others (Markus & Kitayama, 1991). In this vein, priority is given to "discovering, actualizing, and confirming one's internal attributes" (p. 770, Heine, Lehman, Markus, & Kitayama, 1999), which can be reflected in feelings of self-worth (Markus & Kitayama, 1991). Positive self-regard is often viewed as fundamental to successful adjustment in independence-oriented cultures (Heine et al., 1999). Consequently, Western parents may view supporting children's self-worth as a central goal in raising children. Indeed, Miller, Fung, Lin, Chen, and Boldt (2012) describe European American parents as subscribing to a "folk theory of childrearing" (p. 10) that places a premium on cultivating children's self-regard. Notably, there is much evidence that American mothers hold self-worth goals for children to a greater extent than do Chinese mothers in that they place more value on children's self-esteem, seeing it as more of a priority in children's development (e.g., Chao, 1996; Ng, Xiong et al., 2019).

East Asian countries such as China, in contrast, are oriented toward interdependence with individuals defining themselves largely in the context of their social relationships, roles, and duties (Markus & Kitayama, 1991). A premium is placed on operating harmoniously and responsibly within the collective. This often involves vigilance to one's shortcomings, with continual efforts to overcome them so as to contribute effectively to the group (Heine et al., 1999). The emphasis on improving the self is also evident in Confucius philosophy, which has had a pervasive influence in East Asia since ancient times. Value is placed on continuous learning, the purpose of which is to morally and socially perfect the self to contribute constructively to society. Thus, East Asian parents may place much importance on children's constant striving to improve themselves. In fact, Chinese (vs. American) mothers are more likely to hold self-improvement goals for children in that they see such striving as more of a priority (e.g., Chao, 1996; Ng, Xiong et al., 2019). Parents' self-improvement goals may be driven not only by cultural norms and values but also by China's societal structure given the substantial educational tracking involving high-stakes national examinations.

The role of parents' goals in their responses to children's performance

Goals have been argued to be major drivers of parenting (e.g., Bornstein, 2006) such that parents' self-worth and self-improvement goals for children may shape how parents respond to children's performance. When parents hold self-worth goals, their central concern is with supporting children's positive self-regard. Consequently, parents may adopt a success orientation in responding to children's performance, highlighting the positive while refraining from critical feedback. Supportive of this idea, the more both American and Chinese mothers endorse self-worth goals, the more they report using success-oriented responses (Ng, Xiong et al., 2019). Moreover, in an experimental study in which mothers' responses were observed, mothers induced to hold a self-worth goal (i.e., via information indicating that children feeling good about themselves can lead to success in the academic domain) gave children more positive feedback than did mothers induced to hold a self-improvement goal, with this pattern evident in both the United States and China (Ng, Ng, & Pomerantz, 2020).

When parents hold self-improvement goals, in contrast, their main focus is on helping children identify their shortcomings and working to overcome them. Thus, parents' responses may be failure oriented in that they emphasize what children did wrong. Indeed, the more both American and Chinese mothers endorse self-improvement goals, the more they report using failure-oriented responses to children's successes and failures (Ng, Xiong et al., 2019). When mothers were induced to hold self-improvement (vs. self-worth) goals (i.e., via information that children's constant efforts toward improvement can lead to success in the academic domain), they provided more negative feedback in the United States, but not China where such feedback was already quite high compared to the United States (Ng, Ng et al., 2020).

As a consequence of such processes, American (vs. Chinese) parents' greater tendency to hold self-worth over self-improvement goals may translate into a greater tendency to use success- over failure-oriented responses. Indeed, American parents use more success-oriented responses than do Chinese parents who use more failure-oriented responses (e.g., Hess, Azuma, Kashiwagi, Holloway, & Wenegrat, 1987; Miller et al., 2012; Ng, Xiong et al., 2019). For example, in observations of mothers interacting with children after they succeeded or failed in the laboratory, Ng and colleagues (2007) found that American (vs. Chinese) mothers gave more positive and less negative feedback, regardless of children's performance. In a similar vein, laboratory observations in the context of free play and waiting tasks show that American mothers respond more positively to children's accomplishments than do Japanese mothers living in the United States (Dennis, Cole, Zahn-Waxler, & Mizuta, 2002). Importantly, the differences in American and Chinese mothers' self-worth and self-improvement goals appear to contribute to the differences in their success- and failure-oriented responses (Ng, Xiong et al., 2019).

Even after taking mothers' goals into account, however, sizeable differences in American and Chinese mothers' responses to children's performance remain (Ng, Xiong et al., 2019). Thus, other forces are also likely to play a role in the differences. For example, descriptive norms (i.e., perceptions of how parents typically respond to children's performance) may provide a decisional shortcut about how to respond, simply requiring that parents notice how others respond and follow suit (Cialdini, 1988). Prescriptive norms (i.e., expectations for how parents should respond to children's performance) may also shape parents' responses. In the United States, parents may feel pressure to praise children as it is viewed as an integral part of normative child-rearing to support a key cultural priority (Miller et al., 2012). In China, parents may feel pressure to use failure-oriented responses; Fung (1999) argues that shaming—which is a failure-oriented response—is viewed in China as a functional practice that teaches children to be attentive to societal standards and the perspectives of others for which parents are viewed as responsible (Chao, 1996).

The role of parents' responses to children's performance in children's development

Given that the differences in American and Chinese parents' self-worth and self-improvement goals for children set the stage for differences in how they respond to children's performance, such goals may ultimately produce differences in American and Chinese children's adjustment. The heightened success-oriented responses that ensue from parents' self-worth goals may buffer children against emotional distress by conveying they are competent and worthy. However, such benefits may not always be realized because some types of success-oriented responses have costs (for a review, see Henderlong & Lepper, 2002). For example, the unrealistic expectations of continual exceptional performance conveyed by inflated praise appear to undermine children's self-esteem over time (Brummelman, Nelemans, Thomaes, & Orobio de Castro, 2017). The more parents use success-oriented responses, the happier children feel after success, which partially accounts for American (vs. Chinese) children feeling happier about their successes (Ng et al., 2007). Nonetheless, the evidence to date suggests that over time, mothers' success-oriented responses do not necessarily contribute to children's emotional (Ng, Xiong et al., 2019) or academic (Ng et al., 2007) adjustment.

The heightened failure-oriented responses that accompany parents' self-improvement goals, in contrast, appear to undermine children's emotional adjustment but facilitate their academic adjustment. Parents' failure-oriented responses may put pressure on children, conveying they can never do well enough, thereby heightening children's emotional distress (e.g., anxiety and depressive symptoms). Indeed, both Chinese and American mothers' failure-oriented responses predict children feeling more distressed after failure (Ng et al., 2007) and being at greater risk for emotional distress over time, adjusting for their earlier emotional distress, which accounts for Chinese (vs. American) children's heightened emotional distress (Ng, Xiong et al., 2019). At the same time, however, parents' failure-oriented responses may focus children on where they need to improve while supporting them in this endeavor (e.g., via accompanying instruction). In line with this idea, Ng and colleagues (2007) found that the more both American and Chinese mothers provided children with negative feedback, the better children's subsequent performance on a logical reasoning task, over and above their earlier performance, particularly when children had succeeded.

The differences in American and Chinese parents' responses to children's performance appear to place children on trajectories of emotional and academic adjustment in line with cultural priorities. Specifically, the tendency for American parents to be more success- and less failure-oriented in their responses appears to enhance children's emotional adjustment, but detract from their academic adjustment, which is in line with the emphasis placed on self-worth in the United States. In contrast, the tendency for Chinese parents to be more failure-oriented in their responses appears to detract from children's emotional adjustment, but enhance their academic adjustment, which is in line with the emphasis placed on self-improvement in China. Thus, both American and Chinese parents appear to be supporting children in developing the characteristics necessary to thrive in their culture. Notably, it is not that American parents do not care about children's academic adjustment or that Chinese parents do not care about children's emotional adjustment; rather, to support children's development such that it is in line with cultural norms and values, parents often use socialization practices that prioritize one type of adjustment over the other. It may also be that cultural priorities lead to the view that one type of adjustment is more essential. For example, in the United States, emotional adjustment may be viewed as fundamental to fostering academic adjustment and ultimately a "good" life; conversely, in China, it may be that academic adjustment is seen as fundamental in begetting emotional adjustment and a "good" life.

Cultural change

Although the focus of the model we propose is on how parents' responses to children's performance maintain cultural priorities, parents' responses may also foster cultural change. Culture, as well as societal structure, is dynamic in that it is constantly changing due to a variety of forces. Greenfield (2009) makes the case that throughout the world, there is a trend toward greater urbanization, commercialization, technology use, and formal schooling, which can lead cultures to be more independence-oriented. In China, such change may be particularly rapid as there has been major reform toward a market economy. Moreover, with increased Internet accessibility comes increased exposure to Western culture. These kinds of changes appear to influence children's development. For example, consistent with a trend toward a heightened independence orientation in which self-confidence in social interactions is valuable in urban areas of China, Chen, Cen, Li, and He (2005) found that in 1990 urban Chinese children's shyness had positive correlates (e.g., peer acceptance), by 1998 this was no longer the case, and by 2002 it had negative correlates (e.g., peer rejection), although in rural areas it still had positive correlates (Chen, Wang, & Wang, 2009).

Parents' goals for children are likely to reflect changes in cultural orientation and societal structure, which may set the stage for changes in their responses and ultimately children's adjustment. In line with this idea, Ng, Xiong, and colleagues (2019) found that although Chinese parents endorse self-worth goals less than do American parents, they endorse them to the same extent as self-improvement goals. Such dual priority may be useful in preparing children for success in a society in transition in which interdependence continues to be valued, but independence is also valued (Keller, 2012). Cultural change may come not only from downstream consequences of parents' goals for their responses to children's performance and ultimately children's emotional and academic adjustment, but also from children themselves who may be some of the earliest adopters of new norms and values as they may be less culturally entrenched and more likely to gain access to Western culture via technology. Children may, for example, become less accepting of their parents' failure-oriented responses, showing reactance rather than strivings for improvement, which may disrupt the benefits of such responses or lead parents to use alternatives.

Conclusions and future directions

In the cultural socialization model we propose, parents' responses to children's performance act as key mechanism by which parents assist children in developing in line with cultural priorities. In the United States, priority is placed on children's self-worth and ultimately their emotional adjustment; in China, priority is placed on children's strivings toward self-improvement and ultimately their academic adjustment. Because parents' responses to children's performance are driven by their goals which reflect their cultural orientation and societal structure, such responses can serve as mechanisms of cultural maintenance as well as change.

As is clear from the large body of theory and research on responses to performance, particularly praise, such responses can differ on a variety of dimensions (e.g., ability vs. effort emphasis, autonomy-supportive vs. controlling, inflated vs. not inflated; for a review, see Henderlong & Lepper, 2002), it will be key for future research to identify if and how these dimensions play into the cultural socialization process, with attention to regions of the world other than the United States and China.

References

Bornstein, M. H. (2006). Parenting science and practice. In A. K. Renninger & E. I. Sigel (Eds.), *Handbook of child development. Vol. 4. Child psychology in practice* (6th ed., pp. 893–949). Hoboken, NJ: Wiley.

Brummelman, E., Nelemans, S., Thomaes, S., & Orobio de Castro, B. (2017). When parents' praise inflates, children's self-esteem deflates. *Child Development, 88*, 1799–1809.

Chao, R. K. (1994). Beyond parental control and authoritarian parenting style: Understanding Chinese parenting through the cultural notion of training. *Child Development, 65*, 1111–1119.

Chao, R. K. (1996). Chinese and European American mothers' beliefs about the role of parenting in children's school success. *Journal of Cross-Cultural Psychology, 27*, 403–423.

Chen, X., Cen, G., Li, D., & He, Y. (2005). Social functioning and adjustment in Chinese children: The imprint of historical time. *Child Development, 76*, 182–195.

Chen, X., Wang, L., & Wang, Z. (2009). Shyness-sensitivity and social, school, and psychological adjustment in rural migrant and urban children in China. *Child Development, 80*, 1499–1513.

Cialdini, R. B. (1988). *Influence: Science and practice* (2nd ed.). Glenview, IL: Scott, Foresman.

Dennis, T. A., Cole, P. M., Zahn-Waxler, C., & Mizuta, I. (2002). Self in context: Autonomy and relatedness in Japanese and U. S. mother-preschooler dyads. *Child Development, 73*, 1803–1817.

Fung, H. (1999). Becoming a moral child: The socialization of shame among young Chinese children. *Ethos, 27*, 180–209.

Greenfield, P. M. (2009). Linking social change and developmental change: Shifting pathways of human development. *Developmental Psychology, 45*, 401–408.

Greenfield, P. M., Keller, H., Fuligni, A. J., & Maynard, A. (2003). Cultural pathways through universal development. *Annual Review of Psychology, 54*, 461–490.

Gunderson, E. A., Gripshover, S. J., Romero, C., Dweck, C. S., Goldin-Meadow, S., & Levine, S. C. (2013). Parent praise to 1- to 3-year-olds predicts children's motivational frameworks 5 years later. *Child Development, 84*, 1526–1541.

Heine, S. J., Lehman, D. R., Markus, H. R., & Kitayama, S. (1999). Is there a universal need for positive self-regard? *Psychological Review, 106*, 766–794.

Henderlong, J., & Lepper, M. H. (2002). The effects of praise on children's intrinsic motivation: A review and synthesis. *Psychological Bulletin, 128*, 774–795.

Hess, R. D., Azuma, H., Kashiwagi, K., Holloway, S. D., & Wenegrat, A. (1987). Cultural variations in socialization for school achievement: Contrasts between Japan and the United States. *Journal of Applied Developmental Psychology, 8*, 421–440.

Hoffman, M. L., & Salzstein, H. D. (1967). Parent discipline and the child's moral development. *Journal of Personality and Social Psychology, 5*, 45–57.

Keller, H. (2012). Autonomy and relatedness revisited: Cultural manifestations of universal human needs. *Child Development Perspectives, 6*, 12–18.

Lamm, B., Keller, H., Teiser, J., Gudi, H., Yovsi, R. D., Freitag, C., … & Lohaus, A. (2018). Waiting for the second treat: Developing culture-specific modes of self-regulation. *Child Development, 89*, e261–e277.

Markus, H. R., & Kitayama, S. (1991). Culture and the self: Implications for cognition, emotion, and motivation. *Psychological Review, 98*, 224–253.

Miller, P., Fung, H., Lin, S., Chen, E., & Boldt, B. (2012). How socialization happens on the ground: Narrative practices as alternate socializing pathways in Taiwanese and European-American families: III. Interpretive frameworks in routine practices. *Monographs of the Society for Research in Child Development, 77*, 28–58.

Ng, F. F.-Y., Pomerantz, E. M., & Lam, S.-F. (2007). European American and Chinese parents' responses to children's success and failure: Implications for children's responses. *Developmental Psychology, 43*, 1239–1255.

Ng, J., Ng, F. F.-Y., & Pomerantz, E. M. (2020). *Mothers' goals influence their responses to children's performance: An experimental study in the United States and Hong Kong.* Manuscript in preparation.

Ng, J., Xiong, Y., Qu, Y., Cheung, C. S., Ng, F. F.-Y., Wang, M., & Pomerantz, E. M. (2019). Implications of Chinese and American mother's goals for children's emotional distress. *Developmental Psychology, 55*, 2616–2629.

Pomerantz, E. M., Ng, F. F.-Y., Cheung, C. S., & Qu, Y. (2014). Raising happy children who succeed in school: Lessons from China and the United States. *Child Development Perspectives, 8*, 71–76.

INDEX

Printed in Great Britain
by Amazon